UNDERGRADUATE TEACHING

CHALLENGES, ANALYSIS, SOLUTIONS...

VEENA KUMAR

Ph.D., Doctorat (Sorbonne, Paris)
Executive Director, IUCEE International Educator Certification Program
Ex-Professor Humanities & Head, Education Technology,
Indian Institute of Technology (IIT), New Delhi, India

ISBN 979-8-89026-881-5

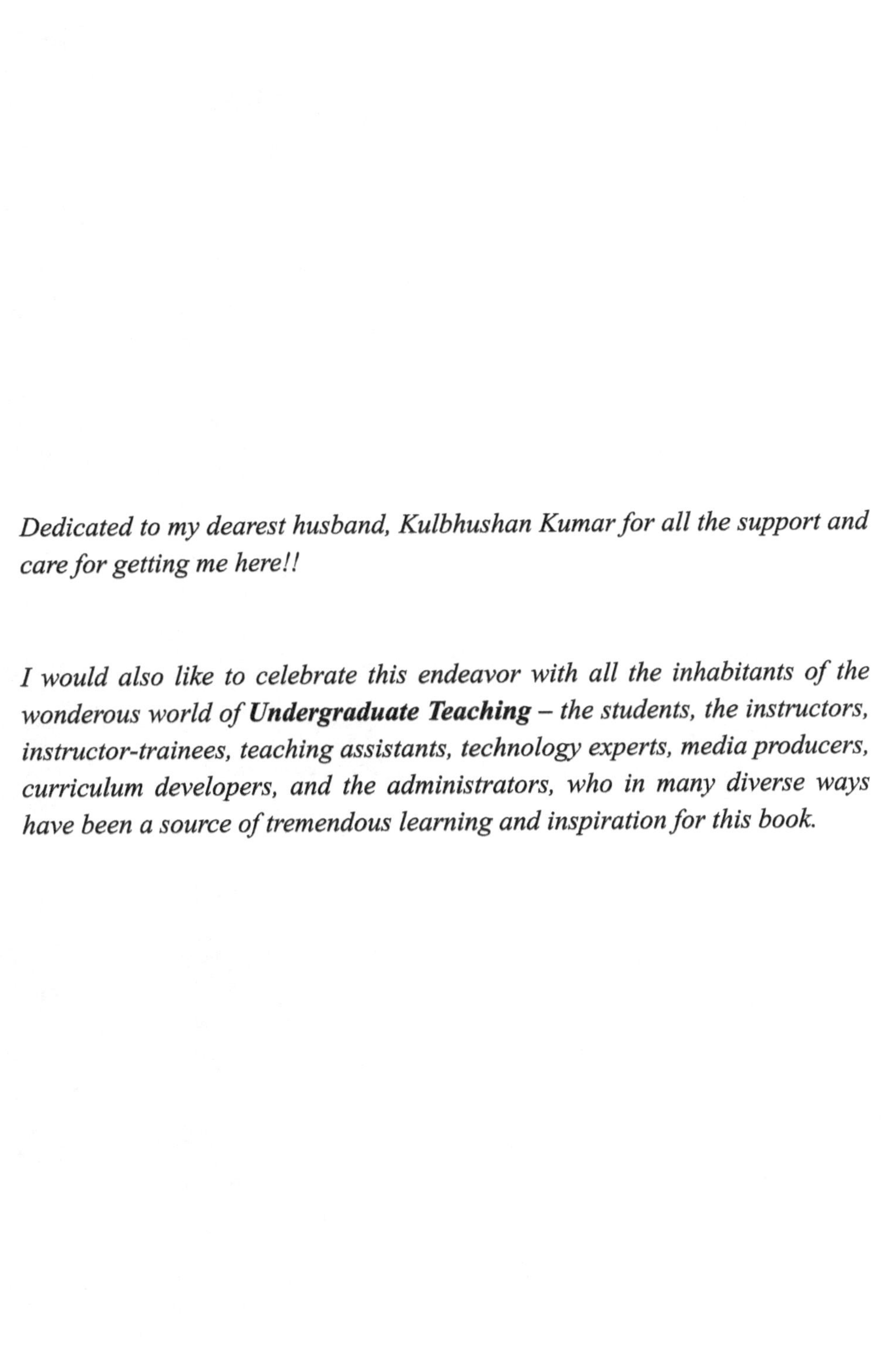

Dedicated to my dearest husband, Kulbhushan Kumar for all the support and care for getting me here!!

*I would also like to celebrate this endeavor with all the inhabitants of the wonderous world of **Undergraduate Teaching** – the students, the instructors, instructor-trainees, teaching assistants, technology experts, media producers, curriculum developers, and the administrators, who in many diverse ways have been a source of tremendous learning and inspiration for this book.*

Table of Contents

Acknowledgements

This book has been in *curing* for several years and during those years, several people have added *something special* which has facilitated the curing process. Sincere thanks are due to several different sets of people who have influenced my thinking and have been a source learning for me. The list is long and includes authors of books and research papers read over the years; outstanding speakers heard at the conferences; and colleagues and instructor/participants from my own workshops whose feedback and informal conversations have stimulated and churned my thought process. I must also thank my students and faculty trainees in France, India and the USA who have been, at times knowingly but more often unknowingly, the source of much wisdom through their assignments, comments, and feedback.

My grateful thanks are due to a number of people who have been a part of the review process. I would like to specifically thank Dr. Neeraj Buch (*Dean Undergraduate Studies & Associate Provost for Student Success, Rochester Institute of Technology, USA*), Dr. Archana Mantri (*Vice Chancellor, Chitkara University, Chandigarh, India*), Dr. Amit Lathigara (*Vice Chancellor, R.K. University, Rajkot, India*), and Dr. Javeed Kittur (*Associate Prof., Ohio State University*), and Sanjeev Kavale (*Research Scholar, Arizona State University, USA*) for taking the time to review the manuscript and provide invaluable feedback.

I am especially indebted to Dr. Samir Khullar (*Head, CSE, Northwestern University, USA*), and Dr. Sara Owsley Sood (*Assoc. Chair for UG education in CS, Northwestern University, USA*) for organizing a brainstorming session with undergraduate faculty to share their views on the challenges and strategies discussed in the book. I feel fortunate to have the opportunity to get feedback and different perspectives from scholars and active practitioners. Another interesting perspective was added to the review process by Salina Kumar who reviewed the text from a TA's point of view.

I am grateful to Prof. Krishna Vedula, Executive Director of Indo-Universal Consortium of Engineering Education (IUCEE) for giving me the opportunity to design and direct the *IUCEE International Educator Certification Program (IIECP)* which is my dream project and has grown to be a signature program of IUCEE in making tangible contribution towards transforming higher education in India. We acknowledge with a lot of humility and pride that the IIECP has been recognized by IGIP, Austria for joint certification with their Ing.Paed. IGIP (IGIP *Diploma in Engineering Pedagogy)* program.

The other set of people whose help I would like to gratefully acknowledge are the silent supporters who believe in you and your endeavors. They lend meaning to the entire exercise and help you keep going. I am truly grateful to my wonderful family for their affectionate and enthusiastic support throughout my professional journey, and during the writing of this book.

Finally, I would like to thank all the resource persons and organizations who generously share pictures, cartoons, and graphics freely as an open source that beholden authors like me can use to enrich their readers' learning experience. All photos and cartoons taken from the internet and Wikipedia are gratefully acknowledged.

Preface

Why a Book on Undergraduate Teaching?

Undergraduate teaching in the 21st century is becoming progressively more challenging. The motivation to write this book is driven by two very important but neglected realities about undergraduate teaching. The first one relates to the fact that teaching at the undergraduate level is different from teaching at any other level and faces unique challenges. The second relates to the fact that most undergraduate instructors have *no* training in pedagogy and are not well-prepared to manage these challenges. Since undergraduate instructors are hired based on their academic credentials, they do not view *teaching* as a specialized skill that needs time and effort to be learned and mastered. ***Undergraduate Teaching*** serves as a practice guide to directly address these two realities. The book aspires to introduce undergraduate instructors to the science of teaching (and learning) and prepare them to identify the challenges, analyze them within the theoretical context, and suggest solutions that are simple, research-validated, and easy-to-implement.

Let us begin by identifying the unique challenges of undergraduate teaching by comparing them to those faced while teaching at the high school or graduate levels. Table 0.1 brings out these in terms of *Learning Environment; Learners' Sense of Security; Teaching Methodology and Assessment Pattern;* and *Instructor Preparedness*.

Table 0.a – Unique Challenges of Undergraduate Instruction

Aspect	High School Instruction	Undergraduate Instruction	Graduate Instruction
Learning Environment	Small class size, familiar learning environment; known peer group; and familiar set-up.	Large to very large classes, unfamiliar learning environment; unknown peer group; each course delivered differently.	Small class size; mature interaction with the instructor & peers; familiar learning environment.
Learners' Sense of Security	The learners feel secure, reassured, and confident in a familiar and safe set-up that they have *experienced* over several years.	The learners are transitioning into a new, unfamiliar set-up and feel vulnerable, lost, and overwhelmed because of unpredictable academic and emotional pressures.	The learners feel secure because they are in a familiar university environment. Being older they are more confident in taking charge of their academic needs.
Teaching Methodology & Assessment Pattern	Structured coursework, familiar methodology across different subjects; known assessment patterns; and a lot of handholding with close interaction with teachers.	Overwhelming quantum and complexity of the coursework. The course design and delivery can change from course to course, and from instructor to instructor; no handholding and little contact with the instructor. Assessment patterns can be unfamiliar and perplexing.	Experienced and confident university learners with high level of self-efficacy. In control of their own learning. Coursework generally focused on research & independent work.

Aspect	High School Instruction	Undergraduate Instruction	Graduate Instruction
Instructor Preparedness	Specific academic qualification and training in pedagogy required for employability. Structured format provided for mentoring and support.	No qualification in teaching is required. No formal training in pedagogy. No facilities for mentoring. Confused priorities – hired to teach but recognition/promotion awarded on the basis of research and publications.	The instructor is more in the role of a facilitator. Courses focus on personal research and/or project work. Mature students with a high level of self-reliance.

The above comparison brings out only some of the challenges. There are many other issues that require special skills to successfully manage undergraduate courses and the aspirations of undergraduate students.

The quality and effectiveness of teaching become very important considering the significant role undergraduate education plays in building the future of not just the young graduates but also of the community and the country in which they live. Students step into undergraduate programs with a lot of aspirations and anticipation and look forward to joining the workforce after graduation. On the other end, communities depend on undergraduates to fill the largest sections of the workforce in most sectors. Clearly, the quality of undergraduate instruction has far-reaching consequences The stakes at this level are very high for all stakeholders: the students *(in terms of time, money, and academic success)*, the instructors *(in terms of personal satisfaction and professional success)*, and the institutions *(in terms of student placements, rating, reputation, and business viability)*. The burden of fulfilling the aspirations of all stakeholders rests squarely on the shoulders of the undergraduate instructors. According to a UNESCO report, *"The number of students in universities has more than doubled globally in the last two decades to 235 million. And, it's expected to double again in the next decade, along with international student mobility"*

(UNESCO World Higher Education Conference, 2022), which indirectly emphasizes the magnitude and seriousness of the importance for instructor preparedness.

In recent years, the task of an undergraduate instructor has become even more challenging due to *four* main developments: i) the changed profile, needs, and expectations of the Generation Z students entering the university; ii) the quantum and complexity of the course content; iii) the arrival of new methodologies and technology tools; and iv) the increased accountability of undergraduate education for preparing students for a fiercely competitive job market. Not long ago, undergraduate teaching was centered around textbooks covering the prescribed curriculum and ensuring that a majority of the students successfully completed their course(s). Today, new content is added every year, and instructors need to constantly upgrade their knowledge base as well as their teaching methodologies. In addition, many universities today expect or allow instructors to design their own courses and create their own assessment, which makes the list of challenges and the competencies required to cope with them, longer every academic year.

Undergraduate Teaching is designed to fill this gap by providing a good balance of theory and practice that should prepare undergraduate instructors to be more professionally competent, whether they are new to the profession or have been teaching for years. The practical strategies provided are time-tested and research-verified, and they work equally well across all disciplines.

What is Special about this Book?

There are three main features that make this book special: the focus on purpose, the scientific approach, and the reader-centric layout. The overarching purpose of this book is to get instructors ready to manage the pedagogical intricacies of undergraduate instruction. In the absence of any formal training, the preparatory process must be simple and systematic. Using a focused approach, the book adopts a structured pathway to walk the instructors through their professional preparation process.

<table>
<tr>
<td>Break the instructional process down to core components & associated</td>
<td>Identify challenges associated with specific pedagogical tasks.</td>
<td>Analyze the manifestation of challenges within the theoretical framework.</td>
<td>Propose effective, research -validated solutions that work across disciplines.</td>
</tr>
</table>

Fig. 0.1 – Conceptual Structure of the Undergraduate Teaching

The content organization is based on the premise that all concerned parties (instructors, curriculum designers, and institute heads) recognize that undergraduate teaching is a specialized, serious undertaking that calls for meticulous planning and skillful implementation. Here, the pedagogical process cannot be intuitive; it needs to be intentional and carefully orchestrated to address the specific challenges.

In order to effectively manage the undergraduate instructional process, the instructors must have an in-depth understanding of key constructs such as the *expectations of the students and their academic, emotional, and employability needs; how learning happens in young adults; what is the best way to design* and *deliver an undergraduate level course; and how to manage (design and implement) the assessment process.* This in-depth understanding needs to be paired with the development of competencies to design and implement time-tested, research-validated practices that hold good across all levels and disciplines, ranging from the humanities, social sciences, pure or applied sciences, engineering, medicine, law, management etc.

As for the approach, the book opts for a highly scientific approach. Teaching, we are told, is both an *art* and a *science*. While the *art of teaching* is a natural gift given to a chosen few, the *science* of teaching is within reach for all. Adopting the practices that are based on scientific principles, everyone can learn to teach skillfully because these principles can be explained, analyzed, verified, and applied. This book focuses on the *science of teaching a specific community of learners: the undergraduates.* This is accomplished by structuring the input to address both the *theory (why)* and the *practice (how)* of individual components of the undergraduate instructional process. The generous use of tables (40) and figures and graphics (30) reinforces the scientific approach and helps to facilitate easy comprehension and assimilation of the concepts discussed.

The layout decisions of the book are primarily guided by the desire to be reader centric. The structure chosen for the book is a judicious mix of the formats of a textbook and a practice manual. Keeping in mind that most undergraduate instructors can squeeze out only a limited amount of time for working on their personal and professional development, an all-out effort is made to present the input, analysis, discussion, and guidelines in a reader-friendly manner. The author opts for an unadorned, inclusive, and conversational style of writing. The input for each section is laid out in an easy-to-read manner. Each section focuses on one specific key component. Every section begins by identifying *major challenges* associated with a specific aspect of undergraduate teaching and ends with a set of *tips for managing them*. An additional feature *Recommendations for the instructor* is included to guide the instructors bring out the relevance and practical implications of the different theories discussed. The self-assessment instruments provided at the end of the book can help instructors to keep track of their personal and professional growth.

How is the Content Presented?

The content of the book is structured according to the pathway illustrated in Fig. 01. The undergraduate instructional process is first broken down into its key components, sub-components, and associated tasks. Then, the anatomy of each component is examined in detail, focusing on not only the *what* and the *why* components but also the *how* component of the undergraduate instructional process. **Undergraduate Teaching** is designed as a practice guide and aspires to provide the knowledge and practical skills required to effectively address the specific challenges of undergraduate teaching. The deconstruction of challenges and the solutions proposed are validated by the author's extensive research, teaching, and training experience in this field. Figure 02 attempts to visually capture the key components, sub-components, and related tasks that the undergraduate instructors must learn to manage competently and confidently.

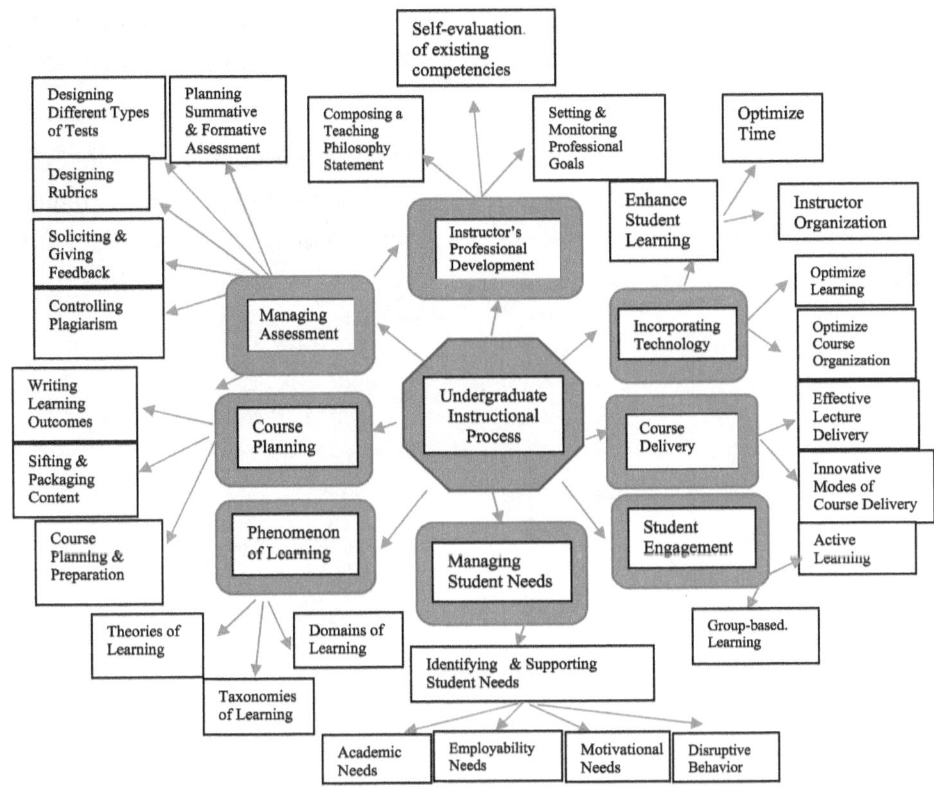

Fig. 0.2 – Key Components of the Undergraduate Instructional Process

In Fig. 02, we can see the key components: *The Phenomenon of Learning; Managing Student Needs; Managing Course Content; Managing Course Delivery; Student Engagement; Partnering with Technology; and Managing Assessment.* Along with the key components, we see some of the sub-components and associated tasks that every undergraduate instructor is expected to understand and manage competently.

The book starts aptly by encouraging instructors to begin by ***Looking Inwards and Taking Stock*** of their existing competencies and taking stock of their personal and professional growth. Two instruments have been provided for instructors to start the process of self-evaluation and to identify their strengths and areas needing attention. Based on the findings of this self-analysis, the instructors are guided to create a systematic action plan through a *Teaching Philosophy Statement.* Keeping the focus on instructors' personal and professional growth, the book ends with an ***End Note*** which is a short section that closes the instructor-readiness loop by revisiting the self-appraisal process initiated in Section 1.

All resources used in the text are cited under ***References*** using the APA format. The book ends with a well-designed ***Glossary*** that provides extended definitions of the key terms that are essential for providing university educators, a solid pedagogical background.

 1 # Looking Inwards and Taking Stock!

The fact that you have this book in your hands confirms that you are involved in college instruction and, clearly, take your profession seriously. In recent years, teaching undergraduate students has become progressively more challenging due to several new developments, such as the changed profile and expectations of Gen Z students entering universities, the ever-increasing quantum and complexity of curricula, and the emergence of potent technology tools and innovative methodologies. Not long ago, undergraduate teaching was centered around prescribed curricula and textbooks, but now the challenges are very different. Today, as more and more universities expect instructors to design their own courses and create their own assessments, the list of challenges and required competencies to cope with them is getting longer every year.

As undergraduate instructors, we have high professional aspirations and want to be the best at what we do, but more than often, it does not happen. Being a competent college instructor requires two sets of related but different competencies: i) managing course content (*what to teach*) and ii) managing course delivery (*how to teach it*). In the university environment, it is taken for granted that if you know *what* to teach, you will automatically know *how* to teach it. This is far from being true. The fact is that there is a whole lot of science behind the *how* component, which needs to be learned and mastered. This book is designed to fill this gap by identifying the challenges, examining them in a theoretical context, and proposing strategies for overcoming them effectively.

A good starting point is to look inward, take stock of your current competencies, and identify your strengths and shortcomings at this point in time. To achieve this, you must set a trajectory that takes us through a clear pathway involving the following steps:

- Getting to know your professional self.

- Self-evaluating your current competencies, and

- Drawing up an action plan and composing a *Teaching Philosophy Statement.*

1.1   Getting to Know Your Professional Self

Any effort to enhance one's professional competencies involves being clear about one's professional ideology, goals, and capabilities. This is not an easy task because to know your professional self, you need to follow a structured reflective process that generally, most of us are not exposed to. The reflective process requires introspection and a systematic approach to analyzing one's ideology, aspirations, and professional strengths and shortcomings. The reflective process involves asking yourself questions, thinking about them objectively, and responding to them honestly. If you do not have a reflective mindset or are not used to the reflective process, the immediate worry is what questions to ask. Given below are a few sample prompts that can trigger your thinking process. Create a short list of questions, think seriously about each question, and write down the response. The responses will guide you for creating an action plan for monitoring your professional growth.

Why am I in the teaching profession? Think about the reasons that made you choose the teaching profession. Was the decision dictated by *choice, chance,* or *compulsion*? What do you love about being a teacher? What would you like to change?

What are my professional goals and aspirations? Think about your professional ambitions and how you want the world to see you as an expert. What special efforts, if any, have you made to achieve your goals? What are the constraints that obstruct you from achieving your goals?

What is my vision for an outstanding undergraduate educator? Begin by listing attributes and competencies that you think are required for becoming an outstanding college educator. One way of doing this is to think of a teacher from your school or college days who could be your role model. It is true that many of us are inspired by our professors to follow in their footsteps. Where do you see yourself in your own eyes?

Responses to the above or similar prompts help us to get a better understanding of ourselves as educators. Unfortunately, we seldom take the time to meditate on these issues. However, now that you have decided to take charge of our teaching effectiveness, this is a good time to dig deeper, find some answers, and start your journey towards becoming an outstanding college educator.

1.2   Taking Stock of the Current Competency Level

Any endeavor related to mastering a professional skill must begin by taking stock of the current level of your competency in the targeted skill. The very first step of the trajectory is to determine where you currently stand on the professional excellence ladder – what are your strengths and shortcomings, and how to channel this awareness to upgrade your competencies to achieve the desired level of proficiency. This is best realized by self-evaluating your current competencies by using appropriate instruments.

Here, two well-designed instruments are suggested that use different approaches and criteria to evaluate teaching effectiveness. The objective is to get a holistic, comprehensive self-assessment. Both instruments are very powerful and help us get an objective self-evaluation of our current competencies. Instrument I is a teaching effectiveness matrix based on *Joseph Lowman's 2-D Model of Effective Teaching*, while Instrument II is developed by the author on the basis of feedback received from a focused survey administered to university instructors and students.

1.3   Instrument I – Lowman's 2-D Model of Effective Teaching

There is a lot of literature out there that attempts to capture the profile and competencies that may define an effective college instructor. The choice of the Joseph Lowman *2-D Model of Effective Teaching is* based on the fact that it sums up the entire debate with two qualifiers. According to Lowman, the two dimensions of exemplary teaching lie in the instructors' ability to: i) generate *Intellectual Excitement* (IE), and ii) develop good *Interpersonal*

Joseph Lowman
(Credits: Internet)

Rapport (IR) with students. Each dimension includes a number of components that require specialized skill sets, which the instructors need to be cognizant of. Both these dimensions are closely related to student motivation and must be managed skillfully. Undergraduate classes are rather large, and building good interpersonal rapport with individual students can be arduous. Similarly, the content of the undergraduate courses is complex, and creating intellectual curiosity across all topics can be daunting. However, a sustained effort to focus on both these dimensions can indeed make teaching more effective and joyful. *(Morse, A. et al, (2017)*

The figure below (Fig. 1.1) explains the *2D Model of Teaching Effectiveness* by further breaking each dimension into qualities and competencies that must be developed and assessed. Both these dimensions will be revisited in subsequent sections while discussing other aspects of the undergraduate instructional process.

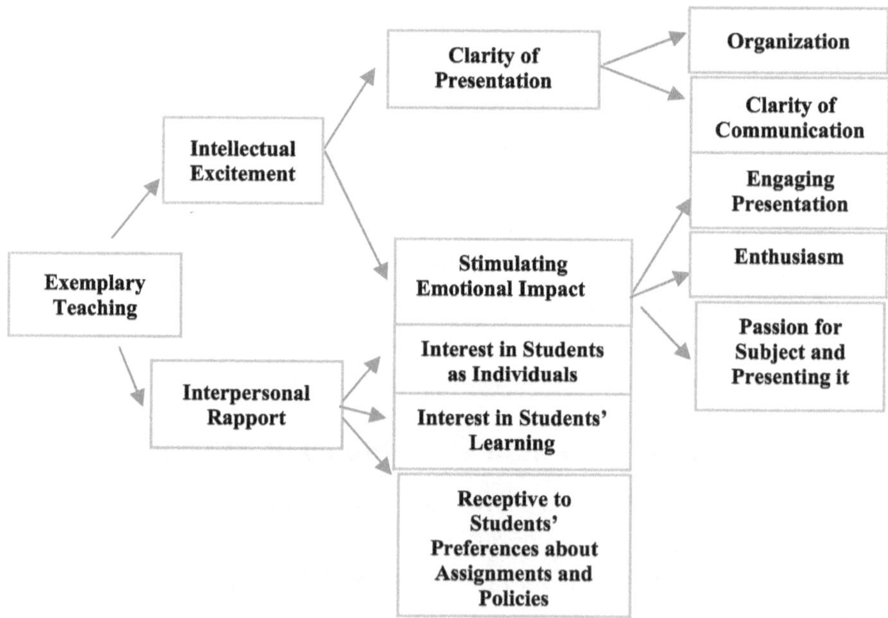

(Lowman, Joseph, Mastering the Techniques of Teaching, Jossey-Bass, San Francisco, 1995)

Fig. 1.1 – Joseph Lowman's 2 D Model for Effective Teaching

1.3.1   Measuring Teaching Effectiveness

Based on this 2D Model of Teaching Effectiveness, a matrix was developed that can help individual instructors to take stock of their own teaching effectiveness. This instrument presents a mapping of the two dimensions of *Intellectual Excitement* (IE) and *Interpersonal Rapport (IR)* in nine categories, represented by nine tiles. Each tile has been given a label that explains the proportion in which the two dimensions are combined as low, medium, and high. The instructors are invited to introspect and self-evaluate themselves by selecting the tile (one of the nine categories shown in Fig. 1.1) that collectively represents their current level of proficiency in both the IR and IE dimensions.

		Interpersonal Rapport		
		Low	Moderate	High
Intellectual Excitement	**High**	6. Intellectual Authority	8. Exemplary Lecturer	9. Complete Exemplar
	Moderate	3. Adequate	5. Competent	7. Exemplary Facilitator
	Low	1. Inadequate	2. Marginal	4. Socratic

(ASCE ExCEEd Teaching Workshop – 2010)

Fig. 1.2 – Matrix for Evaluating Teaching Effectiveness

As you look at the matrix, you are likely to be confused by the unfamiliar terminology or labels used for different categories. Before starting the self-evaluation process, it is important to understand what each title represents. Descriptions provided in Table 1a can be very helpful.

Table 1.a – Levels of Teaching Effectiveness based on Lowman's 2D Model

Title	Implication	Interpretation/Conclusion
Inadequate	The instructor is ***Low in both IE*** and ***IR*** dimensions.	Both dimensions are weak, and a lot of effort is required to come up to the acceptable level. You need to seriously review your command over the subject content as well as your connect with the students.

Title	Implication	Interpretation/Conclusion
Marginal	The instructor is *Low in IE* and *Medium in IR* dimension.	While the instructor's rapport with students is acceptable, a lot more work is needed to upgrade the domain knowledge.
Adequate	The instructor is *Medium in IE* but *Low in IR* dimension.	You need to really focus on strategies to connect with your students. The command of the course content also needs constant monitoring.
Socratic	The instructor is *Low in IE* but *High in IR*. The term *Socratic* comes from a teaching methodology that depends on questioning used to develop critical thinking and logical reasoning.	This shows that the instructor has a good connect with the students and has earned their love and confidence. But a lot of work is needed to update the domain expertise.
Competent	The instructor is *Medium in both IE* and *IR* dimensions.	Most instructors feel they belong here. However, this is rather tricky because it is very easy to get complacent and accept mediocrity.
Intellectual Authority	The instructor is *High in IE* but *Low in IR* dimension	This is a very common situation in the university milieu. There are instructors who are award-winning researchers and celebrated subject experts but are not very successful as teachers, mainly because they are unable to communicate at the students' intellectual level.
Exemplary Facilitator	The instructor is *High in IR* but *Medium in IE* dimension	This type of instructor is a great facilitator and helps to motivate the students through personal attention and care. However, there is scope for more work in developing domain expertise.

Title	Implication	Interpretation/Conclusion
Exemplary Lecturer	The instructor is ***High in IE*** and ***Medium in IR***	This is a very happy position. The instructor is in excellent control of the course content and enjoys a fairly good connect with the students.
Complete Examplar	***High in both IE*** and ***IR dimensions***	This is where we all should aspire to be. No doubt that this is a very difficult task but each one of us can get there by determination, diligence, and following a scientific approach.

1.3.2　Self-assessment Exercise Using Instrument I

Study the matrix carefully. If you are unsure about any label, refer to Table 1.a. to get clarity about different labels. Evaluate yourself as objectively and honestly as possible. Experience shows that majority of instructors tend to take the easy path and rank themselves as No. 5 – *Competent*. A more thorough examination of our connect with the students and domain knowledge should be attempted.

While our ultimate dream is to be a *Complete Exemplar* where both dimensions are at the highest level, we need to be as objective as possible without overestimating or underestimating our competencies. The instrument promotes reflection and makes us aware of where we should be directing our efforts and in what proportion.

1.4　Instrument II – Seven Attributes of an Outstanding University Educator

This instrument requires undergraduate instructors to self-evaluate themselves on seven key attributes that have been identified as being essential for becoming successful university educators. For constructing this instrument, the first step was to determine the key attributes to be included in the instrument. A number of different lists developed by researchers and university teaching-learning centers were examined. Seven attributes were selected based on the results of a large anonymous survey conducted with over 300 instructor-trainees and 450 students. The participants were given a list of ten personal qualities and ten professional competencies considered desirable for an outstanding university instructor. They were asked to pick five qualities in each category that they thought were the most important. The qualities and competencies chosen by participants from different batches, irrespective of their academic qualifications, country of origin, or cultural differences, were quite similar. Under personal qualities, the top five listed were *diligence, patience, empathy, accessibility,* and *passion for excellence.* Under professional competence, *content expertise, being technology-savvy, good organization, enthusiasm for using innovative methodologies,* and *effective communication* made the top-five list. These top choices were regrouped as seven key attributes. Participants confirmed recognizing many of these attributes in teachers whom they remembered as being outstanding. The attributes that made the final-seven list are: *Content expertise, Accessibility & Student Connect, Good Organization, Positive Approach to Technology, Enthusiasm for Using Innovative Methodologies, Good Communication,* and *Passion for Excellence.*

However, before proceeding to self-evaluation, it is important to know what each attribute stands for and what is the best way to reflect and self-evaluate yourself. Let us get a better understanding of each of these seven attributes selected to be included in this instrument:

Attribute #1 – Expertise in the Domain Knowledge: This is clearly the first and most important requirement for excelling at college teaching. No doubt that most undergraduate instructors have a good level of content expertise, but it is also true that most of us tend to overestimate ourselves and tend to become complacent (especially if we are teaching the same course most of the time). The questions to ask here are: *how updated am I? When did I read or review a new book or a research paper on the subject? What new input have I added to my lectures in the last semester or year?*

Attribute #2 – Accessibility and Student Connect: This is a tricky area because most instructors feel that they are very accessible, and students are welcome anytime. However, the fact is that students (especially the ones who need help) are very reluctant to ask for help. The instructor needs to demonstrate accessibility by setting up office hours, online study groups, etc., and ensuring a very open and welcoming environment. The questions to ask here are: *do I really know my students well? Do I have a system for office hours? Do I have a system to identify and support students who need help?*

Attribute #3 – Good Organization: Given the diverse set of duties that a college instructor is called upon to fulfill, being well-organized is crucial. Between course planning, preparing in-class and collaborative activities and projects, correcting assignments, and working on research, the instructor is forever hard-pressed for time. In addition to the professional duties, there are personal and family commitments that need their share of time and energy. The questions to ask here are: *am I able to manage all tasks on time and to my satisfaction? Do I have a system (paper or technology-based) for planning and monitoring different activities? How well is the system working?*

Attribute #4 – Using Innovative Methodologies: This attribute refers to open-mindedness towards experimenting with new teaching and student engagement methodologies inside and outside the classroom. In the past few years, the profile, expectations, and needs of undergraduate students have evolved a great deal. The quantum and complexity of course content have also become more demanding, and these developments warrant new methodologies. An enthusiastic instructor is always thinking of new ways to ensure that the content is delivered in a way that promotes understanding and makes learning more meaningful and joyful. The questions to ask here are: *how much time do I spend preparing my lectures? What new methodologies have I experimented with to enhance teaching in the past semester or year? What new in-class activities have I tried? How successful am I at keeping the students engaged and motivated?*

Attribute #5 – Good Communication Skills: One attribute that appeared in all lists was the instructor's ability to communicate well. It is believed that irrespective of the profession, 80% of success depends on the professional's ability to communicate well. This is even more true for a college instructor who is required to constantly communicate with a large group of young individuals. If you are not fully satisfied with your spoken communication and think you need to do better, do not brush it aside. There are many ways of addressing this with full privacy (See pp - 133-134) The questions to ask here are: *can students understand me clearly? Am I audible to the last benches? Does my spoken communication project confidence? Is my voice pleasant and well-modulated?*

Attribute #6 – Positive Approach to Technology: Presence of technology has added a new dimension to undergraduate teaching. The service rendered by technology during the COVID-19 years (2020–22) has earned it a permanent place in the realm of college instruction. Every day, new apps and technology tools are becoming available that are not only user-friendly but also free of charge. An instructor teaching tech-savvy Gen Z students cannot afford to not partner with technology. The questions to ask here are: *do I believe in the power of technology to support undergraduate instruction? What is my current competency level? Am I willing to spend the required time and effort to learn and use technology in my classes?*

Attribute #7 – Passion for Excellence: It is hard to become an outstanding professional unless you have the passion to excel at what you are doing. This becomes even more important if you are a university instructor because you are a role model for young people who are getting ready to enter a profession themselves. In the university arena, people tend to become complacent once they get tenure and reach a certain position. Getting out of the comfort zone of mediocrity requires constant monitoring of one's professional goals and the required matching competencies. The questions to ask here are: *what is my dream destination? In which field do I want to make a name for myself? Do I have well-defined short-term and long-term plans for my professional growth? Do I have a plan to monitor my professional growth?*

1.4.1   Self-assessment Exercise Using Instrument II

We will use this simple and non-judgmental instrument to assess ourselves on the seven attributes. Please study the explanation for each attribute (given above), reflect carefully, and using the instrument given below (Table 1.b), self-evaluate yourself. Think about each attribute carefully and evaluate yourself as objectively as possible. The idea is to get a clear picture of your strengths and shortcomings, which will help you direct your efforts in the right direction for planning and monitoring your professional growth.

Table 1.b – Self-evaluation on Seven Attributes of an Outstanding University Educator

Evaluate your satisfaction level in the following <u>seven</u> areas on a **scale of 1 to 4 where <u>1 is the lowest and 4 is the best.</u>** Please give yourself a score and add a rationale or comment.

No.	Attribute	1	2	3	4	Rationale/Comments
1.	Content Expertise					
2.	Accessibility & Connect with Students					
3.	Good organization					
4.	Using Innovative Methodologies					
5.	Effective Communication					
6.	Positive Approach to Technology					
7.	Passion for Excellence					

Self-evaluation exercises using Instruments I and II helps us to take stock and get clarity about where we stand on the professional excellence ladder at this point in time. This important information about our strengths and shortcomings helps us identify the specific competencies that we need to work on and, accordingly, create an action plan that will serve as a tool for monitoring our personal and professional growth. Use the blank format of Instrument II provided to help you assess yourself (See p - 254) Try and do this exercise once every year.

1.5   Setting Priorities

We know that college teaching is a demanding profession, and to keep progressing, we need to prepare well and set priorities. This is true for all instructors, whether you are new to the profession, or have been teaching for years. We need to set priorities to achieve two sets of objectives: first, to *strike a productive balance between teaching and research*, and second, *to draw up a viable plan for of our own professional development*.

1.5.1   Striking a Balance Between Teaching and Research

A dilemma all undergraduate instructors face is balancing priorities between teaching and research, that are viewed as the two important facets of their profession. In the real-world, instructors are hired to teach. Research is important too, but their primary responsibility is to their students, and teaching should be their main focus. Unfortunately, there is an inherent anomaly in the system: university instructors are hired to teach, but their professional advancement depends on their achievements in research (the number of publications, presentations at conferences, etc.). When the time comes to apply for promotion, a new job, or a grant, the evaluation criteria are heavily loaded towards research output. Hardly ever, excellence in teaching is considered the prime qualifier for the award.

There is absolutely no debate about the important role research plays in an instructor's professional growth. But it must be taken up by choice and not under duress. Like teaching, undertaking research is a specialized activity that requires a certain bent of mind and passion. However, in the current academic tradition, along with teaching, the instructors are forced to undertake research because their future depends on it. This complex situation prevents college instructors from excelling at either. Both teaching and research require undivided focus, time, and dedication, and faced with confused priorities, the instructors are forever struggling for time and often end up doing a mediocre job of both.

To rise above mediocrity, you need to decide in which field you want to make a name for yourself: in teaching or in research. If you are a passionate researcher, you should take up a position that focuses primarily on research. But as an instructor, your first and prime responsibility is to teach. It is important to remember that you are hired to teach and are paid to teach students who have made heavy investments of time and money and have blindly put their future in your hands. As long as you carry the title of *professor*, your top priority must be teaching, and your top professional goal must be to become an outstanding instructor in your field. Research must be undertaken along with teaching, but not at the cost of teaching.

1.5.2   Taking Charge of Your Own Professional Development

The second area where instructors need to set priorities and create an action plan is taking charge of their professional development. In the absence of proper training, pre-service and in-service instructors must find ways to learn about each of the seven key components of the undergraduate instructional process: *the learning process, student needs, course design, course delivery, student engagement, incorporating technology, and assessment.* Each of these components and the related tasks (Fig. 02 at p- 21) is a specialized field in itself and needs to be learned in a scientific manner with a proper understanding of the theoretical principles and practical implications.

The task of an undergraduate instructor becomes more challenging because he or she is dealing with a large group of young adults who are themselves passing through a difficult time. As discussed in the preface, undergraduate students have their own fears and apprehensions. They are entering a new, unfamiliar learning environment and are overwhelmed by the complexity of the content and the new patterns of course delivery and assessment. They suddenly find themselves among a peer group that comprises students from other states and countries. Added to all this is the fear of failure. An undergraduate instructor has to be not only a domain expert but also a philosopher, psychologist, sociologist, and motivation manager. Managing all this efficiently can be very daunting. In the absence of any training, most instructors work intuitively and depend on their personal experiences of how they were taught by their teachers. However, the entire instructional process as well as student needs and expectations are undergoing rapid changes, and practices need to be updated to get the desired results.

So, how does an instructor take charge of his or her own professional development? The instructor will need to adopt a scientific and systematic approach and identify suitable resources. Fortunately, today, a number of resources are available, including books, scholarly articles, faculty development workshops, and professional courses. ***Undergraduate Teaching*** is also designed for this specific purpose. It aspires to serve as an effective and user-friendly resource. It identifies the challenges generally experienced in the different areas of college teaching and provides practical solutions for managing them efficiently.

Once you have identified a resource, you need to carefully plan your professional development as a proper project. The following six-step plan yields excellent results:

Fig. 1.3 – Plan for Personal Professional Development

The starting point is always defining your vision for yourself—how do you want the world to see you? Once you have clearly spelled out your professional goals, you need to self-assess your competencies and identify areas that need attention. For this purpose, you may choose instruments I and II that help you get a comprehensive evaluation of your strengths and areas that need attention. Now, create a plan with clear deadlines. These deadlines are often very difficult to keep, but having a deadline is an important part of the plan. Depending on your plan, you will identify the most suitable resource and work on the identified areas. It is highly recommended to work on one aspect at a time. Supposing you feel you need to work on your course planning, student engagement, and designing better assessments, choose one aspect to focus on at a time. At the end of the semester, self-assess yourself for improvement and update your plan. Often, when we decide to work on attending to one shortcoming, a number of other things fall into place as well. A set of practical tips for taking charge of your professional development is provided at the end of this section.

1.6   Teaching Philosophy Statement (TPS)

What is a *Teaching Philosophy Statement* (TPS)? A TPS is a statement of your personal ideology about what education at the level you are teaching should aim to achieve. It is a reflective document about your beliefs, values, and approach to teaching. TPS allows you to reflect and communicate your views about the role of an educator in managing the course content, student needs, and other related aspects. Your TPS is a personal benchmark for your aspirations and performance, but it must align with the mission statement of the institution you work for.

Your TPS is also a part of your professional plan. It guides you to set and achieve your short and long-term goals. A clear and comprehensive TPS serves as the blueprint that details out the different milestones to be achieved in a timely manner. It helps to monitor your progress and provides clarity to yourself and others about your goals and methodology. It helps you improve teaching as well as learning.

Moreover, a TPS comes in very handy when you are applying for promotion, a new job, a research grant, or an international collaboration. Most institutions and funding agencies require a TPS attached to the application dossier.

1.6.1 Composing a Teaching Philosophy Statement

The *Teaching Philosophy Statement* is a personal document and must be based on your own personal opinions and observations. It is natural that the Teaching Philosophy Statement of every instructor is different. Typically, a *TPS* has two areas of focus: one on personal ideology, beliefs, and aspirations, and the other on professional goals, performance, and plans for advancement.

To describe the personal ideology, beliefs, and aspirations, asking yourself the following questions can be very helpful:

- What are my professional aspirations? How do I want the professional world to see me?
- What should be the qualities of an outstanding university educator?
- How should an educator engage with the students?
- How do I fare on my own vision?

To capture the professional goals, performance, and plans for advancement, you need to examine the *on-the-ground* requirements for being an outstanding college educator in terms of managing the different responsibilities assigned to you (your courses, the academic and motivational needs of your students, and administrative responsibilities). The following questions can facilitate the brainstorming process:

- Do I have the academic proficiency required to teach the courses well?

- What is my relationship with my students? Am I supporting them well?

- How well am I managing the different responsibilities? Which areas need immediate attention?

- What are my short-term goals? What do I want to do this semester or this academic year?

- What are my long-term goals? Where do I want to be in two to three years?

If you are serious about your performance and professional growth, your TPS can serve as an indispensable tool. It is like your professional diary, which is both your companion and your guide at the same time. Of course, it is a dynamic document that needs to be reviewed and updated regularly.

1.7   Section 1: Wrap-Up and Tips for Planning Your Professional Growth

As can be seen, there are two clear objectives for this opening section. First, to look inward and self-evaluate yourself on how you are faring as an undergraduate instructor at this point in time, and the second objective is to create a plan of action (with a schedule) for fixing the deficient areas.

Two instruments have been provided for instructors to self-evaluate themselves and take stock of their strengths and shortcomings. The first instrument is based on Joseph Lowman's *2-D Model of Effective Teaching*. Lowman claims that an instructor's effectiveness is dependent on how well the two dimensions of the model—*Intellectual Excitement* (IE) and *Interpersonal Rapport* (IR)—are managed. The second instrument, *Seven Attributes of Outstanding Undergraduate Instructors,* is developed in-house and is based on the feedback received from instructors and students. Each of the seven attributes has been explained in detail. Both instruments complement each other and together, provide a holistic view of where we stand on the professional excellence ladder at this point in time. Based on the knowledge gained through the two self-evaluation exercises, the participants are guided through the process of creating an action plan by composing a personalized *Teaching Philosophy Statement* which further stimulates the reflective process and helps the instructors to create a plan of action for becoming an outstanding university instructor. Given below are some tips for monitoring your professional growth.

Table 1.c – Tips for Monitoring Your Professional Growth

Tip	Recommendations
1.	Take time to reflect and understand your deeper aspirations as an academician and set your personal and professional goals and aspirations.
2.	Get clarity about your current competencies by self-evaluating yourself. Use the Instrument I (based on *Lowman's 2D Model of Effective Teaching)* and Instrument II – *Seven Attributes of Outstanding Undergraduate Instructor* to identify the dimension/s and attributes that need attention. Based on the results of the two self-evaluations, make a list of your strengths and shortcomings. Draw up a time-bound action plan for working on your weaknesses and reinforcing your strengths.
3.	Create a *Teaching Philosophy Statement* that documents your ideology about your profession and lists your goals in terms of who you want to be and how you plan to contribute to the lives of your students and the profession at large. Reinforce your commitment by specifying deadlines and creating a calendar for reviewing your progress every semester or every year.
4.	Substantiate this by creating a detailed weekly plan for yourself that will include time allocation for managing different activities for i) course preparation, ii) student management, and iii) personal growth. Please note that often you may not be able to follow this plan but having a plan is in itself an important first step.
5.	Maintain a course file to keep notes about what difficulties were faced; how certain parts of the course were received, and assimilated by students; and which activities worked, and which did not.
6.	Spend time to familiarize yourself with the theoretical background of all key components of the teaching-learning process. Knowledge of theories deepens the understanding, helps to refine the practice, and build confidence.
7.	Plan to read at least two research papers every semester – one related to your discipline and the other related to best practices and innovations in teaching methodologies.

2 # Understanding the Phenomenon of Learning

2.1   I Am an instructor, and My Job is to Teach

All professions involving human interaction are bilateral in nature; so is teaching. Whether you are a doctor, lawyer, psychologist, a religious head, or teacher, your success depends not only on your expertise in the domain knowledge but also on your competency in identifying and meeting the needs of the beneficiaries. As college professors, we are in the business of teaching, but what do we know about how students learn? It is true that as instructors we take our profession very seriously and put in sincere effort to update our domain knowledge and prepare well for our classes, but our entire focus is on teaching. The general attitude is that *my job is to teach*, and it is the *students' job to learn*. What we forget is that teaching is meaningful <u>only</u> when it leads to learning. The question we should be asking is: *I am teaching: are my students learning?* This crucial connect between teaching and learning is often ignored. Even though the two terms: *teaching and learning*, are often used in unison, in practice, we seldom connect the two. This section is devoted to understanding the phenomenon of learning so that the teaching can be made more effective. The objective is to get full clarity about the phenomenon of learning: how it happens, what factors promote or thwart it, and, above all, what we as undergraduate instructors need to *know* and *do* to ensure that learning happens in their classes.

2.2   Learning Defined

It seems obvious that any discussion about *Teaching* must start with a clear understanding of the phenomenon of *Learning*. The term *learning* is both general and specific and has been defined in different ways. Definitions of the term range from '*gain knowledge of a subject or of how to do something*' (*Longman Dictionary*) to '*modification of behavior through practice, training, and experience'* (*Dictioary.com*). In the academic context, the term learning becomes more complex and may be defined as a highly structured, intentional process for imparting knowledge and higher-order skills like interpretation, application, analysis, evaluation, etc. A different definition of learning comes from *Ambrose et al.* who define learning as a *"direct result of how students interpret and respond to their experiences – conscious and unconscious, past and present."* (*Ambrose et al. (2010)*. Learning has also been explained as "…. *shorthand for encoding and storing information in long-term memory from where it can be retrieved and used."* (*Felder-Brent, 2016*).

In recent years, neuroscientists have brought out new facts about how the human brain learns and stores information. Our attention is drawn to the role of short-term and long-term memory, and their connection to learning. A simple way to explain this connection is to analyze the difference between *information* and *knowledge*. When new input is received passively, it is stored in short-term memory as information, but when it is analyzed and internalized, it is stored in long-term memory as *knowledge* that can be retrieved and used as and when needed.

2.3   The Science of Learning

To get an in-depth understanding of the phenomenon of learning, we need to take a scientific approach and take guidance from the enormous body of research on the topic. Also referred to as education psychology or cognitive psychology, the science of learning focuses on deciphering the process by which human beings learn and the related aspects that influence the process of learning. Once we understand how learning happens, we can structure instruction to be more effective. To get an in-depth understanding of the phenomenon of learning, we need to examine some of the major theories that provide a scientific explanation of the phenomenon.

2.4   Some Theories of Learning that are Relevant for Undergraduate Teaching

We know that every practice, significant or insignificant, simple, or complex, is based on a theoretical framework. Similarly, learning theories help instructors to understand the scientific principles on which most teaching practices are based. Knowledge of learning theories not only explain why a certain practice works or does not work, it also empowers the practitioner to master, modify, and refine the practice. A confident practitioner is, by default, well-grounded in theory. Innovation is impossible without a clear understanding of the theory behind the practice. Knowledge of theories helps to connect teaching to learning and improve both teaching efficiency and student learning experience.

Plato
(Credits: Internet)

Understanding the phenomenon of learning has been a subject of great interest to educationists for centuries. As early as 400 BC, Plato raised the question about how humans learn. He believed that human soul had innate knowledge, and when it came across familiar experiences, learning happened as a recall process. Even though Plato's explanation did not find much acceptance, he believed that learning must be a continuous process and to this end, he established the first institution of higher education, *The Academy*, a philosophical school in Athens.

Over the centuries that followed, thinkers, educationists, and psychologists continued to present different explanations to decipher the mystery of human learning.

Edward Thorndike
(Credits: Internet)

It was not until the mid-nineteenth century that Edward Thorndike brought a scientific approach to the study of learning and laid the foundation of *Educational Psychology* as a discipline. He proposed that learning is incremental and that it is important to *"structure the environment to ensure certain stimuli that would 'produce' learning". (Hilgard & Bower, 1975).* Once Thorndike initiated the scientific approach to the study of learning, there was no looking back, and today, a substantial body of research is available on every possible aspect of learning as it happens in different age groups, in different disciplines, and in different learning environments (traditional, online, independent study etc.).

One can spend years studying these theories. However, as practicing undergraduate instructors, our main interest is to use the scientific knowledge to sharpen our teaching methodology. We want to use the knowledge to design and deliver our course content so that learning is maximized. For that purpose, we will look at *four* major theories that are of special relevance to undergraduate instruction. Here, each theory will be discussed briefly, mainly from the point of view of its practical impact. A large number of scholarly resources are available for each of these theories, which can help a serious investigator get a more in-depth understanding. The four learning theories that every undergraduate instructor should be familiar with are:

- Theory of Constructivism

- Zone of Proximal Development Theory

- Social-Emotional Learning Theory

- Brain-based Learning Theory

Many of the practices recommended in this book are informed by these theories, and we will be revisiting each one of them in different context across different sections.

2.4.1 Theory of Constructivism

The theory of constructivism is attributed to Jean Piaget, a Swiss educationist, and provides a scientific explanation of how learning happens. According to this theory, learning happens only when the learner is actively engaged in working with the new input (reflecting, analyzing, manipulating, applying, etc.) rather than just receiving it passively by listening to a lecture or watching a video lecture, etc.

Jean Piaget
(Credits: Internet)

Piaget believed that learning happens in the context of the learner's *schema* (the existing cumulative knowledge base comprising of ideas, beliefs, experiences, perceptions, etc.) that each one of us carries within us. To fully understand the theory of constructivism, we need to understand the constituent principles on which the theory is built. According to Piaget's theory of constructivism, once the learner receives the new input, a two-step process takes place that includes i) ***Assimilation*** – how the new input is added to the learner's pre-existing knowledge base (*schema*), and ii) ***Accommodation*** – how the schema is modified through interaction with the new input. This results in learners constructing a personalized understanding of the new knowledge, which is stored in their long-term memory.

The theory of constructivism is explained clearly by Catherine Fosnot in her book *Constructivism: Theory, Perspectives, and Practice*. In the Preface of the book, she explains: "*Constructivism is about knowledge and learning; it describes both what "knowing" is and how one 'comes to know*". Later, she goes on to say that *"...a constructivist view of learning suggests an approach to teaching that gives the learners the opportunity for concrete, contextually meaningful experience through which they can search for patterns; raise questions; and model, interpret, and defend their strategies and ideas"*. *(Fosnot, 2005).* In other words, *Constructivism* can be best described as a learning theory that holds that knowledge is best gained through a process of reflection and active construction in the mind of the learner *(Mascolo & Fischer, 2005).*

Recommendations for the Instructor

- Once the new input is delivered, create opportunities for students to interpret, reflect and manipulate the new knowledge provided so that they can re-construct and internalize the new input in their own minds.

- Even though learning happens when the new input is manipulated by thinking, reflecting, analyzing etc., the critical importance of the initial delivery of the new input must not be underestimated. This is the most important ***first step*** of the learning process. It is essential that the initial input is properly packaged and delivered so that maximum number of students can understand it for further processing.

2.4.2   The Zone of Proximal Development Theory

This theory was proposed by Lev Vygotsky, a Russian education psychologist. The theory focuses on the social aspects of learning that involve acquiring, interpreting, and internalizing knowledge.

Lev Vygotsy
(Credits: Internet)

Vygotsky claimed that all learning happens in a socio-cultural context and involves social interaction. The theory of *Zone of Proximal Development (ZPD)* claims that the learner can achieve higher levels of performance while working with a more knowledgeable one, whether it is a peer, a facilitator, or the instructor. In ZPD, Vygotsky brings out the difference between what students can achieve by themselves and what they can achieve while working collaboratively with others *(Vygotsky & Cole, 1981)*. This extended learning with a *more knowledgeable one* is the reason why social interaction (student-to-instructor or student-to-student) becomes so important for reinforcing learning, especially at the undergraduate level, because of the sudden jump in the quantum and the complexity of the content that students have to cope with.

Recommendations for the Instructor

- Provide opportunities to students to work together so that they can learn from each other and improve their academic performance.

- Ensure that the ambiance in class is relaxed where students are comfortable to ask questions, offer critiques and comments to promote active engagement and in-depth understanding.

- Develop a culture of giving and taking open and continuous feedback to encourage incremental learning (*Scaffolding*).

- Set up an effective system where students can help each other (*peer-tutoring* or *buddy system*).

2.4.3   Theory of Social-Emotional Learning (SEL)

The *Theory of Social-Emotional Learning* (SEL) is a relatively new addition to the inventory of learning theories. This theory is not attributed to any one individual scholar but seems to have evolved over a period of time as a result of work done by several different scholars and educators. Certainly, Albert Bandura's *Social Learning Theory (Bandura, 1977)* seems to have played an important role in laying the foundation for this theory. The Social Learning Theory claims that *learning occurs through observation, imitation, and modeling and is influenced by factors such as attention, motivation, attitudes, and emotions (Hammer, 2011)*. The theory focuses on how learning is affected by interaction between environmental and cognitive elements.

Taking a broader view, SEL proposes that academic and professional success is enhanced when students are trained to take charge of their social and emotional well-being. SEL emphasizes that the acquisition and application of skills to manage their emotions, make responsible decisions, and build positive relationships help students succeed in life and contribute effectively to the community. The work of two other well-known scholars, *Howard Gardner* (through his *Theory of Multiple Intelligences*) and *Daniel Goleman* (through his research in *Emotional Intelligence*), has also made important contribution in shaping this theory.

In 1994, a group called *Collaborative for Academic, Social, and Emotional Learning* (CASEL) was created to undertake serious research in SEL. CASEL identified five skills that form the core of SEL – *Self-awareness, Self-management, Social Awareness, Responsible Decision-making,* and *Relationship Skills*. This implies that instructors must recognize the importance of SEL and incorporate strategies that help students to understand and manage their emotions and social interactions.

Clearly, the SEL theory is of immense value to the undergraduate student population in building self-efficacy and self-confidence, which in turn helps them to enhance their academic performance. Moreover, these skills are of paramount importance for young men and women who are getting ready to step into the real-world as young professionals and need to learn how to manage their emotions, build positive relationships, and make responsible decisions.

Sustained efforts are required from both the institutions and the faculty to incorporate elements of SEL into regular classroom teaching. The institutions need to put in place some special programs to generate awareness about the need for developing core SEL skills. Peer-support programs or workshops on topics such as interpersonal communication, emotional intelligence, conflict resolution, effective negotiation, etc. can be invaluable for undergraduate students.

Recommendations for the Instructor

- Include activities that involve self-evaluation and reflection so that students become aware of their own emotions, strengths, and areas for improvement.

- Create opportunities for students to work together, and learn to accommodate, and nurture good relationships.

- Be a role-model and demonstrate good social-emotional behavior demonstrating control over your own emotions and showing respect to one and all.

2.4.5   Brain-Based Learning Theory: What Neuroscientists Tell Us

Since the 1980s, neuroscientists have presented some amazing findings about how the human brain learns. We are told that learning is an automatic process: as long as the brain is functional, learning will happen. Learning happens when the brain encodes and stores information in long-term memory *(schema)* so that it can be retrieved and used when required. As a result of these studies, a new discipline called 'brain-based learning' is fast gaining recognition. The importance of this discipline can be assessed by the fact that Harvard University, USA, offers a master's and a Doctoral degree program in this field ("Mind, Brain, and Education (MBE)" program), and there is a peer-reviewed scientific journal on brain-based education as well as a professional society called the *International Mind, Brain, and Education Society* (IMBES).

Brain-based learning helps us to understand the relationship between learning and the two types of memory – short-term memory and long-term memory.

Some of the key findings registered by brain-based learning that are relevant to undergraduate teaching are:

- Learning happens when the brain creates new neural networks. Active learning interventions (when students are engaged in doing rather than listening) promote the creation of new neural networks.

- The brain processes information in small chunks.

- Repetition enhances long-term memory.

- Emotions strengthen memory.

- Our brains are programmed to focus on new and unusual input.

- Social interaction promotes learning.

Renate Caine
(Credits: Internet)

The new insights provided by brain-based learning have encouraged educators to research and develop strategies that can be applied in regular classroom teaching. Educators like, *Renate Caine, Geoffery Caine,* and *Eric Jensen* have developed practical strategies that attempt to incorporate findings of the brain-based learning in classroom instruction.

In their book, Renate Caine and Geoffrey Caine elaborate upon the neuropsychological functions of the brain during learning and suggest how the information can be used by instructors to create a more meaningful and effective learning experiences for their students *(Caine, R. N., & Caine, G., 1991).* Similarly, using the findings of neuroscience, biology and psychology, Eric Jensen has developed practical strategies for creating a favorable environment that motivates students to actively participate and take charge of their academic, social, and emotional success. *(Jensen & McConchie, 2020)*

Geoffery Caine
(Credits: Internet)

Eric Jensen
(Credits: Internet)

Even though there is still much to be learned about how brain learns, stores, and retrieves information, there seems to be a system for prioritizing what information gets stored in long-term memory. Information, events, and applications that are logical, meaningful, and connected to one's experience are more easily understood and stored in long-term memory. This implies that the instructor must choose explanations and examples that are well within the experience range of the learners so that they are easily understood and retained.

It is interesting to see that many findings of the brain-based learning theory confirm and validate constructs proposed by academicians centuries earlier when nothing was known about how the brain functions. Based on the input provided by different theories (the *Brain-Based Theory*, the *Constructivist Theory*, and the *Zone of Proximal Development Theory*), we can identify a five-stage process that scientifically explains the process of learning. Each of these five stages is important, and the instructor must navigate through them carefully so that student learning is maximized.

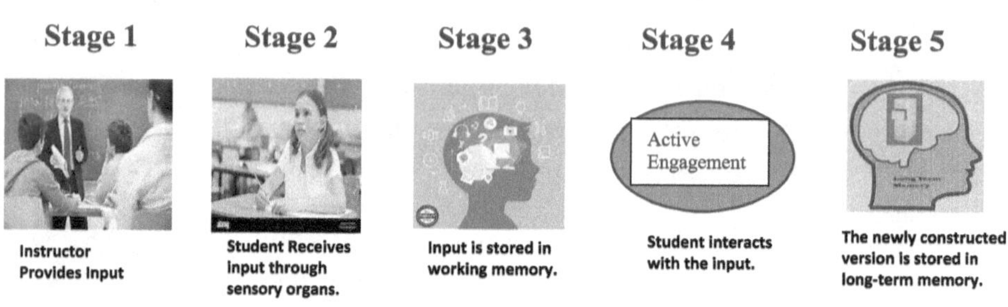

(Photos Credits: Internet)

Fig. 2.2 – A Simplistic Representation of How Learning Happens

The process of learning begins with the instructor providing the input (stage 1). This is an important first step in the process, without which nothing can happen. However, contrary to what many of us instructors believe, this is not the end of our responsibility; a lot more remains to be accomplished. Students receive the input provided in class through sensory organs (by listening to the lecture or viewing a PowerPoint presentation or a video) (stage 2). The received input is stored in *working memory* (stage 3). It is known that an estimated 50–80% of input stored in working memory is lost over 24 hours. To ensure that the input provided is fully internalized and assimilated, the instructor must create opportunities for the students to manipulate the new information alone or in small groups, inside the class or outside the class, so that they can work with the input and internalize it (stage 4). Once the students get an opportunity to manipulate and work with the input through active learning activities (by analyzing and applying it for problem-solving), they re-construct the input that is stored in long-term memory (*schema*) to be recalled as and when needed. (stage 5). The *schema,* we are told, is stored in clusters of neurons spread across different parts of the brain. If the information is repeated often, the schema becomes stronger making it easier to retrieve the information. *(Mastascusa et al., 2011).*

There is little doubt that a clear understanding of how learning happens can guide the instructors to structure and implement instruction more effectively. A substantial amount of information about each of the theories discussed above is available, and a serious investigator can readily access to delve deeper and learn more about any one or all theories discussed in this section.

Recommendations for the Instructor

- Brain-based theory tells us that learning happens when new neural networks are created, and new and unusual input help to develop new neuron networks. Make sure to include new and interesting input in the form of explanations and examples.

- Plan to deliver instruction in small bites to match the brain's capacity for processing and retaining new knowledge. This will avoid overload and promote learning.

- Ensure that key concepts are repeated in different forms (in-class activities, quiz etc.) because repetition strengthens the neural pathways and deepens the understanding.

- Once the initial input is provided, create opportunities for students to interact with it and internalize it.

- As students learn differently, use different modes to deliver content.

- Finally, ensure that the environment in your class is welcoming, pleasant, and relaxed.

2.5 Domains and Levels of Learning

Two other aspects of learning that every college instructor must be conversant with are the domains and levels (taxonomies) of learning. There are three domains of learning:

1. ***Cognitive domain*** –This domain relates to knowledge and includes intellectual processes of learning and acquisition of new knowledge by using skills such as interpretation, analysis, problem-solving, and evaluation.

2. ***Affective domain*** – This domain relates to emotions and involves the development of emotional responses to instruction at large (ideas, content, process, and peers). It focuses on the impact of feelings (positive or negative) on a learner's motivation, attitude, and joy of learning.

3. ***Psychomotor domain*** – This domain relates to kinesthetics and includes the development of a whole range of physical activities, ranging from basic motor coordination to complex maneuvering skills.

Speaking in a more casual way, the three domains are respectively linked to the *head*, the *heart*, and the *hand* of the learner. Scholars believe that instruction that includes more than one domain of learning promotes richer and more wholesome learning experiences.

Of the three domains, the role of the *affective domain* is often undermined in the learning process. As emphasized in brain-based learning, there is a strong connection between emotions and learning. We know from experience that students perform well in subjects that they like. Students also perform well when they feel comfortable in the learning environment and experience an emotional bond with their instructor. A positive learning environment is inclusive and promotes a sense of belonging. The impact of this positive affective environment is directly reflected in students' academic performance.

2.6 Levels (Taxonomies) of Different Domains of Learning

Each domain (Cognitive, Affective, and Psychomotor) operates at several levels at which learning takes place. These are described in terms of Taxonomies. The term *Taxonomy* refers to "the science or technique of classification into ordered categories" (*dictionary.com*). The taxonomies provide crucial guidelines for defining course outcomes and designing assessments. Clarity about the taxonomies used for each domain allows the instructor to differentiate and manage different levels (lower to higher order) of learning. The graphic below provides a comprehensive view of the different levels of learning in each of the three domains.

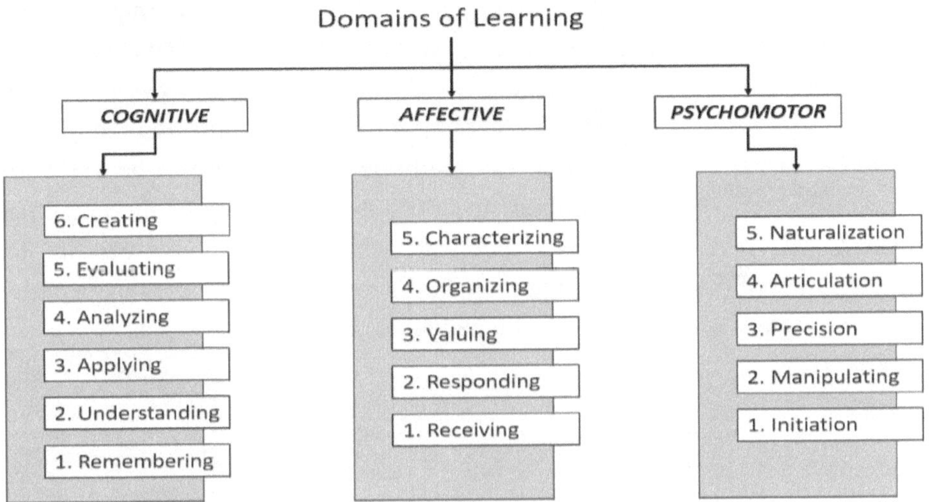

Fig. 2.3 – Taxonomies of the Three Domains of Learning

While each domain and its hierarchical set of levels (described by the specific taxonomy) has its own importance in higher education, the curriculum designers normally rely on the taxonomy of the cognitive domain especially when it comes to composing learning outcomes and assessment. Taxonomies of the affective and psychomotor domains are used for a specific range of learning activities. Taxonomies of the affective domains are used for disciplines such as sociology, philosophy, or the fine arts that involve subjective perceptions or values. Taxonomies of the psychomotor domain are used mostly for courses that have a practical component or deal with manual operations such as conducting laboratory experiments or setting up or operating equipment etc. For a better overall control, it is important for undergraduate instructors to be fully conversant with all three domains of learning and their respective taxonomies.

2.6.1 Taxonomy of the Cognitive Domain

The credit for developing taxonomies of different domains of learning often goes to Benjamin Bloom, but in fact, a number of people were involved in this research and contributed towards this body of knowledge over a period of 1956 to 1971.

Benjamin Bloom
(Credits:Internet)

The taxonomy of *Cognitive Domain* was proposed by Benjamin Bloom in 1956. He proposed that learning can be classified into six hierarchical levels: *Knowledge, Comprehension, Application, Analysis, Synthesis,* and *Evaluation.* The value of this taxonomy was recognized immediately especially as it was found to be valid for all disciplines. In 2001, this taxonomy of the cognitive domain was revised by L.W. Anderson, who was also involved in the development of the original taxonomy. In the revised taxonomy, the *Synthesis* level was taken out, and a new, higher level, *Creating,* was added above *Evaluation.*

The revised Bloom's Taxonomy of Cognitive Domain also has six levels: *Remembering, Understanding, Applying, Analyzing, Evaluating,* and *Creating (Anderson and Krathwohl, 2001),* and has fully replaced the earlier version. In this book we will be also using the revised Bloom's taxonomy. Table 2.a explains each of these six levels with the help of competencies associated with it.

L.W.Anderson
(Credits:Internet)

Table 2.a – Taxonomy of Cognitive Objectives

Level	Description
Level 1 – Remembering	The learner is able to recognize, recall, or list facts and related information.
Level 2 – Understanding	The learner is able to describe, explain, or translate the learned facts and information.
Level 3 – Applying	The learner is able to apply, employ, or demonstrate new knowledge to explain a phenomenon or solve a problem.

Level	Description
Level 4 – Analyzing	The learner is able to break down complex information to explain how parts relate to each other and the whole.
Level 5 – Evaluating	The learner is able to judge, compare, or assess the newly learned facts, and information.
Level 6 – Creating	The learner is able to use the newly learned fundamentals, facts and principles to design, assemble, construct or create.

As mentioned earlier, undergraduate instructors need to be conversant with taxonomies of all three domains. However, for structuring the course content and designing assessment, the knowledge of the taxonomy of cognitive objectives is critical. We will be revisiting this taxonomy in subsequent sections to learn how to use it most effectively for writing course outcomes (pp - 100-103), and designing assessment (p -239).

2.6.2   Taxonomy of Affective Domain

This taxonomy was published in 1964 by David Krathwohl, who was also a joint author of Bloom's initial version of the cognitive domain. The affective domain

deals with feelings and emotions, and theories of brain-based learning and SEL highlight the importance the importance of emotions in learning. The taxonomy of this domain is classified into five hierarchical levels, as discussed in Table 2.b.

David Krathwohl
(Credits:Internet)

Table 2.b – Taxonomy of Affective Objectives

Level	Description
Level 1 – Receiving	The learner passively receives information. However, this is a very important first step without which no learning can happen.
Level 2 – Responding	The learner is actively involved in the learning process.
Level 3 – Valuing	The learner attaches value to the acquired information and knowledge.

Level	Description
Level 4 – Organizing	The learner organizes different ideas and values within her own schema and consolidates her learning.
Level 5 – Characterizing	The learner interprets and builds abstract knowledge.

2.6.3   Taxonomy of the Psychomotor Domain

This taxonomy addresses the learning objectives specific to kinesthetics (body movements) and reflexes for interpreting and furthering knowledge and skills. All laboratory work and activities, such as creating a field survey or a model of a building, looking through a microscope, driving a car, baking a cake, etc., fall under this domain. We can see that a thorough knowledge of the taxonomy of the psychomotor domain is important while planning experiential learning activities.

The Taxonomy of the Psychomotor Domain was initially proposed by Anita J. Harrow in 1964. That version had seven levels: *Perception, Set, Guided Response, Mechanism, Complex Overt Response, Adaptation, and Origination*. This taxonomy was revised several times till a simpler, widely accepted version was proposed by R.H. Dave in 1970. The revised taxonomy has five levels – *Initiation, Manipulation, Precision, Articulation*, and *Naturalization* that are explained in Table 2.c.

Table 2.c – Taxonomy of Psychomotor Objectives

Level	Description
Level 1 – Initiation	The learner is able to see and directly copy the action.
Level 2 – Manipulating	The learner is able to complete the action under guidance or by following instructions.
Level 3 – Precision	The learner is able to independently execute the action.
Level 4 – Articulation	The learner is able to use the acquired expertise to complete the action under different situations, parameters, and conditions.
Level 5 – Naturalization	The learner is able to complete the action automatically and confidently without guidance or instructions.

Over the years, studies have continued in this domain. An even simpler taxonomy of psychomotor objectives was proposed by Moore in 1998. This one had only three levels: ***Imitation*** (perform by imitating the demonstration), ***Manipulation*** (perform by following instructions), and ***Precision*** (perform accurately, efficiently, effortlessly, and automatically without help).

2.6.4   Fink's Taxonomy of Significant Learning

It is interesting to note that research in the field of learning domains is ongoing, and from time to time, modifications and adaptations of the original taxonomies are proposed. One taxonomy of interest is the *"Taxonomy of Significant Learning"* proposed by Dee Fink, in 2013. This new taxonomy includes components from Bloom's original taxonomies of the cognitive and affective domains. The model is easy to understand. This taxonomy has three components from Bloom's taxonomy of cognitive domain: *fundamental knowledge* (facts, information); *application* (critical thinking, applying fundamental knowledge to solve problems), and *Integration* (making connections with facts, people, and the real-world). It has three components from the affective domain: *the human dimension* (metacognition, knowledge about yourself and others), *Caring* (attention to others' needs and being available for help), and *Learning to Learn* (working on being a self-directed learner or researcher).

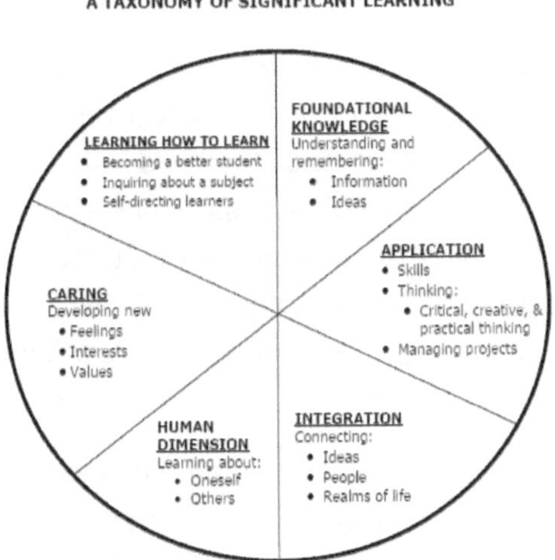

[Source – Fink, 2003: 30; image from Google Images]
Fig. 2.4 – Components of Fink's Taxonomy of Significant Learning

Despite being based on Bloom's taxonomies of cognitive and affective domains; Fink's *Taxonomy of Significant Learning* is radically different in format. Unlike earlier taxonomies, these components are non-linear. As can be seen from Fig. 2.2, the different components of Fink's *taxonomy* are independent and yet closely connected with each other. The non-hierarchical structure offers more flexibility and interactivity. Fink's taxonomy is found to be particularly useful when instructors want to develop courses using the backward design discussed in detail in Section 4 (p - 98).

2.7 Section 2: Wrap-Up and Tips for Harnessing Learning

The main objective of this foundation module is to make instructors aware of the need to connect teaching with learning. As instructors our focus is mainly on teaching, and we forget that teaching is meaningful only when it generates learning. It is, therefore, very important for instructors to study how learning happens. To this end, four important theories of learning that are of direct relevance to undergraduate instruction, are discussed. Each of the four theories—the *Theory of Constructivism* (Jean Piaget), the *Theory of Proximal Development* (Lev Vygotsky), the *Social-Emotional Learning Theory*, and *Brain-Based Learn*ing – explains one or more aspects of learning. Some key recommendations based on these theories are shared that the instructors can adopt to ensure that learning happens in their classes.

Other important dimensions of learning that college instructors must be cognizant of are the domains and levels of learning. The three domains of learning – *Cognitive, Affective,* and *Psychomotor* and the corresponding taxonomies are introduced. Given their importance in the pedagogical process, these taxonomies, especially the Taxonomy of Cognitive Objectives, will be revisited several times in different contexts in which they are used. A new and well-accepted taxonomy, – *Taxonomy of Significant Learning,* is also discussed.

The table below lists some practical, research-validated tips and strategies that instructors can adopt to ensure that their teaching translates into learning. The rationale, formats, and methods for successfully implementing each of these strategies will be further reviewed in the subsequent sections. Table 2.d lists recommended teaching strategy along with the theoretical frameworks that validates each strategy.

Table 2.d – Tips for Harnessing Learning and Identifying Supporting Theories

Tip	Teaching Strategies	Supporting Theoretical Framework
1.	Prepare content in small learning bites so that course content is easily understood and assimilated.	Brain processes information in small chunks. (*Brain-based Learning*)
2.	Punctuate passive listening in class with active learning where students have the opportunity to revisit, discuss and manipulate the newly acquired knowledge.	Learning happens when learners are actively engaged in manipulating newly acquired knowledge and create their own version of knowledge that is stored in long-term memory. (*Theory of Constructivism – Jean Piaget*).
3.	To promote learning, plan activities where students are asked to work together. The activities can be in-class or outside the class, and can be completed in pairs, small groups, or large groups.	Social interaction promotes learning. Students perform better when they are working with peers. (*Theory of Proximal Development – Vygotsky* and *Brain-based learning*).
4.	Do not hesitate to experiment with new tools and methodologies.	Brain is programmed to focus on new and unusual input and processes (*Brain-based Learning*).
5.	Make sure that proper mechanisms are put in place for taking regular feedback. This must be followed by providing constructive and encouraging guidance.	Regular review and repetition promote retention. Positive reinforcement and emotions strengthen learning. (*Brain-based Learning*)
6.	Keep the affective filter low by creating a relaxed classroom environment. Recognize and compliment students on their performance and progress, however small.	Emotions strengthen learning. Students learn best in a relaxed environment. (*Brain-based learning*)

Tip	Teaching Strategies	Supporting Theoretical Framework
7.	Make sure to explain the most important/core concepts using different modes – lecture, visuals, simulations etc.	Students process information differently. Also, repetition reinforces learning (*Brain-based learning*)
8.	Become familiar with the different domains and taxonomies of learning. Make sure to fully master Bloom's Taxonomy of Cognitive Objectives because it is used for designing learning outcomes as well as assessment.	Knowledge about domains and levels of learning helps the instructor to organize teaching as well as assessing learning in a more scientific manner.

<table><tr><td>3</td></tr></table>

Managing Student Needs

3.1 Meet Your Gen Z Students

Most undergraduate students are in the age group of 18–22 years and belong to what is popularly known as Generation *Z (Gen Z)*. Much like their predecessors, the *Millennials (students born after 1990 – after the advent of the internet)* the *Gen Z* learners (*students born after 2000 – after the advent of social media*) share common personality traits that have a strong bearing on the way they learn. As instructors, we must know our students well so that the instruction is designed to maximize learning for the maximum number of students in class.

A substantial body of research is available about the personality traits and learning needs of this generation of learners. Some of the well-recognized personality traits of Gen Z learners are that:

- They have a strong affinity for technology,
- They enjoy autonomy,
- They enjoy social interaction,
- They enjoy researching information,
- They have a very short attention span, and
- They work best in a relaxed environment.

Because of their atypical behavior, the students are often judged as being *indifferent, disinterested,* and at times, even *disrespectful.* Clearly, we need to readjust our glasses and view our Gen Z students as individuals who have different learner profile and aspirations. Their academic, emotional (affective), and employability needs are also very different. Educationists agree that the specific learner profile and learning needs of Gen Z students warrant substantial modifications in teaching methodology. Understanding these needs and devising strategies for meeting them is the main objective of this section.

3.2　Managing Student Needs: Major Challenges

Gen Z students have high expectations from college education. Most students expect to enter the job market after completing their undergraduate studies. On the other end, the expectations of the job market from graduating students have become much more demanding, which puts new pressures on undergraduate instruction and instructors alike. Consequently, the success parameters for 21st-century undergraduate instructors have expanded beyond mere course completion. Today, undergraduate instructors are faced with several challenges arising out of changes in learner profiles as well as the demands of the job market. Meeting these challenges successfully requires substantial rethinking and re-planning on the part of the instructors as far as teaching methodology and the management of student needs is concerned.

Listed below are some of the main challenges that most undergraduate instructors face while managing their Gen Z learners:

- Establishing a close rapport with the students.
- Identifying their individual needs
- Integrating skills to get undergrads ready for the job market.
- Managing student differences.
- Keeping students motivated.
- Managing disruptive behavior.

All these are real challenges, and a close examination shows that all of them are interconnected in some way or the other. Let us examine each of these challenges to understand the reasons and consequences so that suitable strategies can be adopted for managing them.

3.3   Building a Rapport with Your Students

In Section 1 (p - 26), we learned from Joseph *Lowman's 2-D Model of Effective Teaching* that *Interpersonal Rapport* (IR) is one of the two dimensions essential for promoting learning; *Intellectual Excitement* being the second dimension. We also know that the environment in which students work impacts their motivation and emotional well-being, which in turn, impact their academic success.

If we were to calculate the number of hours a typical undergraduate student spends in college over four long years, it becomes obvious that providing a warm, empathetic, and caring relationship with their students becomes an important responsibility of undergraduate instructors. This implies that the instructors must set aside time and make the effort to know their students well.

Two strategies that work well for establishing a close rapport with the students are: i) learning their names; and ii) getting to know them as individuals (as opposed to a class).

3.3.1   Learning Your Students' Names

The best formula for establishing rapport with your students is to be able to call them by their names. This implies that we need to learn their names, which, given the large class size, is not an easy task. However, we should treat this as a 'no option' situation and be prepared to invest the time and effort to make it happen. The practices proposed below are found to be very effective.

Using Student Introduction Cards

One of the most effective tools for remembering students' names is using a *Student Introduction Card* (see sample below). How it works is that instructors request students to bring a passport-size picture on the first day of class while s/he carries a bundle of 5" x 7" (or 4" x 6") index cards and a few glue sticks. Ask students to fill out the intro cards as shown in the slide: name, birthday, contact number, email address, hobbies, and respond to one multiple-choice question about their preferred learning style: *I learn best by i) reading and making my own notes. ii) watching videos, and iii) working with friends.*

The introduction cards are very helpful in memorizing the names. The memorization process can be further facilitated by using different color cards for girls and boys. The photos on the index cards help the instructor to link the name to the face. Start by remembering the names of five girls and five boys. During the first 5–7 classes, bring these cards to class and begin calling students by name (it doesn't matter if they see you consulting the cards).

<table>
<tr><td>

Name:
Birthday:
E-mail:
Mobile No.

I learn best by (Circle the applicable option)
a) Reading & making my own notes
b) watching videos
c) working with friends,

</td><td>

Photo

</td></tr>
</table>

Fig. 3.1 – Student Introduction Card

The *Student Intro Card* provides valuable information (the birth date) that can be used to further the interpersonal rapport with the students. The instructor can create a tradition of wishing birthdays in class. Use the cards to develop a spread sheet listing the birthdays (it should not take more than 2 hours to do that). Before going to class, note the names of the students who have their birthdays on that day or in – between classes. The few minutes spent here will go a long way in promoting positive vibes in the classroom.

An effective alternative to using the introduction cards is creating a *virtual photo roster*. Require each student to send you a 'Greetings' email message with a photo and personal information like name, birthday, their hobbies, their preferred learning mode, and their expectations from the course. To ensure conformity, post the information you want included in the email, along with your email address. An initiative to learn students' names does wonders in setting up a communication channel and helping students get over their initial hesitation to approach you. Once you have the intro-cards or e-mails, you can create a plan to memorize names of students in your class.

Creating a Seating Chart

Another effective strategy for remembering names is to create a weekly seating chart for the first three weeks or so. Explain to the students that the seating chart is your personal strategy to get to know them well, and everyone will get a chance to sit in the first two rows by rotation. On day 1, come prepared with the seating chart for the first two rows. Call each student to come and sit in the specific space indicated on your chart. Make sure you have a good mix of boys and girls. Tell them that these are their seats for the next two classes. You will be surprised to learn that you will be able to call at least a few students by name immediately. Next week, rotate the seating chart and remember the faces and names of the new set of students. Later, once you have a better idea of students' academic levels, you can create ***mixed-ability seating,*** which is extremely useful for promoting effective student engagement and learning.

3.3.2   Getting to Know Your Students as Individual Persons

Given the size of undergraduate classes, this is also a major challenge. Students in a typical undergraduate class have different academic and motivational needs, and to address them efficiently, we need to know them as individuals so that more personalized and focused support can be provided to them.

As instructors, we want to provide the best possible support to our students, and for that we need to first identify the area where help is required. It is a fact that there are many different reasons why students may perform poorly. For example, there may be one student who does not have sufficient background knowledge, and another student may not have the right analytical and problem-solving skills to manage college-level content. There may be another who has poor linguistic proficiency and may have difficulty understanding the lectures. Once the instructor has a general idea about the learning needs of different sets of students in class, a suitable support system can be put in place.

In addition to academic support, some students also need help with motivational adjustment. We should not forget that these students are new to the college environment and are struggling with their own set of challenges. We saw in Section 2 (p - 52) that the affective domain (emotional connect with the content and environment) is very important for academic success. This is reinforced by Brain-based Learning that tells us that *emotions strengthen learning*. We know that when a student says, 'I hate Physics or Geography', it is understood that either he has failed in the subject or does not like the instructor. To provide motivational support to the students, it is important that the instructor identify the students who need assurance that the best possible support will be provided. Observation shows that there is a close connection between motivational needs and academic performance. When students have poor academic performance, they lose motivation and get emotionally disconnected, at the same time, when students are unhappy or stressed, they generally do not perform well, and the strategies used for providing academic support can also help in building emotional strength and overall confidence.

The simple practice of celebrating student birthdays mentioned earlier is a very simple and effective strategy for establishing rapport with individual students. The practice not only helps the instructor remember students' names but also works wonders in breaking the communication barrier and encouraging students to open up and participate more actively in class.

Of course, the main avenue to get to know your students as individuals (as opposed to a group of learners completing a course) is through the effective use of office hours. In a normal university setting, most instructors have declared office hours but, in most cases, these are underutilized. Even when instructors make it a point to be available, hardly anyone shows up. As instructors, we feel we have done our share, and if the students do not want to avail of this facility, it's up to them. While it is true that students are not always excited to take advantage of office hours, we should not forget that students have much less free time than we do. On average, undergraduate students attend 3–5 courses, and it is quite possible that they have other classes at the times your office hours are scheduled.

Clearly, the office hours need to be better organized. We instructors should begin with the premise that students have limited free time and are reluctant to ask for help (especially when they need it most). This means that we need to set up a system that will encourage them to connect with you so that you can get to know them and provide both academic and motivational support.

One strategy that generally works well is to ask students to pick up their *first* graded quiz or assignment during office hours. By slotting about 4-5 minutes for each student, you can go over the feedback and make a personal connection with them. Experience shows that this exercise, though a bit tedious for the instructor, is very helpful in breaking the hesitation barrier and encouraging students (even the shy ones) to feel more comfortable to interact with the instructor.

One important point to keep in mind is that connecting with high-performing students is equally important. This small population of students is often neglected because we are so busy taking care of average or below average performers. Bonding with high performers can be very rewarding for both the students and the instructor. These students can be prepared to undertake research and participate in inter-college competitions. They can also help the instructor by supporting students who need academic help.

If your class is very large, you may have to make special accommodations by holding additional *online* office hours. These are especially effective for small group interaction. To allow wider access, you may schedule one or two online office hours over the weekend. The online office hours can also be converted into small study groups.

3.4   Getting Students Ready for the Job Market

Today, the mission of undergraduate education is not limited to just degree completion but also making graduating students employable. Consequently, the responsibility of an undergraduate instructor goes well beyond course completion. We know that every student entering the university aspires to be suitably employed after the completion of the degree program, and we also know that completing the degree program does not automatically prepare a student for employment. Data from labor departments in different countries projects a high rate of unemployment among graduating students. This is mainly because a substantial percentage of graduating students lack proper preparation for the job market. It is important for undergraduate instructors to recognize that their responsibility does not end with just completing the course. A conscious effort is needed to incorporate methodologies and activities that will help the students develop skills required to be job-ready.

The required skills and competencies for becoming employable have been identified by corporations, employers, and university accreditation bodies. During its meeting in Devos in 2016, the *World Economic Forum* (*WEFORUM Meeting Overview, 2016*) listed the following ten skills for 21st-century graduates to become competent to successfully participate in the fourth industrial revolution:

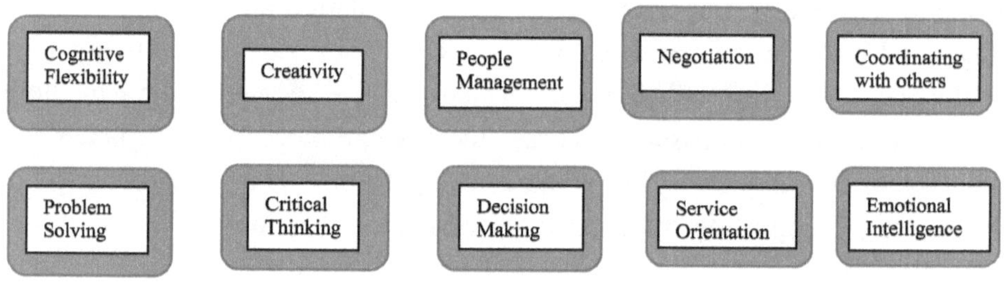

(https://www3.weforum.org/docs/AM16/AM16_MeetingOverview.pdf).
Fig. 3.2 – Employability Skills for 21st Century Graduates

The Accreditation Board of Engineering and Technology (ABET) recommends a slightly different list of skills that graduates in STEM disciplines need to acquire to become employable. This list includes skills such as: *In-depth knowledge of concepts, Complex problem-solving, Using technology tools, Analyzing, and interpreting research data, Applying knowledge for societal good, Concern for the environment, Professional ethics, Working in teams, Communication skills, Project management,* and *Lifelong learning.*

It is crucial for undergraduate instructors to not only recognize the importance of these 21st century employability skills and graduate attributes but also make the development of these competencies an integral part of their course planning and delivery. At the same time, the instructors must make students aware of the importance of developing these skills early in the program. Strategies discussed in subsequent sections keep a sharp focus on this very important additional dimension of undergraduate teaching.

3.5   Understanding Student Differences

The other major challenge that undergraduate instructors face is managing the heterogeneity of their classes. Diversity comes in many forms and shapes, but the four main areas are:

- Students have different academic and motivational needs.
- Students have different socio-cultural profiles.
- Students have different learning styles.
- Students have different levels of course readiness.

3.5.1   Students Have Different Academic Profiles

A typical undergraduate class is heterogeneous, with a mix of students with different intellectual capabilities and levels of motivation. One of the best rewards of investing time and energy to get to know your students at the individual level is that you are able to plan the right type of support needed by different sets of students. Identifying and addressing these needs is essential for keeping your class productively engaged in learning.

It normally takes a couple of weeks of class interaction and at least one formal assessment to get clarity about the academic profile of the class and identify the needs of the different sets of students. Broadly speaking, four different sub-sets of students can be typically identified in almost any undergraduate class. Using the metaphor from athletics, the sub-sets may be classified as the *Winners*, the *Active Runners*, the *Survivors,* and the *Outsiders.*

Table 3.a – Academic Profiles found in a Typical Undergraduate Class

Type	Characteristics
The Winners  (Credits:Internet) 15-20% of class strength	These are highly motivated, <u>high-performing</u> students who have a high level of self-efficacy and commitment. These students have clear goals and know how to work towards them. All work is submitted on time and is of high quality. Unfortunately, this set of students gets the least amount of attention from the instructors. *Recommendations for the Instructor – This is a special sub-set of your class that needs a different kind of support. The instructor can keep these students challenged by setting up special research and innovative projects. Their leadership qualities can be nurtured by allocating them a couple of students to be mentored from the low-performing group.*
The Active Runners  (Credits:Internet) 60-65% of class strength	This is the largest sub-set and students here are dedicated and mostly diligent. They are actively engaged in class activities and try to do their best. They have clarity about their goals but do not always know how to work toward them. Assignments and class work are submitted on time but may be of inconsistent quality. These students are well-adjusted and motivated but clearly, they need help in managing their learning so that their academic performance matches the effort. *Recommendations for the Instructor – Generally, instructors tend to pitch their course delivery at this level of learners. However, additional effort is needed to plan interaction at the personal level to support them more effectively..*

Type	Characteristics
The Strugglers  (Credits:Internet) 10-15% of class strength	The performance of these students is <u>below average</u> due to several different reasons. They want to participate in class activities and perform better but are reluctant to. They lack confidence and feel limited. They hesitate to ask questions and the work submitted is of 'below expectations' quality. *Recommendations for the Instructor – Clearly, these students need support in both the academic and motivational areas. Begin by organizing a separate office hour for this group that can be used as a study group. Teach them how to help themselves through self-correcting materials (handouts& quizzes) posted in the virtual classroom. It may also help to assign them a team leader from the Winners' group.*
The Outsiders  (Credits:Internet) 3-5% of class strength	This is the smallest and most challenging sub-set of the class. These are generally disengaged and low performers. Due to several different reasons, they feel de-motivated and disconnected from the instructor, peers, and the content being taught. They do not like to participate in class activities and at times, may be disruptive. Often, the work is not submitted on time, and when submitted, it is of poor quality or plagiarized. *Recommendations for the Instructor – Clearly, these students need support in both academic and motivational areas. The instructor should meet privately with individual students and identify reasons for their attitude. It may be best to set up a buddy system for these students. If needed, the instructor may take help from the college counsellor.*

Once you have clarity about the needs of different sets of students, you can plan strategies to address them by setting up very focused support activities.

3.5.2 Students Have Different Demographic and Socio-Cultural Profiles

In a typical university class, it is not at all uncommon to see students coming from a variety of demographic and socio-cultural backgrounds. There are students who come from cosmopolitan, urban, semi-urban, and rural backgrounds. They have different socio-cultural and economic backgrounds. In addition to the demographic and socio-cultural differences, the parental educational profile also plays a big role in the level of students' self-efficacy and self-confidence. In a typical class, you may find one student whose parents are both high-profile professionals (doctors, engineers, lawyers, etc.), another whose father has college education, but the mother has barely attended school, and yet another student who is a first-generation college student (the first one in the family to enter college). Strange as it may seem, even in very advanced countries, there are still a fair number of first-generation college students. Instructors need to be aware of these differences that directly impact students' motivation and approach to learning.

The demographic, socio-cultural, and economic background often determine the type of schooling the student has experienced, and the study skills acquired during schooling play an important role in determining their success in college. The impact of the socio-cultural and economic background can be observed during in-class participation, peer interaction, and knowledge management, which in turn impacts their self-esteem and academic performance.

3.5.3 Students Have Different Learning Styles

Learning style may be defined as the preferred method of an individual learner for acquiring, structuring, processing, and assimilating new information or a skill. The origin of the term *learning style* is often associated with the *Theory of Multiple Intelligences,* proposed by Howard Gardner, a professor at Harvard University.

Howard Gardner
(Credits: Internet)

For a very long time, the ability to learn and apply the learned knowledge was measured in terms of the "Intelligence Quotient" aka IQ. In his *Theory of Multiple Intelligences*, Gardner suggested that human beings have not one but many different intelligences (*Gardner, 1983*). He listed seven of them: ***Linguistic, Logical, Spatial, Musical, Bodily, Interpersonal, Intrapersona***l. In 1993, Gardner added an eighth intelligence called ***Naturalistic Intelligence*** *(*the ability to recognize and classify patterns in nature). In 1996, a ninth intelligence, ***Emotional intelligence*** was added by Daniel Goleman who believed that emotional intelligence has direct bearing on a person's performance *(Goleman, 1996)*. There is a strong recommendation that another intelligence, ***Spiritual Intelligence,*** should be added to this list.

The *Theory of Multiple Intelligences* established that different intelligences impact the way people learn and perform. Based on personal strength, every learner learns differently or has a different learning style. The subject of learning styles drew a lot of attention of the 20th-century academicians, and a number of instruments have been developed that can help both the learner and the instructor to identify different learning styles. Each instrument has a different format and focuses on some or all of the following seven styles:

Table 3.b – The Seven Universally Accepted Learning Styles

Learning Style	Modes and Materials
Visual learner	Learns best through pictures, videos, drawings, graphics.
Aural – Auditory	Learns best by listening to lectures, presentations, discussions.
Verbal learner	Learns by writing and negotiating through words.
Logical/Analytical Learner	Learns by deciphering patterns and connecting concepts using an analytical approach.
Social learner	Learns best through interaction with others; is sensitive and empathetic. This category of learners has strong verbal and non-verbal communication skills and work well in teams.
Solitary learners	Learns best by thinking and reflecting alone; prefers a quiet Environment

Learning Style	Modes and Materials
Physical or Kinesthetic Learner	Learns best by "hands-on". Instead of observing, learning happens by doing. The learner prefers to work with hands and feels the need to move around.

In 1984, David Kolb proposed the *Experiential Learning Theory,* which suggests that individual learners have a preferred way of processing learning through their experience. He calls it the *Kolb Experiential Learning Profile* (KELP). Kolb identified nine different ways in which learners can process the experiential learning cycle – ***Initiating, Experiencing, Imagining, Acting, Balancing, Reflecting, Deciding, Thinking***, and ***Analyzing***. A lot of material is available on *Experiential Learning Theory,* and it would be worthwhile for instructors to examine some of the scholarly articles and get background knowledge about it.

Some Commonly Used Instruments for Identifying Learning Styles

To measure different learning styles, Neil Fleming proposed the VARK model in 1987. The VARK model included four main learning styles: ***Visual, Auditory, Reading-Writing***, and ***Kinesthetic.*** This was followed by a spate of models, tests, and inventories proposed by different researchers. Most of them are built around different combinations of the basic components mentioned above. Most of these instruments are free, though some ask for a nominal fee. Some of the very popular instruments are:

1. ***Learning Style Quiz:*** *The* instrument has 40 questions, and the participants can get immediate results with recommendations.

2. ***What's your Learning Style?*** The instrument has 20 questions focusing mainly on learners with visual, auditory, or tactile preferences.

3. ***Learning Style Quiz*** by ThoughtCo: The instrument has only 10 questions and focuses mainly on learners with visual, auditory, or tactile preferences.

4. ***What's my Learning Style***? by Quizterra: This instrument has 10 very interesting questions and goes beyond the learning style; it considers some of the personality traits.

5. ***Felder-Silvester Inventory of Learning Styles:*** This is perhaps the most scientific of the learning style tests *(Felder, R.M.; Silverman, L.K., 1988)*. This 44-item questionnaire is based on 8 learning styles: *Intuitive, Sensory, Visual, Verbal, Active, Reflective, Sequential,* and *Global.*

More information about each one of them is available, and many more such instruments may be available by the time you decide to recommend one of them to your students.

Should Students Know Their Learning Style?

There is some evidence that being aware of one's learning style helps to manage one's own learning better. It is true that a student's learning style is often shaped by a student's cognitive ability, emotional connect to the content being studied, and the environment in which it is being studied. However, we must look at different learning styles objectively because no one style is better or worse; each one of them is different.

As for instructors, it is observed that their teaching style is unconsciously influenced by their own learning styles, so in order to overcome this limitation, it is useful for instructors to have clarity about their own preferred learning style. Being aware of your own learning preferences and the learning preferences of your students can help you design instruction more intelligently. Even though there is no solid evidence to support that tailoring classroom instruction according to different learning styles impacts students' overall performance, it seems logical to recommend that instruction be delivered using a variety of modes and formats so that everyone benefits irrespective of his or her preferred learning style. This strategy is especially effective for undergraduate courses that deal with a diverse student population and multi-layered, complex content.

Recommendations for the Instructor

- Know that despite all the different labels, it is hard to place a learner in black or white category of learning style. Experience shows that most students use a combination of different styles, and therefore, it is best to just treat them as *learning preferences.*

- Do not fret too much about managing different learning styles. It is almost impossible for an instructor who is managing a class of 50 + students to worry about the learning styles of individual students. It is best to plan to deliver key components of your course using different modes. For example, while teaching a core concept, you may use a PowerPoint presentation, simulation, or demonstration in class, provide the key points or a summary in a handout, and upload additional examples, and practice materials in the virtual classroom. This should take care of the learning preferences of most of the students.

3.5.4   Students have Different Levels of Course Readiness.

In an undergraduate class of 50+ students, it is normal to see students with different levels of preparation for managing college-level courses. This becomes challenging, especially for courses with prerequisites. Differences in class readiness can be observed in three main areas:

- Inadequate background knowledge

- Inadequate study and technology skills

- Inadequate linguistic proficiency

Inadequate Background Knowledge

This is the most common lacuna an instructor is faced with. It is important that the instructor anticipates this and, proactively, plans to address it. To do this effectively, the instructor needs to first identify this group of students who have inadequate background knowledge and then plan to support them right from the beginning of the semester. A simple way to identify this group of students is to conduct a quiz based on prerequisites in the first week of class. Once students needing help are identified, a record should be kept to mentor them closely. A practical strategy is to color-code the names of these students on the roster. This allows the instructor to keep a discrete watch on their participation and performance in class activities.

If, from your previous experience, you can identify key concepts from the pre-requisite courses that students are likely to have difficulty with, you can prepare support materials and make them available in the virtual classroom. Here, technology can be used very effectively and efficiently. Key information, definitions, and formulae related to prerequisites and background knowledge can be posted in the virtual classroom (see *How to Set Up a Virtual Classroom*, pp - 196-199). You can proactively create short worksheets for the key concepts from the prerequisites, create some practice exercises and self-correcting quizzes, and upload them in the virtual classroom.

Inadequate Study and Technology Skills

Depending on their demographic profile, type of schooling, and family background, many students are unable to make a smooth transition from high school to college. Some of the reasons are their inability to manage the quantity of content, type of assignments, group work, problem-solving skills, time management, etc. Some students do not have adequate proficiency in using technology which is fast becoming an integral part of the undergraduate learning experience. Lack of these skills interferes with the academic performance of these students. Two effective ways to address this are: i) using the buddy system; and ii) providing a study-guide.

In the *buddy system*, the instructor pairs up one low-performing student with one high-performing student for peer mentoring. This works wonders for both partners. The high-performing students also benefit a lot from enhanced confidence, leadership qualities, and, above all, the joy of giving.

The practice of providing a *study-guide* benefits all students but is a boon for students who are more comfortable with the written word. The study-guide helps these students organize their study schedule and approach. Here, the instructor prepares handouts that provide additional explanations and examples for the sections of the course that need in-depth processing and are important from the exam point of view. The study-guide also includes important information about examinations – what type of questions will be asked, sample questions, how to prepare for them, and what is expected for *A – grade* responses.

Inadequate Language Proficiency

Success at the college-level requires high proficiency in the language in which the undergraduate studies are being delivered. Lack of language proficiency interferes with students' ability to read, research, participate in class activities, and understand assignments, and this in turn negatively impacts their performance, confidence level, and the joy of learning.

With the globalization of higher education, this problem has become more pronounced because of the increase in numbers of international students. This deficiency is observed mainly in the Anglophone world, where higher education is delivered in English, and the English language is the students' second or even third language. The negative impact of insufficient proficiency in English is noticeable in all disciplines for different reasons. In STEM, Law, and Management, it is because of content that involves the use of technical terms and complex explanations. In Humanities and Social Sciences, linguistic competencies are essential for composing logical and persuasive arguments that are generally presented in long narratives and reports.

This lacuna goes mostly unrecognized (and uncorrected) because of self-denial, though it can be fixed easily if both the instructor and the students take it seriously. The instructors are strongly advised to use simple words and short sentences while designing class presentations, handouts, instructions for assignments and tests, etc. At the same time, they must make these students aware of how the lack of linguistic competence can negatively impact their academic and professional performance.

Some of the strategies that can be used to help these students are:

1. *Explore college resources* – due to the influx of international students, most *Colleges* these days have writing labs or writing centers where programs for helping these students are already available. The instructor needs to take the initiative to help enroll these students in these programs. Help can also be sought from the Institute's or University's *English department* to set up a study group for peer-tutoring these students. If such a system does not exist, the instructor can help the group to hire a graduate student to work with them.

2. ***Use the Buddy System*** – involves identifying a few students with high linguistic proficiency to mentor these students individually or in small groups. The instructor can guide the mentors to provide constructive help by using tasks such as:

   i)   writing short explanations of the concepts learned in class,

   ii) creating a list of the most commonly used technical terms in the discipline, and working on their pronunciation and usage,

   iii) making students practice answering questions or explaining simple concepts, etc.

3. ***Identify and recommend online resources***. Nowadays, a lot of online resources are available that students can use privately to improve their competence in writing and speaking English. Take the time to identify and recommend <u>one</u> suitable program that the students can follow.

3.6   Managing Student Motivation

One of the key challenges for undergraduate instructors is to keep the students motivated so that they are actively engaged in taking charge of their own advancement. In many ways, motivation dictates student success. When students are motivated, the instructor's task becomes easier, more pleasant, and more productive. Therefore, keeping students motivated is an integral and significant part of effective teaching. We have all observed that students are extremely excited and motivated when they first enter college, but as semesters progress, many of them begin to lose motivation.

Motivation has been described as a need or desire to do something well. Motivation is the driving force that helps us reach our goals. In other words, student motivation is the intensity of the desire students feel to excel at their courses. It is the 'engine' of learning (*Paris & Turner, 1994*). Motivation determines the quality of performance: the higher the motivation; the better the performance. According to Schunk & Usher, motivation can influence what we learn, how we learn, and when we choose to learn (*Schunk & Usher, 2012*). Motivation is demonstrated through drive and energy. Many factors impact student motivation, including interest, perception, desire, self-confidence, self-esteem, patience, monitoring, and persistence *(Sass, 1989)*.

To fully understand how motivation can be sustained, it is important to first identify the factors that dampen student enthusiasm and demotivate them. The students' declining motivation and consequent disengagement in coursework is a 'live' problem that is reflected in poor attendance, late and low-quality assignment submission, absenteeism, and active plagiarism.

To prevent this from happening, it is very important for the instructor to be aware of i) the factors that cause demotivation and ii) the type of students who are likely to lose motivation. Clearly, students get demotivated when their expectations are not met. Every batch of incoming students has expectations that may be very different from those of their instructors.

For students, entering college after long years at school is a major landmark event in their lives. They feel they are stepping into a new world and expect everything, including courses, lectures, peer interaction, labs, etc., to be different and exciting. These students are used to a very protected environment and are used to a lot of handholding. The transition from school to college is challenging for most students. It is like asking a young person who is used to swimming in a swimming pool supervised by a lifeguard to jump into an open ocean and deal with the mysteries and unpredictability of the unknown.

For instructors, on the other hand, these students are adults who must take responsibility for their own learning. Both sides have a long list of grudges: instructors find students disorganized, irresponsible, and lazy, while students find instructors apathetic, condescending, and boring. Clearly, this mismatch of expectations is the key cause of student demotivation. It is important for instructors to be vigilant and keep a sharp eye out for catching early symptoms of demotivation so that the reasons can be addressed promptly in a scientific manner.

Table 3.c – Symptoms & Reasons of Student Demotivation

Symptoms of demotivation	Reasons for demotivation
Poor attendance and academic performance.	Confused priorities, poor background knowledge, poor study skills, lack of guidance, etc.
Feeling of isolation and being unwelcome; reluctance to interact with peers.	Diverse socio-economic background; lack of study skills and/or linguistic competencies.
Feel disconnected with the instructor, hesitant to speak or ask questions; reluctant to attend office hours.	Find instructor condescending, inaccessible and apathetic.
Reluctant to participate in class activities and collaborative projects.	Poor language and communication skills resulting in lack of self-esteem and self-confidence.
Worried and stressed demeanor.	Social or financial constraints – loans, family investment in college education; pressure to meet parental expectations.

Along with clarity about the symptoms, reasons, and factors that promote and demote motivation, the instructors must educate themselves about the major theories of motivation that are of direct relevance to undergraduate teaching. Armed with this knowledge, they can develop practices that can help promote and sustain student motivation.

Motivation is of two types: *Intrinsic* motivation and *extrinsic* motivation. *Intrinsic* motivation is what the learner feels from within (*desire to excel*), while *Extrinsic* motivation is dependent on an external trigger (*a reward, bonus marks*). Obviously, *Extrinsic* motivation is temporary, and its effect is linked only to the reward. Intrinsic motivation, on the other hand, is permanent. While both types of motivation are important for students, the instructor must focus on promoting intrinsic motivation.

3.7   Some Relevant Theories of Motivation

There is an enormous body of research available on student motivation. The four theories selected to be discussed here are of direct relevance to promoting motivation in college students as well as in professionals at workplace. Based on the principles proposed by these theories, strategies can be developed to ensure that the students stay motivated and make the most of their time in college.

3.7.1   Theory of Human Motivation: Hierarchy of Needs

Abraham Maslow
(Credits: Internet)

Abraham Maslow, an American psychologist, proposed the *Theory of Human Motivation* in 1943. Maslow's theory claims that humans are motivated by need. His famous model of the *Hierarchy of Human Needs* classifies human needs into five levels in order of importance. Starting with the first and most fundamental need, *Physical Survival* (food and shelter); the model includes *Safety, Love & Belonging, Self-esteem* and *Self-actualization*.

The close connection between need and motivation can be easily observed in the realm of academics. We know that students, especially adult students like our undergraduate students, are motivated directly by *Need*. This is the main difference between how young and adult students learn. If you ask an 8-year-old to memorize a poem, a definition, or a formula, she is not likely to question why she needs to do so. On the other hand, adult learners always question the rationale for every activity they are asked to do. It seems logical to believe that students are likely to be more receptive and motivated to learn if they know why they need to learn a specific concept, theory, or process.

Recommendations for the instructor

- When you start a new topic or a new learning unit, always begin by explaining why the specific content needs to be learned. Place the new knowledge in the context of the course outcomes as well as of the real -world applications.

- Plan instruction to address not only students' academic needs but also their social emotional, and employability needs.

- Set up a discreet and efficient system that encourages students to identify their own academic needs and seek help as early as possible.

3.7.2   Equity Theory of Motivation

J Stacy Adams
(Credits: Internet)

The *Equity Theory of Motivation* was proposed by J Stacy Adams in 1963 and links motivation to the basic human values of fairness and equality. The term *equity* refers to an individual's belief that she is being treated fairly in relation to her peers or colleagues. The theory emphasizes that all individuals want to be treated equally, and adults expect that their efforts to be recognized and rewarded in proportion to the effort made by them and that they will be rewarded in the same manner as others. Students, like employees, are very sensitive and get easily demotivated if they perceive some kind of bias. They are always watching and comparing performances and grades with colleagues and peers. It is, therefore, very important for instructors to be transparent in all interaction with students and ensure that students do not perceive any bias or discrimination.

Recommendations for the instructor

- Ensure that all interaction with the students is open & transparent. Provide grading rubrics for all assignments, and set-up an easy and confidential system for addressing complaints.

- Maintain active communication with your students. It is a fact that we instructors do not take the time to explain our plans and intentions, and the students are often left in the dark with a lot of questions that they are afraid to ask.

> • All policies and performance guidelines must be put in writing and well-publicized either through handouts or postings in WhatsApp or virtual classroom.

3.7.3   The X – Y Theory of Management

Douglas McGregor
(Credits: Internet)

This theory was proposed by McGroger, a social psychologist. Initially proposed for sustaining employee motivation, the theory is equally relevant in the context of managing motivation of college students. The theory talks about two styles of adult interaction: **X** (*Authoritarian)* and **Y** (*Participative)* that directly impact human motivation *(McGregor, 1964)*. Given the profile of our adult Gen Z students, The Y style of management works much better.

It is observed that many instructors, especially young female university instructors, tend to adopt the authoritarian stance (X) because they are afraid to lose control. When an instructor follows the X style (*Authoritarian*) of management, the learners feel alienated, lose motivation, and are reluctant to be fully engaged in the courses.

The class environment is very different when the instructor chooses the Y style of interaction. Recalling the personality traits of Gen Z learners discussed earlier the two characteristics: i) they like autonomy, and ii) they appreciate a closer relationship with their instructors, explain why the Y style of interaction works better for undergraduate students. When the instructor uses the Y (*Participative*) style of management, students feel respected and treated more like partners. This feeling of trust and respect encourages them to be more engaged and motivated to take responsibility for their own success.

Recommendations for the instructor

- Remember, your students are adults and deserve to be respected. Develop good rapport with the students by using some or all of the strategies suggested in the earlier part of this section.

- Make students your partners in the learning process. Request high performing students to help with mentoring other students.

- We know that generation Z students enjoy autonomy. wherever possible, create opportunities to involve them in decision-making however small (e.g. *how many members should we keep in each group,* or *how many days you will need to complete this assignment?*)

3.7.4   The ARCS Theory of Motivational Design

John Keller
(Credits: Internet)

This theory was proposed by John Keller, an academician who has done extensive work on student motivation. This theory is of direct relevance to classroom instruction. Keller recommends that to sustain student motivation, instruction must include four key components: *Attention*; *Relevance*; *Confidence*; and *Satisfaction* leading to the acronym ARCS in the title. Keller's ARCS model proposes a start to end process that can be implemented successfully to plan effective lectures. It is important to understand each of these components well.

Attention: The motivation process begins with a well-designed opening of the lecture that must capture the full attention of the learner and place the new knowledge in the context of the overall course outcomes. A good introduction promotes curiosity and interest. There are many ways to accomplish this that are discussed in Section 5 (pp -126 -127).

Relevance: Students are motivated when they feel that the new knowledge or activity is relevant and deserves the time and effort required to learn it. As can be seen, both these components – *Attention* and *Relevance* – are connected, and one single strategy can be adopted to meet these two requirements.

Confidence: This refers to the learner's perception that she can easily grasp and master the new knowledge or skill being studied. This means that the instructor must design instruction in such a way that every student in class feels that he or she can understand and master it. This is rather challenging and needs to be planned carefully. A sure strategy to manage this is *scaffolding,* which involves making students progress in small steps. For example, instructor teaches a small segment and then asks the class to complete a really simple task based on it. Slowly, the level of complexity can be increased. This builds confidence in the minds of the learners and motivates them to go on to the next level of complexity.

Satisfaction: The fourth and final component of the model implies that the students should leave the class with a feeling of satisfaction from having learned something new and valuable – something they did not know before. It is recommended that a proper closure be planned for each lecture. A number of effective ways of doing that have been discussed in Section 5 (p - 131). In any case, you must plan to keep a few minutes for reviewing and highlighting the new knowledge acquired during the lecture. Lectures (in traditional or online mode) designed using the ARCS model help the instructors ensure that student motivation is sustained from the beginning until the end of the class session.

Recommendations for the Instructor

- While planning your lectures, pay attention to each of the four components of Keller's ARCS model – *Attention, Relevance, Confidence,* and *Satisfaction*

- Introduce every new concept or topic by establishing the relevance and the need for learning it.

- To develop Confidence, ensure that all students feel that they can learn and master the new knowledge or skills being taught. You must be very inventive to design activities/assessment that will help to scaffold learning and build confidence.

- To ensure that students experience *Satisfaction,* provide opportunity for self-evaluation and short group activities. Close every class session by summarizing what new knowledge/skill the students have learned in that specific session, and how the new knowledge is applicable in academics or/and at workplace.

3.8   Managing Disruptive Student Behavior

Along with the academic needs, the Gen Z students also have affective (emotional or motivational) needs that the instructors must watch out for. The student-teacher relationship is like that of a parent and a child. There is a constant struggle between imposing and resisting discipline. It is important for the instructor to maintain a good balance between being compassionate and firm. You want the rules to be followed without being controlling or disrespectful. If the institute does not have the rules, you need to create them for your class, and share them. These should also be posted on the course website for easy access.

Disruptive behavior is symptomatic of a deep-rooted emotional need. It may be defined as behavior that interferes with the smooth conduct of a class. It can be intentional or unintentional, but it always challenges the class norms and rules set by the institution or the instructor. Common examples of disruptive behaviors observed in college classrooms include:

- Talking loudly when the instructor or others are explaining or presenting.
- Making snide remarks to generate laughter.
- Monopolizing classroom discussions.
- Sleeping in class.
- Entering class late or leaving in between classes.
- Using or playing with cell phones in the classroom.
- Eating or sharing food in class.

In most cases, disruptive behavior results from a strong need to attract attention. In most cases, the behavior is not vicious or directed towards anyone personally, though it ends up causing disappointment and a loss of valuable class time. The key is to nip the disruptive behavior in the bud. If it is ignored or allowed to perpetuate (as it often happens because we all tend to avoid confrontation), it is likely to spread and become even more complicated to handle.

Managing disruptive behavior is part of the college teaching package, and it is better to preempt it and take anticipatory steps to control it. The first thing to remember is that you need to be a role model for your students. For example, you cannot expect students to come to class on time if you, yourself, often arrive a few minutes late.

The other thing to remember while dealing with disruptive behavior is that maintaining *privacy* is crucial. Whether it is an individual or a small group of students, the conversation should happen in private. Given below are a few suggestions for successfully addressing disruptive behavior. If we are careful from the beginning and make a genuine effort to connect with the students, this problem will become minimal or non-existent.

Table 3.d – Tips for Managing Disruptive Behavior

Tip	Managing Strategy
1.	Develop clear policies about ground rules related to issues where students are likely to trip up such as *late arrival or leaving in between a class, late submission of assignments, submitting plagiarized assignments, etc.* Share these policies and penalties on the first day of class, post these in writing in the virtual classroom, and keep reminding the students from time to time.
2.	Follow your own policies strictly and consistently across the class. Once the students know you are serious about discipline with no chance of getting away, they will follow it.
3.	Set-up a simple, practical, and confidential system for receiving and attending to complaints.

Tip	Managing Strategy
4.	If the behavior is totally unacceptable, involve someone senior from the department. Make sure you know the university policies and procedures before announcing punishments. If you are forced to take the issue to higher authorities, explain to the student the university policy, procedure, consequences as well as the reason why you are forced to take that action.
5.	Always stay in control. Be polite and respectful but not defensive. If possible, advise the student about the best course of action he/she can take. Never lose temper or shout at the students.

3.9   Participating in the Institute-level Mentoring Program

An additional and important responsibility that some undergraduate instructors may have to take on is to serve as a M*entor* in the Institute-level mentoring program. This is different from the regular practice of overseeing your own students. In this context, *Mentoring* refers to an official requirement of taking charge of *an assigned group of students* and supporting them in a structured manner throughout their entire stay at the university/institute. Many boutique colleges and private universities these days have a formal ***Mentoring Program*** where each full-time instructor is assigned 20 – 25 students whom he or she is expected to mentor. This is a highly structured activity that, if conducted seriously, can be a life-changing experience for the mentee. The process is equally rewarding for the mentor in terms of enriched human interaction and professional satisfaction. The mentor is expected to develop a nurturing relationship and ensure that the mentees achieve their academic goals, learn essential life skills, and maintain emotional well-being. If a student is not doing well, the instructors are expected to communicate with the mentor so that the necessary support and guidance is provided in time.

This is an amazing concept but unfortunately, it has not proven to be very successful. The typical format in which mentoring is conducted in most colleges is that the mentor has a monthly meeting that is open to all the mentees. Most instructors are dissatisfied with the results because most of the students do not come to the meeting, and those who do, have little to share or contribute. The following tips can help achieve a win-win situation:

Table 3.e – Tips for Effective Participation in the Mentoring Program

Tip	Recommendation
1.	Guide mentees to reflect and write down their goals. The goals may be related to academics or personality development. Remember you are also helping them to become employable.
2.	Set expectations right in the beginning and create a clear understanding about shared responsibilities. Create a short document to describe the type and the extent of support you will provide and what are your expectations from the mentees.
3.	The most important goal for you is to build trust. You will need to be an empathetic, active listener. Always provide encouraging, *constructive,* and timely feedback.
4.	You will need to set-up two different modes of communication. One with the entire group and the other with individual mentees. Clearly, the second mode will be exclusive and private. A mix of face-to-face and online interaction can be very effective and efficient.
5.	Plan the monthly meetings carefully. It is best to have a theme where the group will work together on a life skill like effective communications, time management, asking and responding to questions, becoming a productive team member etc.
6.	Plan an efficient way to stay in touch with individual mentees. If you receive negative feedback from any of mentee's professors, organize a private session for consultation.
7.	Guide the mentee to find his/her own pathway to success. Foster independent thinking and decision-making.
8.	At the end of the program, give a proper closure to the relationship. Help the mentees to draw up future plans for themselves.

3.10 Section 3: Wrap-Up and Tips for Managing Student Needs Effectively

This section is devoted to *student* management. Logically, the section begins by identifying the main challenges in managing student needs. Five most observed challenges are: i) establishing rapport with the students; ii) getting students ready for the job market; iii) understanding student differences; iv) keeping students motivated; and v) managing disruptive student behavior, have been discussed. To establish a healthy rapport with the students, the instructor must get to know them as individuals and not only as a group of students. We saw that learning students' names is a magic trick for establishing rapport with the students and merits the instructor's time and effort. Getting to know the personality traits of our Gen Z learners helps the instructors calibrate their expectations and make suitable adjustments to their teaching style.

A typical undergraduate class is by default a heterogeneous group made up of students from different demographic, socio-cultural, and economic backgrounds. Managing these differences requires the instructor to make a conscious effort to know them and their *academic* and *emotional* needs. As instructors, we mostly focus on providing academic support, while the reason for poor academic performance may be emotional. To provide effective academic and emotional support, two things are important. First, identify different subsets of students with similar profiles in your class, and second, plan a support system for each subset for the entire semester, starting as early as possible. Generally, instructors take additional classes and office hours towards the end of the semester or close to the final exams, which does not always bear the desired results.

Equally daunting is the challenge of keeping the students motivated. A number of theories of motivation that are directly relevant to undergraduate students are discussed. The symptoms and the reasons for demotivation have been identified so that the instructors can vigilantly monitor and address them as soon as they are spotted. The section closes with a discussion on the reasons for disruptive behavior by students and how best to manage it.

Table 3.f – Tips for Managing Student Needs Effectively

Tip No.	Recommendations
1.	Try and learn the names of your students and call them by name as often as possible. If you have made the effort to collect the information, create a tradition of calling out birthdays in class. This helps to make the class atmosphere very warm and pleasant.

Tip No.	Recommendations
2.	Establish an open, welcoming, and supportive environment in class. Take frequent feedback from students and keep them involved in their own learning.
3.	Be accessible to your students. Treat students as adults and give them the due respect. Make them partners in the learning process. Be generous with complimenting student achievement, however small. Always keep a pleasant, happy disposition – a smile always works wonders!
4.	Talk to students about 21st-century employability skills/Graduate attributes. Discuss the identified skills, and how you plan to incorporate strategies/assignments/activities that will help to develop these skills. Talk to them about the need to develop self-efficacy and lifelong learning (Section 2 - pp - 67 - 69). This will help you to get better cooperation from students in class participation.
5.	Plan office hours carefully. To address the needs of all students, arrange office hours online. Planning online office hours in the evenings or weekends is strongly recommended.
6.	Carefully study the different theories of *motivation* and follow the recommendations such as i) highlight the need for learning the content being taught (*Maslow*); ii) make content relevant by relating it to the real-world (*Keller*); iii) make students partners in the instructional process (McGroger).
7.	Present content in multi-modal formats using visuals, simulations, and in-class demonstrations so that a maximum number of learning preferences can be addressed.
8.	Try to identify different learning profiles (*Winners, Active Runners, Survivors,* and *Outsiders*) of students in your class. Identify their specific learning needs and create proper strategies to support each type.
9.	Schedule your office hours so that a maximum number of students can take advantage. Keeping one *online* office hour, preferably on the weekend is found to be very effective. Use office hours to provide both academic and emotional support.
10.	Provide short and simple instruments to help students identify their weaknesses and encourage them to take charge of their own learning. Guide students to set small achievable goals for themselves and provide resources for self-help.

Tip No.	Recommendations
11.	In addition to office hours, create online study groups. Here, small groups of students (3-5 students) with similar learning gaps/ needs are put together to work with specially identified/designed study materials. Self-evaluating quizzes may be provided. This strategy works very well for students with inadequate background knowledge required to successfully follow the courses.
12.	Another strategy that is invaluable for providing both academic and emotional support is setting up a *buddy system*. A buddy system involves pairing up a low-performing student or a student who needs emotional support with a high-performing student and a more mature student. The instructor should explain to the high-performing student how time and effort spent will be useful for his/her personal growth and offer to give a letter of appreciation/recommendation.
13.	When faced with an unpleasant situation with students, use a calm, non-confrontational approach/tone to defuse the situation. <u>Never lose your temper</u>. Demonstrate a sympathetic attitude. Listen carefully – ask clarifying questions that help to get to the bottom of the issue. Encourage the student/s to explain his/her stand. Make sure that all conversations happen in private.

<table><tr><td>**4**</td><td></td></tr></table>

Managing Course Content

4.1 Managing Course Content – Major Challenges!

One of the big worries of an undergraduate instructor is how to manage the course content effectively. There are two aspects involved here. The first concerns planning or structuring the course and the second, delivering it competently. This section focuses exclusively on course planning. Discussion about managing course delivery will be taken up in the next section.

Feedback received from participants during several faculty development workshops points to the following four main challenges faced by instructors regarding managing course content:

- Packaging the course content effectively: Most undergraduate students have difficulty coping with the complexity of new knowledge presented in every new course. The challenge is how to present it so that all students can master it successfully.

- Completing the coursework within the semester: the quantum of new information is constantly increasing, and most instructors find it hard to complete the course in time. Most end up having to take additional classes.

- Managing students with a lack of requisite background knowledge: it is observed that a fair percentage of students one inherits in the new course, lack the requisite background knowledge to understand and assimilate the new information.

- Managing students with a lack of collaborative, reflective, or analytical skills: we know how important these skills are for undergraduate instruction but depending upon the schooling these students have experienced, a large percentage of students lack these skills. The challenge is how to incorporate activities that will help develop these skills.

This section attempts to address these concerns and provide some simple and time-tested solutions. But, first, it is important for instructors to get a basic understanding of how curriculum developers design courses. Designing a course is a specialized activity, but as users or practitioners, a basic understanding of the rules, formats, structures, and models associated with the design process, can be very helpful in course planning as well as course delivery.

4.2 Some Popular Models of Course Design

There are several models for course design but the three most commonly used by curriculum developers and instructional designers are:

- **The ADDIE Model** is one of the most established models and comprises five main steps that form the acronym ADDIE: – *Analysis, Design, Development, Implementation,* and *Evaluation.* The model is popular with instructional designers because it is flexible and offers space for experimentation and modifications.

- **Fink's Significant Learning Model:** This model has been described in detail in Section 2 (pp - 57-58). This is a non-linear model that comprises six main components: *Foundational Knowledge, Application, Integration, Human Dimension, Caring,* and *Learning How to Learn.* This model has become very popular in recent years.

- **Design-Thinking Model:** This model is most suitable for courses in STEM disciplines that involve *problem-based* or *project-based learning.* Here, the students work independently or in small groups to analyze, solve problems or develop solution-based products. The model comprises five components: *Empathize, Define, Ideate, Prototype,* and *Test.*

In additions to these three models, there are many other models used by curriculum developers for different disciplines. A lot of research and practical information about each one of them is freely available for further study in case one wants to delve deeper into the subject.

4.3   Designing or Re-structuring a Course

Even though designing courses is the responsibility of curriculum developers or instructional designers, with increased autonomy in the academic space, more and more undergraduate instructors now have the opportunity to design their own courses or restructure existing ones. However, if you are designing a new course or restructuring an existing one as an instructor, there are only four core competencies that you need to be concerned about. These are *designing course learning objectives; selecting and structuring course content; choosing suitable learning resources;* and *creating assessment.* The success of the designed course will depend on how well you have planned each of these four components. This responsibility becomes even more serious if you are designing a required course which you know will be delivered to multiple sections by different instructors.

When we are designing a course, as instructors, we follow a typical sequence of activities. We start by *composing the learning outcomes* (what the students will be able to do at the end of the course), then *choose the learning resources* (textbook, video-lectures, practice manual, handouts etc.), then go on to *identifying content* (list topics/themes to be included in the course), and finally, *design assessment* (assignments, tests, projects, or anything else that can be used as evidence of student learning).

Learning Outcomes	Choose Learning Resources – textbooks, video lecture	Select Content/Develop Lectures/activities.	Plan Assessment

Fig. 4.1 – The Conventional Model Of course Planning

This system is basically focused on the content to be covered: facts, theoretical bases, formulae, etc. Often, the connection between the content to be covered, the outcomes, and the assessment used to measure the outcomes is arbitrary and somewhat unreliable. It is quite possible that learners' performance is not commensurate with the effort they put into completing the coursework and the knowledge/skills they have acquired.

4.3.1   The Backward Design Model

An innovative and improved format for course planning known as *The Backward Design* was proposed by *Wiggins and McTighe* (2005). Here, the four key components are re-sequenced as shown in Fig. 4.2.

| Write Learning Outcomes | Plan Assessment | Select content/Develop Lectures/Learning activities. | Choose Learning Resources – text, video/MOOCs. |

Fig. 4.2 – The Backward Design Model Of course Planning

Starting once again with the *course learning outcomes*, the planning moves directly to *designing assessment* to determine how the achievement of learning outcomes will be measured. Once the assessment pattern is finalized, the planning moves to *selection of content* to be studied in the course ensuring alignment between the outcomes, assessment, and the content to be taught. Finally, the *learning resources* are selected that will provide the desired input to students for achieving the defined learning outcomes. This model makes learning more meaningful because the focus is on achieving learning outcomes rather than on just covering the content. In this model, assessment planning takes priority and directs the selection of the content and selection of learning resources. The model gives better control to the instructor and that is the reason that it is becoming very popular with university instructors.

4.4   Three Levels of Course Planning

To have full control over your course, it must be planned at three sequential levels as depicted below.

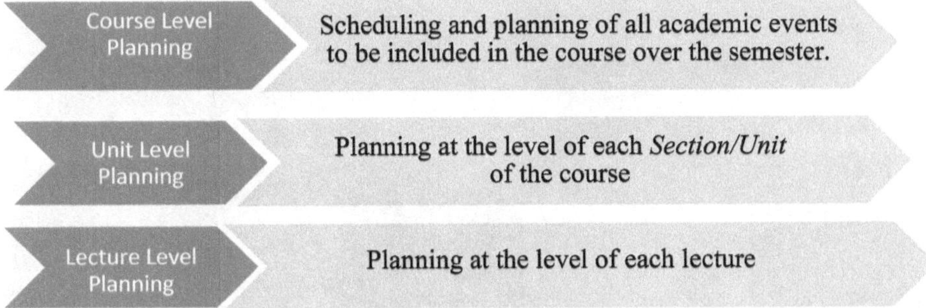

Fig. 4.3 –The Three Levels Of Course Planning

To ensure smooth running of your course, you need to prepare a three-tier plan for it – *Course level, Unit/Module level* and *Lecture-level*. All three levels of planning are important, and each plan furthers your control over the course. It is highly recommended that the master plan and schedule of main academic events along with most of the unit level plan must be completed before the start of the semester.

4.4.1   Planning the Entire Course

The main objective of this planning is to get a macro level picture of the entire course. For planning at the level of the entire course, you need to complete seven main planning tasks which can then be sequenced according to the chosen instructional model – *Conventional* or *Backward Design*.

Key Planning Tasks

The seven planning tasks are:

   i)   Composing course learning outcomes

  ii)   Listing prerequisites and skills required for course completion

 iii)   Creating a draft schedule

 iv)   Segmenting the course content into sections/units

  v)   Selecting learning materials

 vi)   Identifying suitable methodology and special activities

vii)   Planning overall assessment

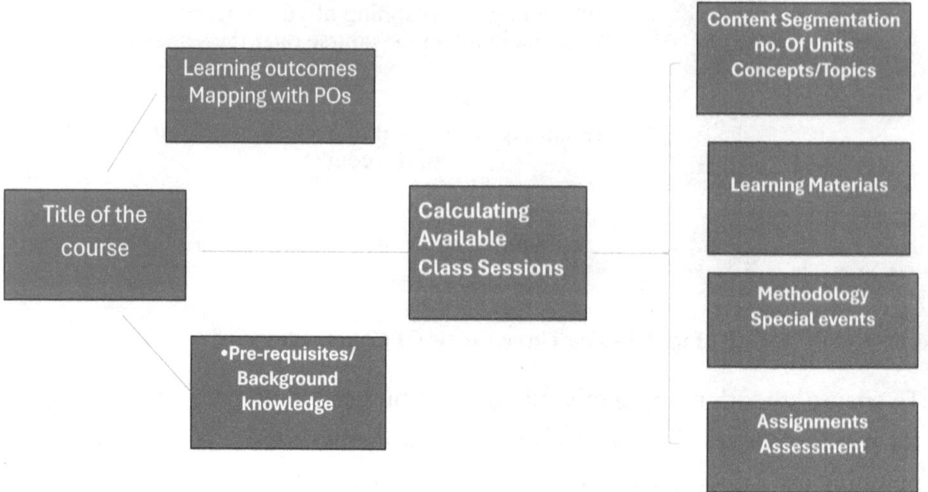

Fig. 4.5 – Key Tasks for Course-level Planning

Let us try to get an in-depth understanding of each of these key tasks for creating an overall, macro level plan for the course.

Task 1 – Defining Course Learning Outcomes (CLOs)

The first step in course planning is composing course learning outcomes. In Section 2, we examined the three domains of learning (*Cognitive, Affective and Psychomotor*) and the taxonomies associated with them. It will be a good idea to review that information (See p-52). We also saw that while all these domains are important, the course learning outcomes are generally structured around the cognitive domain. In this section, we will dig deeper and learn more about learning outcomes and how to compose them.

Course learning outcomes have been defined as *"written statements of what the successful student or learner is expected to be able to achieve at the end of the program module, course unit, or qualification"* (*Adam, 2004*). Often, instructors and students are confused between the two terms: *Learning Objective* and *Learning Outcomes* that are often used interchangeably. Essentially, both define what the learner is expected to acquire at the end of an instructional event in terms of knowledge, skills, or attitude. The only difference is in the usage. We may say that *Objectives* refer to the starting point and *Outcomes*, the endpoint of a course plan. In other words, it may be better to use the term *Learning Objectives* for the planning stage, and the term *Learning Outcomes* for measuring success at the end of the course. Over the years, the term *Outcomes* seems to have gained preference and is used both at the planning and assessment purposes. In this book, we will also do the same, and use the term *Outcomes* for both planning and assessment.

It is natural to start the course planning process by composing course learning outcomes because they are the only means by which the value of a course or any learning event can be described and/or measured. Learning outcomes help both the students and the instructors. They help the students to know what they are going to learn in a particular academic course or a learning event. For the instructor, the learning outcomes serve as a road map to effectively structure the content and plan all instructional activities. Learning outcomes help the instructor (and the learners) to measure acquisition of knowledge and the ability to analyze and apply it.

Measuring the attainment of learning outcomes demands that the learning outcomes are written in terms that are *observable, measurable, and demonstrable.* That is why learning outcomes are framed using *action verbs* (such as *derive, define, list, draw,* etc.) that clearly describe what students can 'do' at the end of the learning event. By the same token, verbs such as *understand, observe, appreciate, reflect* etc., are not suitable verbs for writing learning outcomes. For composing learning outcomes, we mainly depend on the cognitive domain of learning and the taxonomy associated with it (pp - 54-55). This implies that the first step here is to have a complete understanding of the six levels of the taxonomy of cognitive objectives and the performance expectations associated with each of the six levels.

As we know, the taxonomy of cognitive objectives with its six competency levels was developed by Benjamin Bloom in 1956. In 2001, the taxonomy was revised by Anderson who was also involved in formulating the original taxonomy. Now, we mostly use the revised version *(Anderson and Krathwohl, 2001).* The table below describes the performance expectations of each level of the revised taxonomy of the cognitive domain with the help of *doing* or *action* verbs.

Table 4.a – Revised Bloom's Taxonomy of Cognitive Objectives

Level/ Competence	Performance indicators	Suggested Action verbs for composing Learning Outcomes
Level-1 (Lowest level) *Remembering*	The lowest level where the learner is able to recognize, recall or list the facts/information.	*Define, Repeat, Record, List, Recall, Name, Relate, and Underline*
Level – 2 *Understanding*	A lower level of learning where the learner is able to demonstrate understanding by describing, explaining, interpreting or translating the newly learned facts and information.	*Translate, Restate, Discuss, Describe, Recognize, Explain, Express, Identify, Locate, Report, Review, Tell*
Level-3 *Applying*	An important level of learning where the learner is able to apply, employ, or demonstrate the new knowledge.	*Interpret, Apply, Employ, Use, Demonstrate, Dramatize, Practice, Illustrate. Operate, Schedule, Sketch*
Level – 4 *Analyzing*	A high level of learning where the learner examines and breaks down complex information to explain how parts relate to each other and the whole.	*Distinguish, Analyze, Differentiate, Calculate, Experiment, Test, Compare, Plot, Inspect, Debate, Question, Relate, Solve, Examine, Categorize*
Level – 5 *Evaluating*	A higher level of learning where the learner is able to judge, compare, or assess the newly learned facts and information.	*Judge, Appraise, Evaluate, Rate, Compare, Contrast, Criticize, Revise. Assess, Estimate*

Level/ Competence	Performance indicators	Suggested Action verbs for composing Learning Outcomes
Level-6 (highest level) *Creating*	The highest level of learning where the learner is able to use the newly learned facts/ information to design, assemble and construct new knowledge, products, or processes.	*Compose, Plan, Plot, Propose, Design, Formulate, Arrange, Assemble, Construct, Create, Set up, Organize, Restructure, and Prepare.*

Once you have the requisite clarity about the different levels of the taxonomy of cognitive domain, it becomes easy to write learning outcomes that are specific and focused. To ensure that the learning outcomes are observable, measurable, and demonstrable, they are written in a standard format e.g. *"At the end of this learning event, the students will be able to <u>list</u> the parts of an AC motor."*

Please note that the sample action verbs listed for each level (Table 4.a) are only suggestive and not absolute. In other words, just by using a certain action verb does not always place the outcome at that target level of taxonomy. For example, if a learning outcome is composed as, *"At the end of this session, the learner will be able to <u>evaluate</u> the physical features of the three layers of the earth"*, the outcome does not automatically refer to the higher order skill of evaluating (level 5). It is easy to see that the learning outcome is poorly framed because the physical features can be *listed, described,* or *explained* but not *evaluated.* You will need to choose the appropriate verb that can help to correctly measure the targeted cognitive level or skill. The other requirement of a well-composed learning outcome is that it is achievable within the allocated time frame.

A popular myth subscribed to by many instructors and academic programs related to composing learning objectives for undergraduate courses is that only low-order cognitive objectives (*Remembering, Understanding, Applying*) should be used for planning learning and assessment activities for junior-year university students. Higher-order objectives (*Analyzing Evaluating, Creating*) are suitable for senior years. This is not true – all six levels of cognitive objectives can be used for all levels of classes. In the context of learning, *Remembering* and *Understanding* are equally important levels, though for assessment, it is recommended that questions should be pitched at least at the *Application* level.

One question that instructors are often confused about is – how many learning outcomes should be composed for different levels (the entire course, section level, and lecture level) of course planning? Although there is no prescribed number, but the general guidelines can be as follows:

i)   At the entire course level, the learning outcomes are more general and point to overall competencies that the students should be able to achieve at the completion of the course. These are more like the mission statement of your institution. Try to limit them to *six (no more than eight)* outcomes.

ii) At the section or unit level, the learning outcomes are more specific. Here, the number of learning outcomes will depend on the size of the unit/section. Again, the number should be limited to *four-five* outcomes per section/unit.

iii) At the lecture-level, which is limited to one class session, the learning outcome/s must be very specific and should be limited to *one (no more than two)* outcomes.

Task 2 – Listing/reviewing the Prerequisites

Another important starting point for course planning is to determine background knowledge (prerequisites) and skills required to successfully complete the course. In most cases, the department provides the prerequisites for the course allocated to you. You may want to modify them if needed. If you are designing a new course, you must first identify and prerequisites and document them clearly so that learner preparedness can be determined and monitored. To create prerequisites, you may consider the following guidelines:

i)   review the entire course content and the learning outcomes to identify the foundational knowledge required to follow the new course,

ii)   identify the required academic and technical competencies,

iii) review the industry expectations to check if any knowledge or skills need to be added,

iv)   consult colleagues who have experience in teaching or designing courses in the same area.

Task 3 – Creating a Draft Schedule

Whether you are planning an allocated course or designing your own course, a practical way to begin is by creating a comprehensive *draft schedule* for all the activities and academic events to be completed over the semester. The objective is to get a macro level view of how different learning units/sub-section and the associated tasks of the course will be completed during the semester. Most of us do create some sort of plan for the first week or two but after that we just go with planning individual lectures only to discover towards the end of the semester that things are quite out of control. This situation can be easily avoided by completing this step before the start of the semester. The more detail you include here, the more control you will have over the course. The time spent at this stage will pay rich dividends in terms of time management and the overall quality of instruction.

Begin by examining the semester calendar to calculate the total number of available class sessions for the semester. You will find that a few dates will need to be blocked out when all or most of the students will not be available for class sessions because of important university events such as national/ regional holidays, cultural or sports events, institute-level exams, etc. A typical undergraduate course is scheduled to have 42–45 class sessions over 14 – 15 weeks, but you will find that the actual available class sessions may be only 38 – 40. It is within these available class sessions that all academic activities such as lectures, assignments, exams/tests/quizzes, in-class activities/projects, off-site visits, invited lectures etc., must be completed. This exercise is of tremendous value in managing time and monitoring the progression of your course. This draft schedule will put you in the driver's seat and empower you to control the flow of your course.

Task 4 – Segmenting the Content into Units/Sections

Segmentation of the course content can be done either by identifying the key concepts (*Concept/Topic wise*) and associated knowledge or by following the schedule of the course (*Time wise*). The time wise segmentation is generally suitable for online courses where the content is segmented in weekly slots.

Segmenting the course into unites using the content is a two-part process. First, you must identify the core concepts, learning units, topics etc. to be taught in class and second, determine the relative importance of the different concepts/topics to be covered in terms of their complexity and grade-value. This will help you to determine how much class time should be allocated to each one of them. Next, you will need to divide the course in logical segments (sections/units), and the number of class sessions to be allocated for each section/unit. Avoid the common temptation of just dividing the available class sessions equally across the number of identified sections/units (e.g. 6 learning units – 42 class sessions = 7 class sessions per unit). The allocation of class sessions will depend on the complexity of the content to be covered in a particular segment/unit.

Managing to finish course work within the semester is one of the major challenges for undergraduate instructors. Creating a course plan like this allows you to immediately identify the topics that are likely to take more (or less) time to complete. We know that knowledge is multiplying at a stupendous rate while the time for completing the undergraduate degree remains the same. The natural consequence of this is time crunch that we instructors face.

To prioritize the instruction time, it is important for instructors to have clarity about the relative importance of the content to be taught in different sections/units. The relative importance of different topics/themes can be determined based on two criteria. First, the importance of each topic/theme in building the knowledge or competencies required for successful completion of the course and following the next-level course/s for which this course will serve as a prerequisite. Second, the weight each topic/theme carries for evaluation in the final exam. Remember, at the end of the day, your success is reflected through students to perform in terms of grades. Prioritizing content helps you to optimize your class instruction time and monitor the progression of the course.

Experience shows that in most undergraduate courses, the content can be typically sifted into two clear baskets: a) the content that is the core part of the course without which the students will not be able to pass the course and follow the subsequent courses, and b) the content that provides background and peripheral information and helps to reinforce the core concepts.

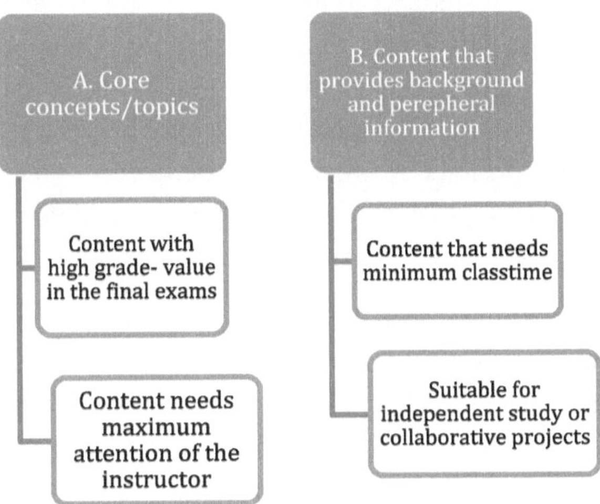

Fig. 4.4 – Sifting the Course Content

Under basket A, list all the topics and learning units that form the heart and soul of the course, and include all the *key concepts* that are important for passing the course. This content is directly related to the specified learning outcomes and must be mastered to successfully complete the course. Nearly 85–90% of the course should fall into this category. Clearly, this portion needs your best attention, time, and energy to ensure that *all* students master it as well as they can.

Under basket B, list topics that you think students can manage by themselves. A survey with over 400 instructors showed that nearly 10–15% of the course content can be comfortably managed by students on their own. A host of different activities can be designed by the instructor for this part of the content to be completed by students on their own. A very effective strategy, Peer-supported Independent Study (PSIS), designed by the author, is discussed in detail in Section 4 (pp - 139 -144).

Task 5 – Selecting Reading and Learning Resources

This involves selecting the main textbook and secondary resources that you want students to use during the course. Most of us take this task for granted and do not spend the time it deserves. When you are designing a course or teaching a pre-designed course, you have the choice to pick the reading/learning materials that you want students to use. If you look at the course description of any undergraduate course, the reading list is very long and intimidating. Clearly, no student is going to have the time to study (or even consult) all the publications on the list. Many departments require instructors to submit a list of reading materials and the instructors are tempted to create a long list of library reference books which can be very daunting and discouraging for the students.

It is important to take time to pick the most suitable textbook and supplementary reading materials carefully. While choosing the prescribed textbook, always think of the academic, cultural, and linguistic profile of your students. It is not necessary that a book written by a world authority will be the most suitable for your students. You want to choose something that they will be able to read and understand easily. A practical strategy is to create a reading guide for each section where you can list out all supplementary materials for specific topic. This may be a chapter or specific pages from the textbook, excerpts from a video lecture with exact minute-readings, or a self-created handout.

An excellent option for supplementing learning materials is offered by ***Massive Open Online Courses (MOOCs)***. These are video or online courses designed and delivered by the known experts in the field and sponsored by prestigious universities or organizations. The best part is that the MOOCs are available in every discipline, and most of them are free.

MOOCs first appeared in 2011. By 2016, nearly 7,000 MOOCs were available, with new ones being added every month. Now, every country has its own local platform to disseminate these international resources to enrich course content. Some better-known platforms are *Coursera* (USA), *edX* (Global), *Udacity* (USA), *NPTL* (India), Udemy (USA), and *Futurelearn* (UK).

Today, the instructors as well as students have a lot of choice of resources as the same course content delivered by different scholars/experts is available, mostly free of cost. In addition to complete courses, smaller video clips explaining a particular concept, phenomenon, experiment, or simulation can be accessed freely. MOOCs are now gaining popularity and researchers are busy experimenting with new ways of integrating them in conventional classroom teaching. The following formats have been found to be quite effective:

- Using excepts from a selected MOOC (examples, explanations, simulation, demonstration etc.) to support regular classroom teaching.

- Using selected portions or exercises of the MOOC for self-study to reinforce the concepts taught in class, and to be used as reading material for a flipped class.

- Asking students to study a selected MOOC like a regular course on their own, for ten of the fourteen weeks. The last four weeks are taken by the instructor to review, reinforce and evaluate the learning. (*Israel, 2015*).

- Asking students to pick a MOOC, study on their own, complete all the required activities. The completion certificate entitles them to earn matching college credits.

Successful use of MOOCs to enrich course content depends a great deal on the correct selection of the MOOC. Often, instructors or curriculum coordinators make hasty decisions about selecting a MOOC depending *exclusively* on the reputation of the authoring faculty or the university. While choosing a MOOC, it is important to ensure that the content covered is compatible with the course it is being used to support. Points that need to be kept in mind are: i) the level of complexity covered; ii) the structure and delivery format; and iii) the cultural affinity (examples, language, and pronunciation of the narrator etc.). However, a lot more research is warranted in this area because, the potential is unlimited but as of now, very few instructors and universities have found an efficient system to effectively integrate these invaluable resources into regular teaching.

Task 6 – Planning the Teaching Methodology for the course

This involves decisions about the approach and methodology to be used for teaching the course. The importance of planning methodology at this point is that it helps you to get organized well in time for implementing different activities and events. For example, if the course has a mandatory practical component, you will need to reserve the lab or a special classroom for it. If you plan to include any site visits or field work, you will need to contact the organization, make reservations, and plan the logistics for taking the students there, etc. If you plan to have invited lectures by academic or industry experts, you will need to send out the invites and make arrangements well ahead of time. If any official permissions are required, you will need to start the process early. Similarly, if you want to include any collaborative activities or mini projects, you will need to have a tentative plan for scheduling them.

Task 7 – Planning the Overall Assessment Pattern for the Course

Planning overall assessment involves decisions such as: i) how many tests or assignments should be administered; ii) what should be the format for each assessment event; iii) what should be the relative grade value of each question or task; and iv) when these tests should be scheduled. If the college or university has a predefined assessment pattern for all undergraduate courses, you will need to plan your assessment around that. If you are designing a new course using the *backward design* model, assessment must be planned immediately after the course learning outcomes have been composed. A number of different aspects will need to be attended to and you will need to spend a lot more time to plan this component.

Please remember that assessment is the most important component of course planning, not only because it measures learning but also because it plays a key role in motivating (or demotivating) the learners. Moreover, the first thing the students want to know is how they will be assessed. Given the importance of this topic, an entire section, (Section 8), has been devoted to the subject of assessment.

4.4.2   Planning Your Course at the Unit/Section Level

Once the course level plan is ready, you are armed with important information regarding the course learning objectives and the number of units to be completed within the available class sessions. Typically, most undergraduate courses can be structured to have 5 – 7 units, and each unit may require a variable number of class sessions. The first step is to study each unit and decide how many class sessions need to be allocated to it. The number of required class sessions depends on the complexity of information and the desired depth of coverage needed for the different concepts/topics included in a specific unit.

Now, it is time to start work on planning individual units. Planning at the unit level is quite intricate and needs your best attention. There are two main approaches that can be adopted for unit-level planning: *time-wise planning* and *topic-wise planning*. Time-wise planning is mostly used for online courses where work to be completed in a week is considered a unit. Each weekly unit is designed to be complete in itself with specific readings, activities, and assessment.

For conventional classroom teaching, *topic-wise* planning works much better. Once the course has been divided into units, the best way to go about this is to plan each unit separately. Fig. 4.6 provides a sample template that should work well as a baseline for all subjects and all disciplines. Additions, deletions, and modifications can be made as required.

At this stage, the course content has already been segmentized into units. The unit level planning process is same for all units. You begin by identifying i) the number of key concepts or the topics included in the unit, and ii) the number of class sessions required for the unit. You must begin by composing the learning outcomes for the unit.

After completing the overall plan for a unit, we need to move to a detailed planning of <u>each</u> core concept/topic within the unit. Let us understand the process by using a sample shown in Fig. 4.6. We can see that the sample unit 1 *has 4 key concepts/topics that will require 9 class sessions to complete.* Now, it is time to plan each of the 4 concepts/topics in detail. The first step is to decide how many class sessions (out of the 9 assigned for Unit 1) will be needed for concept/topic 1. In the sample, concept/topic 1 requires 2 class sessions.

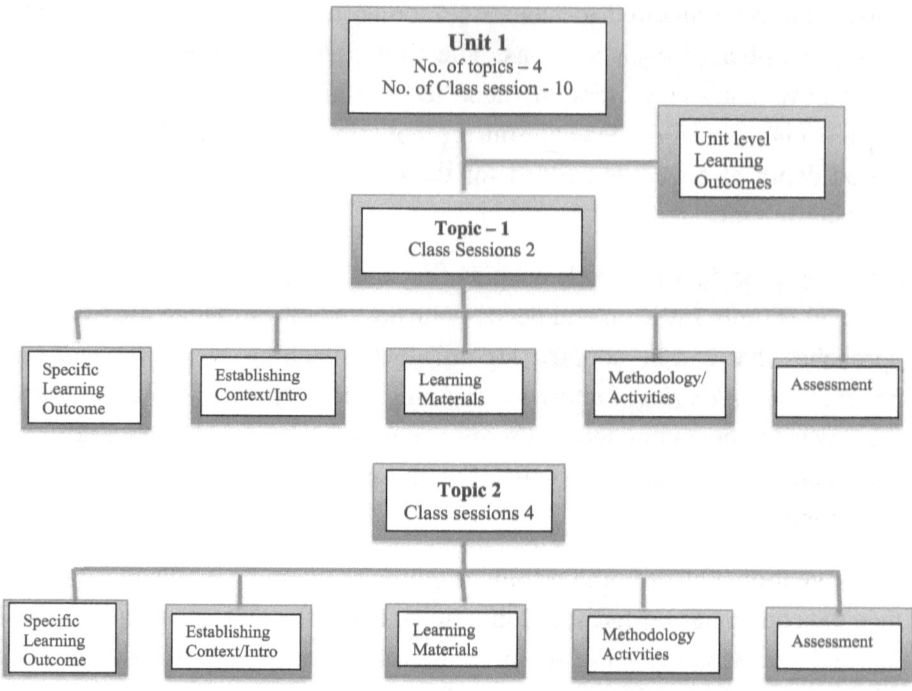

Fig. 4.6 – Sample Template for Unit Level Planning

Let us look at the five main components that need to be worked out for *topic-level* planning. As always, we need to begin by composing the specific learning outcome for the topic. The next step is to plan how the concept/topic should be introduced to generate curiosity and intellectual excitement. Identification of appropriate learning materials comes next which is followed by important decisions regarding the methodology and the activities to be used for teaching the concept/topic. This is the time to decide about any special activities or events like the use of simulation, site visit, invited lecture etc. to be included. Finally, you will need to decide what kind of assessment (graded assignment, quiz, or group work) would be most suitable for evaluating student learning. This is the generic planning process that can be adopted (for the remaining topics (no. 2, 3, and 4) of the unit. Of course, each concept/topic will require different set of activities and number of class sessions, and some modifications.

No doubt that unit level planning appears to be very tedious and time consuming but once you have gone through the exercise, it becomes a lot easier. With this level of detailed planning for each key concept/topic, your preparation, and implementation become very focused and efficient. The time spent on this initial planning will pay dividends throughout the semester by placing you squarely into the driver's seat, and giving you full control over your course.

4.4.3   Planning at the Lecture-Level

Planning at the lecture stage is also very important. Finally, it is through the lectures that all your planning is translated into quality instruction. Lecture level planning includes six key components: *opening, chunking of content, in-class student engagement activities, student feedback,* and *closing.* Effective planning and delivery of lectures is discussed in detail in Section 5.

Looking at all the details provided above, planning a course at three levels may seem like an arduous task. Yes, in the beginning, it may take some time, but every minute invested in planning pays rich dividends. Faculty are advised to keep the planning documents (computer or paper) to review and make accommodations as the course progresses. It will also come in handy if you are asked to teach the same course again.

4.5   Preparing a Course Policy Document

One last, but not the least, task of course planning is composing a policy document for your course. Many institutions and departments do this centrally by posting a long, generic document about each course, giving the structure of the course, main content, outcomes, schedule of exams, etc., which is very helpful, but this customized one-page *Course Policy Document* serves a different purpose, and has a strong impact on the students.

Plan to prepare a short (no longer than one page) *course policy document* that must be distributed to the class on day 1. The success of a course largely depends on how it is introduced to the class on day 1. This is the time to get students excited about the course content they will be studying and to set the tone for the class interaction. Managing the first day of class is discussed in great detail in Section 5 (pp - 144 - 147). If you have a dedicated course website, you should also publish it there, but a hard copy must be distributed in class and more important, read aloud to the students.

What is this document, and why do we need it? Your *Course Policy Document* is a personalized, short, and concise document about the ground rules about your course. It is designed to convey many subtle messages to the students. First, it tells the students that you value your course, that you are well-organized, and that you take teaching seriously. This one-page document tells the students that you take full ownership of the course and have full clarity about how you want it to run.

What should this document include?

There is no fixed list of items for this document. Based on your experience, you can pick issues that are likely to disrupt the sanctity and ambiance of your class. Make sure that the policy is reasonable and applicable. Given below are some of the common items that are generally included in a course policy document:

i) *Attendance and Class Participation Policy:* Most institutions have a standard, well-publicized policy regarding attendance, and it is best to stay with that. However, it is important to emphasize that attendance in your class is not just being physically present but also being fully engaged in class interaction and activities. If any marks are allocated for attendance, you may want to keep a portion of them for participation. In this case, you will need to define clearly what you mean by *participation*.

ii) *Punctuality*: We have all experienced that, unlike school students, college students tend to be less serious about punctuality. You need to make a couple of decisions here, such as: do you permit late arrival? If yes, by how many minutes and how often? For example, my personal policy about punctuality is that I always allow them to come in. Being late up to 5 minutes is excused, but later than that is counted as late, and three late arrivals are counted as one absence.

iii) *Use of Cell Phones* – The cell phone is often seen as a big source of distraction in class. But, with the increasing use of technology in higher education, cell phones can serve as an invaluable tool. You will have to create a policy about when and how cell phones can be used in your class.

iv) ***Classroom Etiquette:*** Instructors often hesitate to include policies about class etiquette, but experience shows that undergraduate students are often unable to handle their new-found independence offered by the university environment and need clear guidelines for in-class behavior as adults. It is important to convey your high expectations about being courteous and respectful to all.

v) ***Plagiarism:*** Plagiarism is an all-pervading phenomenon in undergraduate classes across the globe. The policy regarding plagiarism must be clearly defined. If the institute has a policy, it is best to reinforce that. But if there is no institutional policy, it is very important to create one and impose it strictly and consistently. This topic has been discussed in detail and tips for managing plagiarism in your classes have been provided Section 8 (pp - 241 - 242).

Please make sure that copies of this one-page document are distributed to students on the first day of the class and read aloud by you in class. This conveys a firm message that these policies are important, and you are serious about implementing them.

4.6   Section 4: Wrap-up and Tips for Effective Course Planning

In this section, we looked at the various tasks that need to be completed for effective management of course content. We have looked at a new way of structuring a course using a backward design. We saw how effective course management requires three-level planning. *Course-level planning*; *section or unit – level planning*; and *lecture-level planning*. To gain full control over your course, it is important to understand different component tasks involved in each type of planning.

Starting with writing course learning outcomes, we saw how *Sifting the Course Content* according to the relative academic importance and grade value helps us to identify portions that need our best attention and the portions that students can manage themselves so that more time can be devoted to the core concepts. Another important component of course management is the selection of the most suitable learning resources in a good mix of text and video formats.

Once the planning for course content is complete, the instructor must create a policy document for the specific class. This helps in giving the course a personalized status and promoting a sense of ownership among students. As always, this section will end with consolidated tips for managing course content.

Table 4.c – Tips for Effective Course Planning

Tip No.	Recommendations
1.	If you are teaching a new course, talk to your colleague/s who have taught that course earlier or speak with the Course Coordinator or the Head of the Department. Your questions should be focused on "which part is most difficult for the students", 'the best way to engage the students'; 'what to avoid' etc. If you are teaching the same course again – review your slides, handouts, and activities.
2.	Begin by reviewing the entire course content (can use the main curriculum document or the prescribed textbook) and sift the content carefully according to its importance and weight in the assessment process. This is a very important step that will guide you in deciding how much time needs to be spent on which topics.
3.	Once you have an overall picture of the entire course, create a draft schedule for the entire semester (p- 106). Today, many efficient, flexible, and free technology solutions are available that can be used for the purpose.
4.	Create specific learning outcome/s at the course level (6-8 outcomes) as well as at the unit level (one per lecture). If the outcomes are provided by the Institution, review and if needed, modify them.
5.	The outcomes and master schedule (even though it may change) are invaluable tools for starting the preparation of the course *before the start of the semester.* Try and get as many components as possible (especially class activities, assignments, and assessments) ready ahead of time. These will also facilitate in organizing major events like *site visits* and *guest lectures*.

Tip No.	Recommendations
6.	Identify resources carefully. Instead of depending on just one textbook, you may provide specific resources for each of the core topics. Make these resources available to students. Selected content from MOOCs (selected chapters, examples, exercises, simulations, and video content etc.) can be used to enrich the academic interest and reinforce learning. If you are using resources from the library, have them placed in the reference section so that students can access them easily.
7.	Prepare a brief (no more than one page) policy document to be distributed on the first day of class. Remember that the first day of class is an extremely important opportunity for you to connect your students to the course and yourself. For more detail on managing the first day of class (See pp 144-147).
8.	Finally, think of additions resources (short video clips, simulations, interesting in-class activities, or online projects, etc.) that will not only add value to the course but also promote motivation and learning. Explore ways in which your and students' time and energy can be optimized.

<table><tr><td>**5**</td><td># Effective Course Delivery</td></tr></table>

(Cartoon by Nischal Das, student, Indian Institute of Technology, Delhi)
Fig. 5.1 Planning of an Effective Lecture

In the previous sections, we discussed three important aspects of undergraduate instruction: i) how learning happens; ii) understanding and supporting the academic and emotional needs of our students; and iii) how to manage course content. In this section, we will discuss the next important component: managing effective course delivery.

Today, one often hears that the *lecture era is over* or that *the lecture mode is outdated*. There seems to be some suggestion that it is time to replace the lecture mode with other, more modern, technology-enhanced modes. However, disappointing it may seem to modernists, the lecture mode, much like the blackboard, is here to stay! Of course, given the changed profile of the learner and the availability of new technology-based tools, suitable modifications and enhancements must be incorporated, but the basic structure of the lecture mode is and will remain the lifeline of university teaching. It therefore becomes an important responsibility of every university instructor to master the art of making their lectures focused and engaging.

5.1 The Lecture Mode is Here to Stay!

The lecture mode offers several advantages. First, it is a face-to-face event that allows direct contact between the instructor and the students. It is the most time-and-cost efficient mode for delivering *new knowledge* to a *large body* of students. The mode allows the instructor to customize the content for a specific course and make it more relevant by using different scholarly sources and perspectives. It is easy for the instructor to instantaneously update the content by including the latest findings and developments. It allows the instructor to mix and match diverse modes of delivery, such as verbal, audio-visual, animation, simulation, etc., catering to the different learning needs and styles of the students.

The importance of the lecture mode became most evident during the 2019–2021 COVID pandemic. Suddenly, colleges across the globe had to shut down, and instructors had to resort to the online mode of delivering content. It was during this time that the importance of the traditional lecture mode was most felt. Both the students and the instructors eagerly looked forward to the normalization of the situation so that regular classroom instruction could resume. It confirmed that the lecture mode will always remain indispensable for delivering instruction at the university level.

5.2 Planning Effective Lectures: Major Challenges!

Planning and delivering effective lectures are complex activities that require attention to multiple, diverse components. Based on the feedback collected from participants in faculty development workshops, some of the key challenges experienced by instructors while planning lectures, are:

- Structuring the content,

- Managing class time effectively,

- Sustaining student attention, and

- Completing the set syllabus within the available class sessions.

In this section, we will analyze each of these challenges and examine some successful practical strategies to address them. Planning effective lectures is a two-part process: first, *selecting* and *preparing* the content for the lecture (*what to teach),* and second, *delivering* the prepared content (*how to teach it*). It is a fact that most of us college instructors are focused mainly on the 'what' part and take the 'how' part somewhat for granted. When we say, "*I am well-prepared for my lecture, we generally mean that I am in full control of what I plan to teach"*. Rarely do we have a detailed plan for *how* we are going to deliver it. The fact is that an effective lecture requires a perfect balance of the '*what to teach*' and the '*how to teach*' components.

5.3 Planning the *"What to Teach"* Component

For selecting and preparing content for the lecture, planning is required in the following four areas:

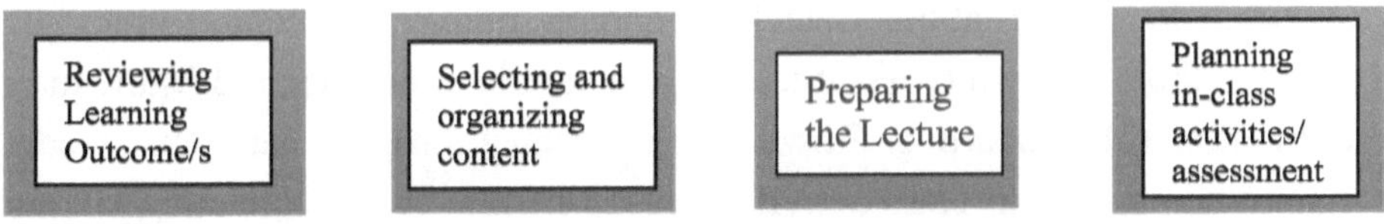

Fig. 5.2 – Tasks for Planning an Effective Lecture

Let us try to understand each of these four planning tasks:

5.3.1 Creating/Reviewing Lecture Outcome/s

In Section 4, we learned that it is essential to have clearly stated learning outcomes at the entire course, unit, and lecture levels. Here, it is important to create/review learning outcomes for each lecture. For a one-hour lecture, normally there should be one (or at the most, two) learning outcome(s). Make sure that the outcome is measurable and written in the standard format (e.g., at *the end of this lecture, the students will be able to apply, calculate, etc.).* This exercise is an important starting point for your own clarity and organization. It helps you to select and structure the content and all associated activities that can be completed within the time frame.

5.3.2 Selecting and Organizing the Content for the Lecture

Once you are clear about the learning outcome(s) of the lecture, you need to select and organize the content to be taught during the lecture. We have learned that the brain processes information in small chunks, so the content chosen for the lecture should be further segmented into smaller *learning bites* according to their relative academic value in scaffolding knowledge and summative assessment. The academic value of a learning event determines how much time and effort you want to spend on it. Typically, a lecture will include at least two learning bites that include part-concepts, explanations, examples, or in-class work. You need to create the sequence in which each learning bite is to be delivered. Clearly, this will need to be adjusted for each lecture.

5.3.3 Preparing Lecture Aids

Once the identified learning bites for the lecture have been logically organized, you need to worry about selecting and/or preparing lecture materials. Typically, there are two types of learning materials to be prepared: i) the main presentation (blackboard or PowerPoint presentation); ii) handouts needed for summary notes, in-class activities, assessments, or for collecting student feedback. Sometimes, you may also need additional materials like models, simulations, realia, etc.

While the presence of blackboard is still dominant, PowerPoint presentations have become the preferred mode for delivering instruction for most university instructors. This is because of two main reasons. First, the classes are very large, and visibility across the class is much better with projection as compared to the writing on the blackboard. Second, the instructor can face the class, which is not possible while using the blackboard. However, if the slides are poorly prepared or used in an unplanned manner, the PowerPoint presentations can become unbearable for the students. Preparing good slides takes planning and time, and instructors are advised to keep the following key guidelines in mind while preparing them:

Table 5.a – Eight Golden Rules for Preparing Effective PowerPoint Slides

No.	Guidelines
1.	Keep the number of slides as limited as possible. Remember, they are there to support you as a speaker. It can be very tiring for the students to be looking at slide after slide for the entire lecture
2.	Keep the slides clean and uncluttered. Do not try to cram too much on one slide. Minimum font size is 28.
3.	Remember the mantra – *6 – 8 lines per slide and 6-8 words per line*
4.	Use only bullet – points – do not include definitions/explanations. Remember, you will provide those to the class
5.	Use the same font for the entire presentation, and respect the blank spaces
6.	Use color meaningfully for a purpose such as classifying or separating information. Colors are strong communicators and using two-three or more colors randomly on the same slide, can confuse the students
7.	Do not use graphics/diagrams/sketches that are directly copied from a textbook or other print material. Re-engineer them by making a copy and then enlarging it several times. Remember, print medium is designed for reading from 10-12, while slides are designed to be viewed from a distance.
8.	Use acronyms judiciously. There are way too many acronyms floating around and it is not necessary that your students recognize each one of them. Always establish the acronym by first using the full form of the title/name and giving the acronym in parathesis.

If you are planning to use the blackboard, make sure that your writing is large enough to be seen from afar. It is always helpful to note down the sequence on an index card to remind you of the order in which you plan to discuss different components of the lecture. If you have complex diagrams, long equations, or important formulae, it is better to distribute them as handouts.

Handouts are a valuable tool for the instructor. Whether they are notes, instructions for in-class activities, home assignments, or instruments for collecting feedback, make sure that they are created in as simple a format as possible. They must be written our clearly and concisely. Of course, you will need to ensure that enough copies are available for the class. Make sure to acknowledge any materials taken from other authors or sources. If you are planning to use any simulation or demonstration in class that need the internet, make sure the internet connection and the equipment are working well.

While selecting and preparing the teaching aids, you need to be extra careful if you are using any pre-existing slides or handouts. If you are using materials that you prepared for another academic event or for the same course taught in a previous semester, it is crucial to review and refresh them. Tell-tale signs like an old date or a reference to an outdated event can really disappoint the students. Remember, you may be teaching that course for the 5th time, but for the students, it is the first time, and they are not very happy to see recycled or outdated materials.

5.3.4   Planning In-Class Activities

Each lecture should include one or two in-class activities that are designed to promote student engagement. These activities serve two very important functions. First, they help to promote motivation and in-depth learning, and second, they help you to assess how the content taught has been assimilated by the students.

Earlier, we have studied that learning happens when students are engaged in navigating through content as opposed to just passively listening to the instructor. To this end, several short (5-8 minute) activities a that the instructor can use in class in the form of short questions or problems to be solved in pairs or threesomes. When students are discussing and analyzing the content learned, they are re-constructing and internalizing the new knowledge. These activities can be used effectively for all levels and all disciplines and are invaluable for ensuring in-depth learning and promoting motivation and the joy of learning. Planning and implementing student engagement is such an important component of undergraduate teaching that a separate section – *Section 6: Ensuring Student Engagement,* where several easy-to-implement *active learning* and *cooperative learning* activities are discussed along with step-by-step instructions for implementing them.

The second important purpose these in-lecture activities serve is to provide feedback to the instructors about how the students are learning. Typically, when we complete a segment of the lecture, we stop and ask the class, "Any questions?" or "Is it clear?" or "Can we go on?" But generally, there is a big silence in class, and maybe a few students attempt to respond. Instead, if we ask them to participate in a poll or solve a problem-based on the content studied, we can get more realistic feedback. This can guide the instructor in deciding whether to go on, or review all or some of the content taught.

5.4   Managing the *"How to Teach"* component.

So far, we have looked at the planning and preparation of *what* we are going to teach; now, we will focus on *how* we want to teach it. This is undoubtedly the most important component of your success as an instructor. A perfectly prepared lecture can be ruined if it is delivered poorly. Planning effective lecture delivery involves the following five key components:

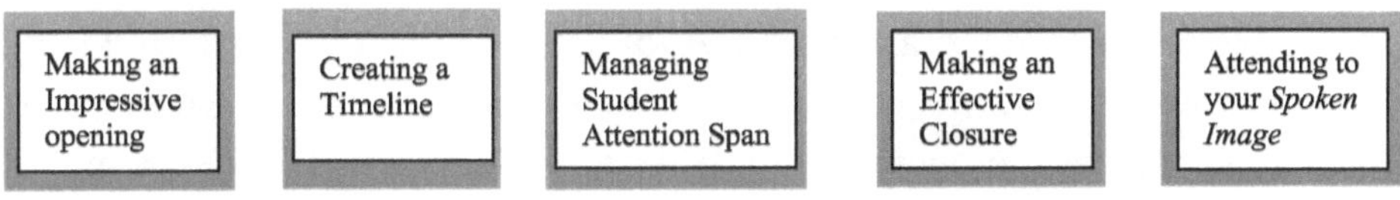

Fig. 5.3 – Tasks for Delivering an Effective Lecture

To ensure a focused and inspiring delivery, we need to keep in mind some of the theoretical constructs learned in the earlier sections. The four principles listed in Table 5.b should always be uppermost in our minds.

Table 5.b – Theoretical Framework for Planning Effective Lecture Delivery

Theoretical Input	Recommendation
The brain processes information in small chunks (Brain-based Learning, - pp - 48 - 51).	Avoid overload. Deliver instruction in small learning bites.
Learning happens when students get an opportunity to construct/re-construct new knowledge (Piaget, - pp 44-45).	After every learning bite, give a small question/exercise that students can work on individually or with peers so that the new knowledge is assimilated.

Theoretical Input	Recommendation
Positive emotions strengthen learning (Brain-based Learning, p - 48 - 51).	Keep the class environment pleasant and relaxed. When students are working on questions/exercises, walk around to help and encourage them.
Social interaction promotes learning (Vygotsky & Social-emotional Learning, p - 46).	As far as possible plan in-class activities to be completed in pairs or threesomes. Do not be afraid of noisy, energetic interaction in class.

Now, let us examine each of the above-mentioned lecture delivery tasks: *Making an Impressive Opening; Planning a Timeline; Managing Student Attention Span; Making an Effective Closure;* and *Attending to Spoken Interaction.*

5.4.1   Making an Impressive Opening

Experience shows that getting a large group interested in a new topic is not an easy task. Most undergraduate classes are 50 + students, with some classes going up to a hundred. A lot depends on how it is introduced. Several theories that we have studied so far confirm the importance of making an impressive opening of a lecture. In Section 2, the ARCS model of motivation tells us that to motivate students to learn something new, we must be able to attract their attention and curiosity by making a strong introduction (A of ARCS stands for *Attraction* (pp - 85 - 86). Maslow tells us that adults are motivated by *NEED* (p - 82). The instructor must create a *NEED* by telling the students why and how this specific concept, theory, or application will help them succeed in college, the workplace, or life. And Joseph Lowman talks about creating intellectual excitement to get students involved in learning process (pp - 26 - 27).

Let us try to understand the phenomenon more scientifically. We know that each one of us carries a unique *schema* or *cognitive map* that holds the entire body of knowledge acquired through academic, social, and cultural input received over years. Now, the instructor needs to add new knowledge to the learner's existing cognitive map. The best way is to create a *Hook* that will help connect the new knowledge to the learner's existing schema. The

Hook can be anything that will trigger the learner's curiosity. It can be a visual, a product, a simulation, a news item, or a story. A common belief in the educational world is that effective instruction moves from *the known to the unknown.* This implies that the instructor must create an introduction or choose an example (*Hook*) that will refer to a context that every student in class is familiar with.

There are a number of ways in which the instructor can make a curiosity-provoking opening and get students immediately involved in the topic of the lecture. In one of the faculty development workshops, participants were asked to suggest different ways in which they could introduce their lectures, several very interesting ways were identified, ranging from sharing a related picture or a news item, a real-world product, application, or phenomenon, to imagining a drastic situation caused or resolved by the concept to be studied.

As instructors, we need to be aware of the two approaches for introducing a new topic: the *deductive approach* and the *inductive approach*. The *deductive approach* is what we instructors normally follow in our classes: begin by defining or explaining the concept, provide supporting examples, facts, or data, and then asking the students to work on assignments or questions to reinforce their understanding of the concept.

In the *inductive approach,* on the other hand, the instructor starts by evoking specific observations, asking a question, examining some facts to establish a specific context and then, linking these to a specific context. The context relates to the concept or content to be studied. The instructor then explains the concept, followed by the usual homework or in-class tasks. Experience shows that the inductive approach works better for promoting curiosity and retentivity, though it may not be suitable for every topic. Instructors must strike a good balance between the two approaches and choose the most suitable one for the topic at hand.

5.4.2   Creating a Timeline for the Lecture

Given that most of us instructors find it challenging to complete the prescribed course work and all other diverse tasks associated with it, in the allocated 42–45 lectures, every minute of every lecture is important and must be planned meticulously. The plan requires sequencing different components of the lecture and the time you propose to spend on each one of them. Clearly, this plan cannot be too rigid because it is hard to predict how different components or events of the lecture will be assimilated by the students and which parts of the lecture may need to be repeated. However, going into a lecture without any sequence or timeline in mind can be disastrous.

A very successful model for planning a timeline for a typical 45 to 55 minute lecture is shared in Fig. 5.5. The model shows how different components of the lecture may be organized with an estimated time allocation. In Section 1, we learned that the brain processes information in small chunks, and consequently, the instructors are strongly advised to break up the selected content into smaller segments and make a general plan for the class session. As can be seen, the model proposes that the class time be divided into several smaller events. Starting with a 4 to 6-minute opening, the instructor addresses the first segment of the content, which is followed by a well-structured peer interaction activity. The activity is designed to get feedback on how the portion covered so far has been internalized by the students. This is followed by the delivery of a second segment of the content which in turn, is followed by a closing activity.

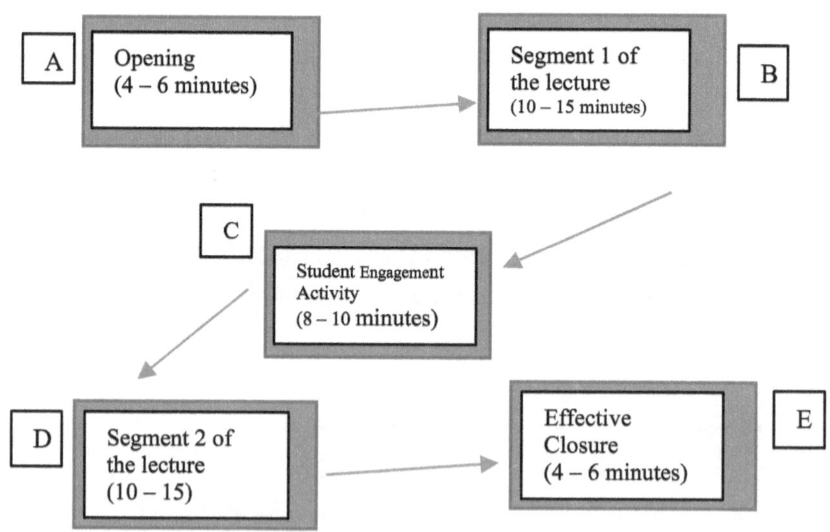

Fig. 5.5 – Suggested Timeline for an Effective Lecture

Please note that this is just a suggested model. Depending on the complexity and academic value of the content being studied, every class session will have to be organized differently.

5.4.3   Managing Student Attention Span

One of the big challenges faced by undergraduate instructors is to sustain the attention span of 50 + students in their classes. The most common comments one hears from instructors are students do not pay attention; they cannot concentrate; they are always distracted; they are not interested etc. The fact, however, is that the human brain has limitations. Science tells us that the typical human attention span is only around 10–12 minutes but a typical undergraduate class session is for 50 – 60 minutes. The challenge then is how to sustain attention during a lecture that is typically scheduled for 50 –60 minutes. Some graduate-level classes run even longer – from 80–120 minutes. To meet this challenge intelligently, we need to understand how human attention works.

Attention span refers to the duration of time a person can continuously focus on a specific activity or task without being distracted. We know that the human attention span is only around 10–12 minutes, which, we are told is progressively getting shorter, thanks to the *remote-control* culture. The limited attention span is also validated by findings of neuroscience that claims that the brain processes information in small chunks. This implies that loss of attention is involuntary, and the instructor needs to be prepared to address it proactively.

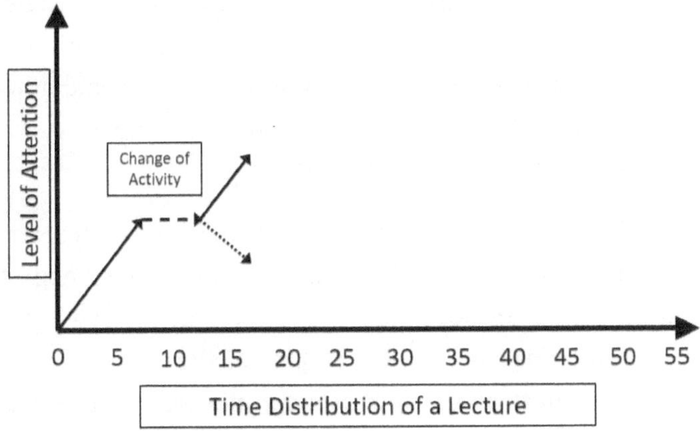

Fig. 5.5– Managing Attention Span

Fig. 5.5 shows how student attention span functions in a typical class. When the class starts, the learners are quite attentive for the first ten minutes or so, but after that their attention begins to wane, and if the instructor continues to lecture without any interruption, students are likely to get completely distracted.

The best solution is to freshen up the air by *changing the activity*. Which means you need to stop talking and make students *do* something. The idea is to shift the class activity from passive *listening* to active *doing* (thinking, writing, discussing etc.). In an ideal scenario, the instructor should not be speaking for more than 75% of the time. The change in activity does not have to be very intricate or complex, but it needs to be content-centric. This could be asking students to write something, see and analyze a visual, or work out a small problem individually or in collaboration with one or two neighboring students.

The main thing is that it should be related to what has *just* been discussed or completed—something that forces the students to reflect on and apply the new knowledge acquired in the class. This intervention must be very short. Depending on the duration of the lecture, it may have to be repeated more than once during the class session to ensure that the attention span is continually activated.

5.4.4 Planning Student Engagement

We learned in Section 1 that it is hard for learners to assimilate new knowledge just by listening to the instructor. Assimilation of knowledge or skill development happens only when students actively interact with the content by thinking, writing, discussing, analyzing, or applying the content being taught. These activities, commonly known as *active learning,* help to sustain attention, motivate learners, and promote in-depth learning.

An important point to note here is that even though in the suggested timeline for effective lectures (pp - 127 -129), the student engagement activity has been placed in the middle of the lecture, it can be planned anywhere during the lecture – in the beginning (A), middle (C), or at the end of your lecture (E). The main decision is how much time you can devote to student engagement activities in a particular lecture. This will dictate your choice of activity and its placement. However, planning an entire lecture by stringing active learning activities one after the other is not practical either and can become very tedious for the students. Well-designed active learning activities can be effectively incorporated into all disciplines and at all levels of university instruction.

The topic of student engagement is such an important component of the teaching-learning process that an entire section (Section 6) has been devoted to it. Here, all different aspects of student engagement and several activities with instructions for step-by-step implementation are discussed in detail.

5.4.5   Giving the Lecture a Good Closure

As instructors, we seldom plan how we are going to end the lecture. Often, we lose track of time and have to hurriedly close and rush out of class to make room for the next incoming class. A well-planned closure is important for not only reinforcing the content learned during the class session but also for helping students to develop confidence in what they have learned. Research shows that motivation comes when students are aware that they have *learned* something new or can *do* something that they did not before *(Merrill, 2008)*. It is important to make students aware of the new knowledge or skill they have gained from the lecture. This is also confirmed by the ARCS model of motivation, where the 'S' in the acronym stands for *Satisfaction,* which comes when students become aware of the new knowledge or skill they have acquired. Therefore, it is important to keep some dedicated time for giving an effective closure to the lecture.

There are many ways to close the lecture. The main objective is to summarize and highlight the new knowledge discussed in class and place it in the context of previous and/or future learning. It is more effective when the summarizing is done by the students rather than the instructor. This activity is discussed in detail in Section 6 (p-164).

5.5   Managing Your Spoken Image

What is *Spoken Image*? In simple terms, we can say that the term spoken image refers to the impression people make about you as a professional, when they hear you speak about a given topic. In life, we care a lot about what people think of us (our image), and to project the desired image, we pay a lot of attention to our physical appearance, grooming, demeanor etc. But, actually, a much more powerful impact is made by our verbal and non-verbal presence. As the wiseman says, *"when we look at a person, we know something about the person; but when we hear the person speak, we know all about the person"*. Your spoken image strongly impacts your students' perception about your self-esteem, empathy, passion, professional engagement, and self-confidence. As instructors our work involves a great deal of speaking about unfamiliar, complex topics to large audiences, which means that we need to be even more attentive about our spoken image.

Can we change or enhance our spoken image? Absolutely! Verbal communication is a skill that can be acquired and refined at any time by following a scientific process. Regretfully, most of us do not take this very seriously. Even when we are dissatisfied with the level of our communication, we seldom do anything about it. As instructors, we need to be cognizant about this very important aspect, and if needed, invest the time and effort to ensure that we are fully satisfied with our level of verbal and non-verbal communication. It is worthwhile to look a little deeper and learn more about the key components (Fig.5.6,) that directly impact our verbal and non-verbal communication.

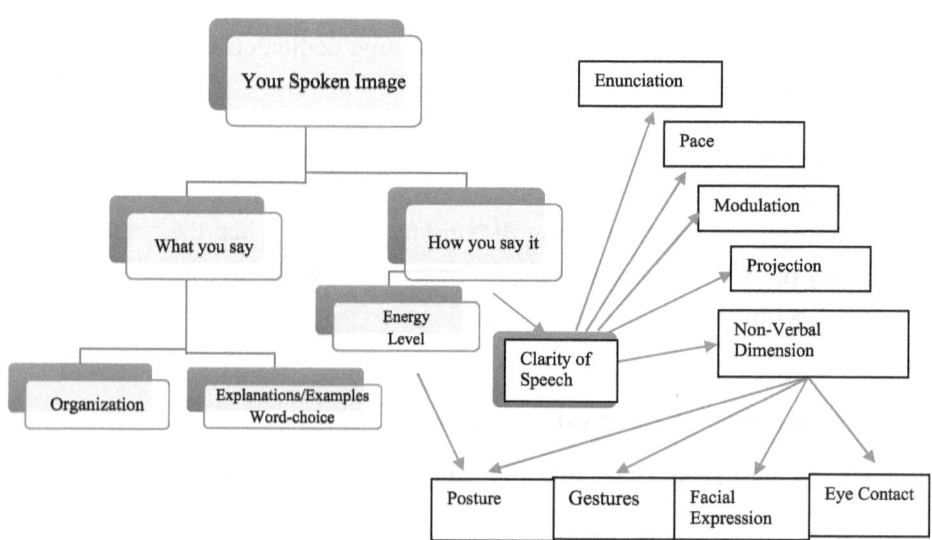

Fig. 5.6 – Managing Your Spoken Image

Take a few minutes to self-evaluate your spoken image and non-verbal communication using the format given below. It could be very rewarding to get a realistic evaluation of i) your overall competence as a communicator and ii) specific area/s that need attention. Armed with a candid evaluation, the instructor could focus on working on just the area/s that are found deficient.

Table 5.c – Format for Self-evaluating Your Spoken Image

Component	Description	Good	Acceptable	Needs Attention
Energy Level	The energy level with which you deliver instruction is perhaps the most important component of your spoken image. Energy level is different from speaking loudly (it is possible to whisper energetically). Energy level conveys many subtle messages to the listener. It conveys your interest in connecting with the listener, your interest in the topic being discussed and most important, your passion for the activity you are engaged in. Make sure to sustain a good energy level throughout the entire lecture.			
Clarity of Speech	Clarity of speech is lost due to several different reasons such as limited competency in the target language, poor enunciation, and poor projection, but mostly, it is due to laziness which becomes a habit in adults. An instructor cannot afford to be a lazy speaker.			
Enunciation	Different from pronunciation, enunciation has to do with the way each sound is formulated n the word. Pronunciation depends on *correctness* of sound/s used in speech. Enunciation focuses on the *clarity* with which each sound is articulated.			

Component	Description	Good	Acceptable	Needs Attention
Pace	Very important for keeping the students alert and engaged. impacts both clarity and listener engagement. As instructors, we need to pay special attention to keeping an optimal pace. If you speak too fast, students may not understand you; if you speak too slowly, they may go to sleep.			
Modulation	Like Pace – the use of modulation impacts both clarity and listener engagement. Modulation helps the speaker to use the voice as a highlighter – emphasizing the parts of speech by using a higher pitch and slower pace			
Projection	Projection refers to your ability to 'throw' your voice to become audible to the last row. Speakers are said to have poor projection if they keep the sound in their mouth which sounds like mumbling. If you have a large class and think, your voice may not reach the last benches, please invest in a microphone. This small, inexpensive device can work wonders in enhancing your spoken image.			
Eye Contact	Eyes are one of the most powerful communicators. One big advantage PowerPoint presentations have over the blackboards is that they allow the instructor to face the students and keep constant eye contact with them			
Facial Expression	Facial expressions are powerful communicators of happiness, unhappiness, irritation, anger, or pain. Be sensitive about your and your students' facial expressions. A smile goes a long way!			

Component	Description	Good	Acceptable	Needs Attention
Posture	Posture controls the energy level and conveys a person's level of confidence. Good posture allows one to breathe well and that in turn impacts the energy level.			

Make a copy of the blank format is provided at pp 255 - 256 to evaluate your spoken image. Identify the areas you need to work on, and actively work on them. You will notice that half the battle is won by just becoming aware of the importance of this aspect of your profession.

5.6   Two Additional Modes for Delivering Instruction

To add variety and stimulate the learning process, the instructors can enliven course delivery by using two innovative modes: the *Flipped Class* and *Peer-Supported Independent Study (PSIS)*. Both these research-validated methods are based on the principles of group-based learning and benefit from social interaction and shared learning. Both these course delivery formats promote academic ownership in students and encourage them to take charge of their own learning. Both promote higher-order learning and graduate attributes like team building, interpersonal communication, and critical thinking. However, the two formats serve very different objectives. While the *Flipped Class* is designed to promote in-depth learning and academic competence, the *PSIS* is designed to promote autonomy, learner confidence and self-efficacy.

5.6.1   The Flipped Class

The Concept

As an innovative course delivery format, the *Flipped Class* is especially suitable for undergraduate teaching because it helps to promote in-depth learning and student accountability. The concept reverses (flips) the normal instructional process. In the conventional course delivery process, students receive new input in class and do practice work individually out of class (homework or assignments). In the *Flipped Class* mode, the students study the content by themselves using the materials provided by the instructor and then in class, work in small groups on a designed practice activities under the supervision of the instructor. Normally, the flipped class is not graded, though some type of student feedback (may be a quiz) must be planned to ensure that everyone has achieved the learning outcome.

Planning and Implementing a Flipped Class

To conduct a successful flipped class, the instructor needs to make several decisions. The following steps can help the instructor plan and implement a successful flipped class.

Table 5.d – Steps for Planning and Implementing a Flipped Class

Steps	Required Action
Step 1 Explain the concept to the students	It is important to begin by sharing the concept of the flipped class and its pedagogical benefits. This will help to get students excited about the process. Clearly explain the concept, the process, their role, and responsibility in learning the material, and the in-class activity. Focus on the benefits and how the mode promotes attributes like in-depth learning, interpersonal communication, self-reliance, leadership etc., that are essential for career building If your students are experiencing this mode for the first time, provide written instructions.
Step 2 Identify a suitable topic & Write outcome for the Session	You want to use this mode judiciously for selected learning units. Identify a topic that students need to master. It could be a core concept/part-concept that is important from the exam point of view or forms a pre-requisite for the next course. Write and share the outcome/s for this specific session.
Step 3 Pick a suitable time	This is an important consideration especially when you are using this mode for the first time. You need to ensure that students are well-settled in class, have had the time to understand the importance of the course and know their peers well. Weeks where major college events or exams are scheduled may not be the best time to use the flipped class mode.

Steps	Required Action
Step 4 Choosing Learning Materials	• Remember, these materials will be studied in self-learning mode, so you need to provide learning materials that are clearly written out and are easy to follow. Including guidelines on 'How to Study' is highly recommended. The learning materials can be in any mode that you think appropriate: • *Text Materials* – could be a chapter from a book; a scholarly article; or a mini lecture prepared by you. Do not randomly assign the reading, instead guide the students by highlighting the specific pages/portions that they should be focusing on. You can provide some reflective or problem-solving questions that students are required to respond as they complete the reading. • *Audio or Video Materials* – can be recorded by you or another expert or selected from an existing video course/ MOOC. • If you are choosing an existing video lecture, do not be enamored by the name of the Professor or the University. Watch the entire video yourself to ascertain its suitability from the point of view of content (relevance of the explanations and examples used) and delivery (the language and pronunciation of the narrator). Identify specific sections that students are required to watch. You can provide a set of small questions to help them check their learning as they go through the video. • Once you have chosen the video lecture, do not ask them to randomly view the entire one-hour video and come prepared to class – identify specific sections that students should focus on. • Upload the learning materials on the chosen online platform. Give students sufficient time to students to complete the reading/viewing the content. A time span of 3-5 days is found to be optimal.

Steps	Required Action
Step 5 Managing the in-class activity	• This is the most important part of the Flipped Class and needs meticulous planning for both the design and the implementation process. The following guidelines are recommended: • ***Design Considerations*** • Based on the reading material provided to the students, create at least two sets of activities/problems of progressive difficulty that the group is expected to work on during the class session. Make sure that these are higher-order learning problems where the groups need to apply the knowledge gained in the reading/s. Remember, just discussing a problem/topic is not good enough. Students must be actively engaged in thinking and doing. For disciplines where brainstorming or constructive discussions are indispensable, require students to write a report or design a presentation. • Make sure that the activities/problems can be completed within the class hour. Keep time for questions and review. If you cannot complete two activities, design one activity/problem that has two parts. • Provide the questions as a handout so that there is a common understanding within the group members. • ***Implementation Considerations*** • Start by asking if they have any questions about the reading, or just ask a few questions to check whether the students have understood the content. • Depending on the type of classroom, make the students sit in small groups (3 for a stadium-type classroom; and 5 for a classroom with movable chairs). If the content to be studied is highly complex, you may want to put students in pre-created, mixed-ability groups and inform them about their group number, etc. ahead of time. • Walk around and glance over groups to monitor if they are headed in the right direction. Provide help if needed.

Steps	Required Action
	• Allocate a time slot for the first problem/activity. After the stipulated time, ask one person from some of the groups to present their solution. Now, give them time to work on the second, more complex activity/problem. Ask for responses from the other groups.
Step 6 Collecting Student Feedback	At the end of the class, collect student feedback. This can be done either by giving a follow-up quiz or asking students to complete a prepared feedback form. Make sure both cognitive (*Did the reading and the in-class activity help you to understand the concept?*) and affective (*did you enjoy the activity? Would you like to have another Flipped Class?*) aspects are covered in the feedback.

5.6.2   Peer-Supported Independent Study (PSIS)

The Concept

The PSIS is an innovative student-centric strategy that focuses on developing learner confidence by promoting autonomy and collaboration. As a learning strategy, the PSIS is very different from the conventional independent study because it is an integral part of regular class work and course assessment. The concept, developed by the author, addresses two very important challenges faced by undergraduate instructors: getting students constructively engaged in coursework and optimizing class time to be able to finish the course on time. The PSIS requires the instructor to identify portions of the regular coursework that students can manage by themselves and design tasks that students complete online independently in small groups. The completed tasks are submitted online by the group as assignments that are graded according to a rubric provided by the instructor at the beginning of the activity.

Based on a solid theoretical framework of social constructivist theory and peer-instruction theory, PSIS promotes student engagement and fosters learning. It combines the benefits of both independent study (accountability, self-reliance, and self-esteem) and collaborative learning. (social interaction, positive interdependence, and peer learning). Surveys conducted after the implementation of PSIS activity over several semesters showed excellent results in terms of enhanced student engagement, an improved class learning environment, and optimized class instruction time *(Kumar, 2023)*.

As PSIS is conducted online, it allows the instructor to save class time and help in completing the coursework on time. Except for the initial introduction of the concept of PSIS, which is done in class, the entire PSIS activity is completed online. Faculty surveys conducted by the author across disciplines confirmed that a comfortable range of 10% to 15% of the course content that is regularly taught in classes can be managed by students on their own and is therefore suitable for PSIS. In another independent survey, the responding instructors claimed that at the end of the semester, they are typically left with about 10%–15% of the unfinished coursework for which they need to arrange additional class sessions *(Kumar, 2023)*. If PSIS is implemented effectively, it will help both the students and the instructors to save some of the end-of-semester rush and stress. As PSIS is a graded activity, the students take it seriously, and the independent work they do helps them to develop self-efficacy and confidence.

Planning and Implementing PSIS

The success of any innovative strategy depends on how well it is planned and executed. PSIS, being a new strategy for both the students and the instructors, requires meticulous planning. Even though the strategy may not bring the desired results in the first implementation, but its potential and positive impact is felt immediately by both the students and the instructors. The following guidelines can help the instructors to plan and implement PSIS successfully.

Table 5.e – Planning & Implementing Peer-Supported Independent Study (PSIS)

Steps	Required Action
Step 1 Explaining the Activity to Students	It is important to prepare the students and put them in the right frame of mind before starting the activity. Begin by sharing the concept, the process, their role and responsibilities, and the evaluation pattern. Emphasize the benefits of working independently with a small peer group. Your objective here, is to get the student excited. Explain how the completed assignment will be evaluated and how you plan to monitor and support the groups.

Steps	Required Action
Step 2 Selecting the content for PSIS	This is an important part of the activity. The instructor must identify sections of the course content that the students can manage themselves. It is best to do so before the start of the semester. Most college instructors confirm that there is a good 10% to 15% content that students can comfortably study by themselves. As this activity is new and will be a part of course evaluation, it is important to choose content that is of low-grade value from the exam point of view.
Step 3 Designing Assignment tasks/ problems based on the selected content.	Once the area/topic has been selected, the instructor will need to design the tasks/problems. Depending on the size of the class, the instructors may choose to give the same assignment task/problem to all the groups or create 3-4 different tasks to give groups a choice. The task/ problem must be open-ended with different ways/approaches for arriving at the solutions. The task should be of medium difficulty level with scope for being divided into sub-tasks so that each member of the group can be given a separate responsibility. Tasks that involve research, analysis, critical thinking and problem-solving are most effective. It is important to ensure that the tasks can be completed within the planned time slot.
Step 4 Setting up an online space for student interaction	PSIS is designed to be conducted online. It is therefore important to set-up the required technology platform where students will interact and post their completed assignments. You can choose a Learning Management System that the students who are conversant with (like Canvas, Moodle, Blackboard, Google Classroom, etc.), or create a special virtual classroom (Google Classroom) for the activity. The LMS or the virtual classroom must have the capability for *creating and mentoring groups* and posting *learning materials and submitting completed assignments*. You will create a special folder for PSIS. (To learn more about setting up a virtual classroom using an LMS, please see Section 7, (pp - 196 -198).

Steps	Required Action
Step 5 Selecting and posting learning resources.	Here, the instructor must take care of three main tasks: i) Identify the suitable resources for completing each task. ii) Upload resources/links along with a brief description and guidelines for using them efficiently. iii) Create and upload guidelines/steps for completing the different assignments. Provide deadlines for each step. All readings/links must be uploaded before the start date.
Step 6 Forming groups	Create small groups of 3 – 5 students. Once again, it is best to create mixed-ability groups so that the stronger participants can help the group advance. To learn about the different types of groups and the process for creating each type, please see Section 6 (pp - 173 - 175)
Step 7 Implementing and Monitoring PSIS	This is an important step and needs to be planned carefully. Once the groups are formed and the tasks have been allocated (or chosen by the groups), The instructor must evolve a suitable and efficient way of monitoring student interaction/progress. Keeping the overall intervention to a minimum, the instructor must provide subtle and timely support to the groups. Two strategies that work best for monitoring the groups are: i) Create a discussion thread ("Ask the Professor") on the work platform. ii) When you create groups on the platform (LMS or Virtual Classroom), include yourself as a sleeping member of each group. That way, you can keep an eye on how the group is interacting/progressing and are able to provide subtle but timely guidance. iii) The instructor can schedule one or two online meetings for the duration of the PSIS and require at least one member of each group to be present. Representation in the meeting can be made a part of the grading rubric. This strategy is found to be very effective.

Steps	Required Action
Step 8 Evaluating PSIS	PSIS is a graded activity, and students must be informed about it right in the beginning. This will help the students to take the activity much more seriously. To ensure a smooth run of the evaluation phase, the instructors must: • Create and post the rubric at the start of the project so that students know how they will be evaluated. • Provide all instructions in simple, clear writing. List the accepted formats – text (docx/pdf), pictures/graphics / videos, PowerPoint presentations etc. • Create a folder where groups will post their completed assignments. • To add seriousness to the assignments, request a colleague or a course alumnus to evaluate them. • Provide access to all students to view and learn from other groups' entries. The best two or three submissions can be applauded in the class.

The PSIS activity offers a win-win solution for both the instructors and the students. It allows students the opportunity to engage in peer study, enjoy autonomy, and gain confidence while developing several much-desired graduate attributes such as team building, critical thinking, problem-solving, improved communication, and lifelong learning. At the same time, by virtue of being an online activity, PSIS offers instructors additional time to focus on more complex and core concepts.

Whenever we plan to experiment with a new methodology, it is normal to think of deterrents that may emerge as big obstructions to the successful completion of the activity. Some of the common apprehensions recorded for the Flipped Class and PSIS are:

- Students will not read or view the assigned learning materials and will not be well-prepared to complete the in-class activity.
- Only some students will participate actively in the group activity.
- The group work will be difficult to manage.
- The entire exercise will be too time-consuming.

Each one of these apprehensions is real, and the instructor must anticipate them and be well-prepared to address them. However, these challenges are common to any group activity. In the final analysis, the exceptional results in terms of in-depth learning, enhanced student engagement, accountability, and learner confidence make it worthwhile for an instructor to invest the time and effort to make these strategies a regular part of the undergraduate instructional process.

A Word of Caution

- Do not expect to get perfect results the first time; the delivery becomes refined with each iteration.

- Do not plan to use these strategies as the principal mode of delivery. They are most effective when used for specific objectives and for selected content.

- For both the Flipped Class and PSIS, success depends on careful planning (*selection of content, timings, preparation of learning materials,* and *design of activities*) as well as on meticulous implementation (*clarity of instructions, group formation,* and *monitoring*). These activities require time and effort but the amazing results in terms of quality and joy of learning that you will witness will make it all worthwhile.

5.7   The First Day of the Class

Experience shows that both the instructor and the students tend to take the first day of class somewhat non-seriously. Instructors feel that not all students will be present, and they will have to repeat much of the information and conversation again. The students feel that nothing important is likely to happen on the first day, so they trickle in half-heartedly or miss it altogether. This perception needs to change because, the opening day of the course is extremely important for communicating several subtle messages and setting clear parameters for delivering your course.

5.7.1   Introducing Yourself and Your Course

Whether you are teaching a course for the first time or for the fifth time, your first class is very important and needs to be planned carefully. Effective management of the first class helps you achieve a number of specific objectives related to establishing rapport with the students and demonstrating the value of the course. It is crucial to generate intellectual excitement and motivation in students for the content to be studied in the course. On the first day of class, undergraduate students have many concerns about the course as well as the instructor. The instructor must plan to mitigate these concerns, make the students feel at ease, and win their confidence.

About the course, the students are concerned about whether it is going to be tough, interesting, and teach something relevant to their future careers. You need to establish that this is an exciting course and that the key concepts they will learn (just the overall picture) will benefit them academically and professionally. At the undergraduate level, each course is designed differently, and this is the time to incite the curiosity of the students about what they will learn and how it will be taught. Share highlights of your methodology and some special activities they will complete. Avoid describing each module or unit; instead, talk about the kinds of skills they will be learning. If you are teaching a theoretical course, explain the importance of the theory in the context of other courses and real-world applications.

Students are equally curious to know whether the instructor will be strict, boring, indifferent, or amazing. You need to plan your introduction to convey several subtle messages (I *am an expert in the subject, I take teaching seriously, it is important for me that all my students enjoy the course and complete it with good grades, etc.*). It is important to show the human and fun side of your personality. Talk about yourself (I am a big foodie; I am a tennis fan, and I am honest and like people to be honest with me etc.).

Table 5.f – The Four Objectives to be Achieved on the First day of Class

Objective	Suggested Plan of Action
Connect with students	Prepare a personal introduction that will establish your expertise and passion for the subject and help to connect with the students. Instead of talking about your biodata – tell the students how you love the subject – what kind of research/projects you have been involved in. What is special about the subject etc.
Get students excited about the course they are about to start!	Prepare an introduction of the course so that students look forward to participating in it. In addition to the key content of the course, talk about the methodology and some special activities they can look forward to – a special project, an off-site visit, a guest speaker etc.
Set the ground rules	Prepare a one-page policy document addressing key disciplinary issues (see pp – 113-115). The same information should be posted also in the virtual classroom.
Demonstrate your seriousness about your teaching and supporting the students	Talk about the different ways in which you plan to stay in touch with the students and what are your expectations of office hours etc. Prepare a short activity related to the academic content of the course. This is also a good time to have a quiz about prerequisites.

Every teacher wants to be liked by his or her students and is often worried about how to present himself or herself to them. This anxiety is even greater in teachers who are new to the profession.

The first decision is about the level of familiarity you want to allow in your interaction with the students. We are told that instructor must act like a facilitator. A facilitator helps the learner to get to his or her own understanding of the content instead of simply explaining a principle *(Bauersfeld, 1995)*. The fact is that you must be both a ***Cop*** and a ***Comrade*** at different times. The *Cop* lays down the high standards to be achieved in the course, and the *Comrade* steps in to ensure that all possible help is provided so that everyone can achieve their set academic goals. The most important thing is to communicate this to the students on the first day of class. Peter Elbow describes these two roles as that of a *Gate Keeper* and a *Coach*:

" ...we have an obligation to students but also to knowledge and society. Our loyalty to students asks us to be their allies ...to invite all students to enter in and join us as members of a learning community. We have responsibility to society – that is to our discipline, our college or university and to other learning communities of which we are members (Elbow, 1986).

5.7.2   Planning an Academic Activity for the First Day of Class

As can be seen, the list of tasks to be completed on the first day of class is rather long. Another important one to be added to the list is to plan a short teaching activity. By beginning the teaching process on day 1, many subtle messages are conveyed to the students. It tells them that you are a well-organized, efficient, and dedicated instructor and that you value time. It is important to come prepared with a small bite from the course that will excite them and raise their curiosity about the course. Another strategy that works well for the first class is to have *a short verbal quiz on course prerequisites*. If you plan to conduct a quiz, the best way is to use PowerPoint. You can create a set of slides where each slide has one multiple-choice question. Project the question, let students think for 1 minute, and then respond by show of hands. You can then reveal the correct answer. The activity sends a positive signal to the students and provides you feedback about the approximate number of students who will need help to boost their background knowledge. This immediate feedback will be very helpful in planning the course. Make sure to tell them how you propose to help the students who need to master the prerequisites and review parts of the previous course.

5.8   Section 5: Wrap-Up and Tips for Making an Engaging Course Delivery

In this section, we have focused on different issues related to delivering courses in a well-organized and effective way. As always, we started by identifying the challenges commonly reported about delivering effective lectures. The main objective of this section is to plan and deliver effective lectures. Five main components of planning and the five components of delivering an effective lecture are discussed in detail. In addition, two very effective alternatives for designing learning activities—*The Flipped Class* and *The Peer-Supported Independent Study (PSIS)* are discussed with step-by-step instructions for planning and implementing them. Input regarding the importance of one's spoken image and how it impacts the communication process is discussed. Finally, effective preparation for the all-important first day of class is discussed. As always, the section ends with tips for ensuring a very forceful and motivating course delivery.

Table. 5. g – Tips for Making an Engaging Course Delivery

Tips	Recommendations
1.	Begin by putting yourself in your students' shoes or thinking of your own student days and list of things that annoyed you or made you uncomfortable in your lectures. Reflect and make sure to avoid them.
2.	Based on the learning from *theories of learning* and *theories of motivation*, plan your course delivery around four important principles i) adults learn by *need,* ii) the brain processes information in *small chunks,* iii) learning happens when students get an opportunity to work together in class to *construct/re-construct knowledge,* and iv) students need to develop *self-reliance and confidence.*
3.	Remember that the key component for a successful lecture is 'preparation'. If an average lecture requires x no. of hours to prepare; a good lecture would need 2x no. of hours, and an outstanding one, 3x. That is the reason why a lot of preparation and identification of resources must be completed *before the start of the semester.*
4.	Plan at least one in-class active learning intervention for each lecture (see sample activities in Section 6 (pp - 162- 169). If you plan to have tutorials/ study groups, plan activities for those sessions too.
5.	Deliver content in small chunks and provide proper transitions by summing up point one and introducing point two. Plan to collect feedback from different sources and use it to refine your strategies (pp - 234 - 238).

Tips	Recommendations
6.	Be sensitive about students' attention span. Keep track of your talking time which should not exceed 65% of the class time. Vary the activities during the lecture. Make sure you are audible to the last bench. If required, invest in a personal microphone.
7.	While delivering lectures pay attention to: i) Your eye contact – do not read from notes or slides. It disrupts eye contact and negatively impacts your image as the content expert. ii) Your energy level – make sure it is consistent throughout the lecture. Keeping a good posture helps. iii) Your pace of delivery. It should be optimal neither too fast nor too slow. Slow down while addressing the more complex parts of the content. iv) Your voice modulation. Use your voice as a highlighter. Complete the self-evaluation form and note down your strengths and weaknesses in the Reflective Report (pp - 256 - 257).
8.	Plan to use the Flipped class mode for a few chosen lectures. This needs meticulous planning and implementation (review input on pp - 135 - 139). Do not plan to deliver an entire course in the Flipped mode.
9.	To optimize your class instruction time, try PSIS where the less-complex portions of the content are converted into mini collaborative projects that students complete by themselves online in small groups. (review input on pp - 139-144). This unique research-validated strategy is much appreciated by both the instructors and the students.

<table><tr><td>6</td><td></td></tr></table>

Managing Student Engagement

6.1 About Student Engagement

What is student engagement? It is one of those phenomena that is easy to spot but hard to define. The Glossary of Education Reforms defines student engagement as *"the degree of attention, curiosity, interest, optimism, and passion that students show when they are learning or being taught."* In other words, we can say that students are engaged when they are seriously involved in their work, despite the challenges and obstacles, and take visible delight in accomplishing their work *(Schlechty, 2001)*.

Looking at the above definition, student engagement and motivation appear to be two sides of the same coin. When students are motivated, they become engaged, and the more engaged they are, the more motivated they become. The motivation-engagement phenomenon seriously impacts learning, which in turn impacts academic performance. There is no doubt that student engagement has a very powerful impact on student success *(Chandler, 2021)*.

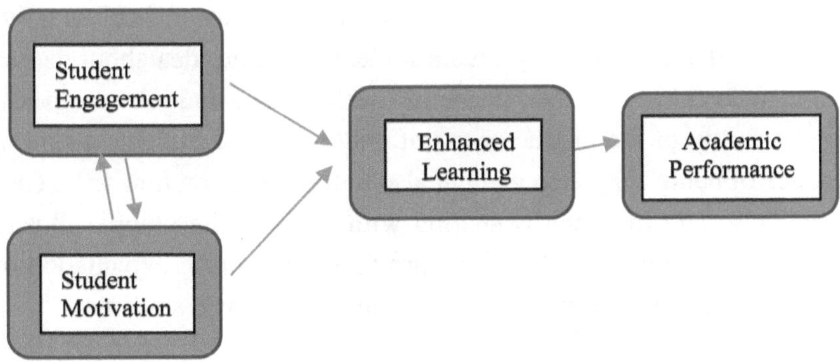

Fig. 6.1 – Student Engagement – Performance Interaction

In the undergraduate learning environment, student engagement can be identified by three indicators: *Cognitive Engagement, Behavioral Engagement,* and *Emotional Engagement. Cognitive Engagement* can be observed when students are actively involved in their learning and are willing to invest the time and effort to master the academic content and complete all required assignments and examinations to the best of their capability. *Behavioral Engagement* can be observed through students' involvement in social, academic, and extracurricular activities, and their willingness to follow the class and college rules. *Emotional Engagement* is displayed through students' attitudes (positive or negative) towards the course, instructor, peers, and the institution. Students are emotionally engaged when they have a sense of belonging and find the class environment pleasant and welcoming. Positive emotional engagement promotes students' intrinsic motivation which in turn positively impacts their academic performance. All these three dimensions are interconnected and closely linked to student motivation. It is very important for the instructor to make a conscious effort to create an ambiance that nurtures all three aspects of student engagement to make learning more meaningful and enriching.

6.2   Dimensions of Student Engagement

As instructors, we have a rather narrow view of student engagement and tend to link it exclusively to student participation during class sessions. But the impact of student engagement is much wider and deeper. Often, we instructors complain about students' lack of participation and engagement in class activities, but the fact is that most undergraduate students have no idea about the impact active engagement has on their academic performance and job readiness. It is the responsibility of the instructor to not only make the students aware of the importance of being fully engaged but also to train them on *how* to be engaged constructively. The first step is sharing with students the graphic illustrating the process of learning (p - 50). This provides a scientific explanation of the interdependence of learning and engagement to our Gen Z students.

Holistic student engagement requires the students to be actively involved in all four dimensions shown below, and it is the responsibility of the instructor to create opportunities for students to do so.

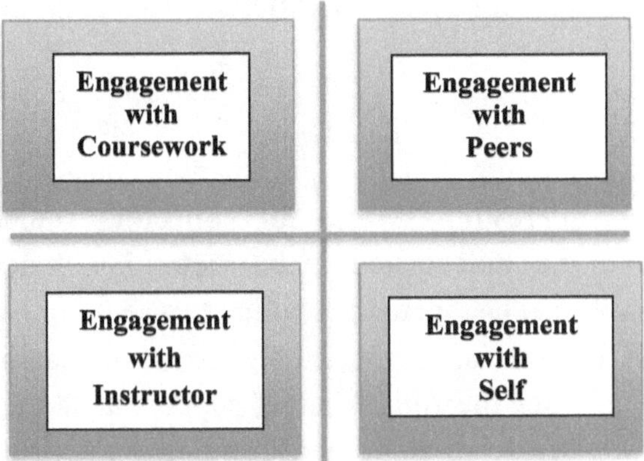

Fig. 6.2 – Dimensions of Student Engagement

All these four dimensions are interconnected and closely linked to students' personal growth and academic performance. It is very important for the instructor to make a conscious effort to create an ambiance that nurtures all four aspects of student engagement and makes learning more meaningful and enriching.

6.2.1   Promoting Engagement with Coursework

This is the most important dimension, and the instructor must devise creative ways to ensure it. Three basic strategies can be very helpful:

- Create additional avenues (a designated virtual classroom) to interact with different sets of students.

- Collecting and incorporating student feedback into regular classroom instruction.

- Avoiding predictability: keep your students surprised.

The first step is to create a *virtual classroom* that will supplement your actual classroom and extend your presence beyond class time. With the availability of many free and readily available resources, this has become a very simple process that takes no more than a few hours. The virtual classroom allows you to communicate individually or collectively and support the learning needs of different sets of students. The process of setting up a *virtual classroom* and how to use it effectively for achieving different goals is discussed in detail in Section 7 (pp - 196 - 198).

Taking student feedback and using it to sharpen your classroom instruction can work wonders in promoting student engagement in coursework. Establishing a functional and interesting system for collecting student feedback is invaluable for both the students and the instructor. For students, it promotes cognitive and emotional engagement, leading to a sense of partnership in the learning process. For the instructor, it helps to refine teaching and provide the opportunity to offer the right kind of support at the right time. Later in this section, we will learn some quick and easy activities for collecting student feedback. In Section 7, some very effective technology options for collecting student feedback are discussed that are very attractive for Gen Z students.

Finally, avoiding predictability and keeping your students surprised is a sure way to keep them engaged in their coursework. What do we mean by avoiding *predictability?* During our college lives, we have all experienced an instructor who operated by the book. You knew exactly how the class would start, how it would end, and what activity would be conducted at what time during the class. Avoiding predictability does not require any specialized tools or activities. All you need to do is to plan every class session a little differently. Making small adjustments, like starting a class with a surprise test or a small group activity, Even just taking attendance at different times during the class can increase student alertness. Using the inductive style to introduce a new topic in a different way (see p - 127) can help to promote curiosity in the content being studied and promotes student engagement.

6.2.2   Promoting Engagement with Peers

Including opportunities for students to collaborate and work together is a sure way of nurturing learning *(Brownstein (2001).* Peer engagement helps in developing effective communication and fostering interpersonal relationships – two competencies that are so important for ensuring both academic success and job readiness. Moreover, we know students enjoy learning together. A large part of this section is devoted to activities that can be used to ensure peer engagement. Peer engagement activities can be divided into two main families:

active learning activities and collaborative learning activities. Later in this section, we will learn about ten active learning activities and six collaborative activities. Earlier, in Section 5, we learned about two different modes of course delivery – the Flipped Class (pp - 134 - 139) and PSIS (pp - 139 - 144) that are great promoters of peer engagement.

6.2.3 Promoting Instructor-Student Engagement

This is a very demanding task for the instructor, as most undergraduate students are hesitant to approach the instructor. Some students are shy, while others are reluctant to impose on the instructor's time. It is for the instructor to be welcoming and proactively encourage the students to connect with him or her. The key avenue for developing enriching interaction is the office hours, where the instructor can interact with students individually or in small groups. For students who have time constraints, arranging one online office hours in the evening or during the weekend can be very useful.

In Section 3, we saw that a typical undergraduate class has four different types of students that, using the analogy of athletics, may be categorized as *Winners, Active Runners, Survivors*, and *Outsiders*. Several tips have been provided for connecting with and supporting students from each of these four categories (p –). The main thing is to have a very relaxed and pleasant class environment where students feel free to ask questions and give suggestions.

6.2.4 Promoting Self-engagement

The most important and challenging task the instructor has is to promote a reflective mindset and self-engagement. We know that real progress comes when students take charge of their own learning. Coming from a school environment, undergraduate students are still very dependent on their instructors. While they may know *where* they want to go, they often do not know *how* to get there. This is the time to promote a reflective mindset. The following strategies work well:

- Encourage them to take a learning style quiz (pp - 74-75). This will allow them to get a better understanding of how they learn best.

- Occasionally, ask students to grade their own assignment using the given rubric and submit a brief report to justify the grade they have given themselves.

- Encourage them to keep a personal progress diary where they can note down situations or habits that help or hinder their learning.

- Teach them to set small personal goals, create timelines, and monitor their own progress.

- At the end of a group activity, ask them to write a reflective report about their experience of participating and learning in a group activity.

- Teach them to keep a record of situations or habits that interfere with their learning and class interaction.

6.3   Student Engagement and Employability Skills

Inclusion of well-designed student engagement activities is of special significance in undergraduate education because it not only promotes in-depth understanding of the content being studied but also helps in developing skills essential for succeeding in the fiercely competitive job market. We know that every undergraduate student is eagerly looking forward to entering the job market after completing the degree program, but it is also true that a degree alone does not guarantee employability. The positive impact of student engagement goes well beyond the classroom and helps students become career-ready, which is the subtle but an important goal of undergraduate education.

Research confirms that activities designed to promote student engagement also help in developing many of the required employability skills. Let us recall the ten 21st century employability skills that have been identified by the World Economic Forum: *Cognitive Flexibility, People Management, Negotiations, Complex Problem-solving, Critical Thinking, Coordinating with Others, Service Orientation, Decision-making, Emotional Intelligence, and Creativity* (pp - 67- 69). Well-designed student engagement activities play an important role in developing many, if not all, of the above-mentioned workplace skills. Strategies recommended in this book keep a sharp focus on developing these essential skills.

6.4   Learning Through Collaboration

Now that we have clarity about student engagement, the next question is: how can we ensure that students in our classes are fully engaged in their course work, their peers, and themselves? We have also seen the two-way relationship between student engagement and motivation. When students are motivated, they are fully engaged, and when students are engaged, they become motivated. In Section 3, we have learned a great deal about the theory of *motivation* and how it can be sustained through different practices. Before we start to plan strategies for promoting student engagement, it is important for instructors to know why we need to do so. As always, theory must guide practice.

6.4.1   The Theoretical Perspective

Motivation is important for learning. When students are motivated, they are engaged, and are inspired to take charge of their own learning. The close relationship between student engagement, motivation, and learning is strongly supported by the following theories discussed in earlier sections.

In the *constructivist theory*, Jean Piaget tells us that learning happens when the learner are seriously engaged in thinking, interpreting and manipulating the new input. This personal understanding gets assimilated into students' existing cognitive map. In other words, to learn new content, the student must be seriously engaged with the content to be learned.

In his famous theory of *Zone of Proximal Development theory*, Vygotsky tells us that social interaction promotes student engagement leading to learning (p –). Vygotsky brings out the difference between what students can perform by themselves and what they can do while working collaboratively with others *(Vygotsky & Cole, 1981)*. A well-designed group learning task 'allows the group members to combine different abilities, skills, knowledge, or other physical or cognitive resources that are more than any group member can produce alone' *(Chi, M. 1994)*. This is also confirmed by *brain-based learning* theory. In recent times, Eric Mezur's work has established the positive impact that peer-instruction has on learning. *(Mezur, 1997)*.

We have also seen that student engagement is crucial for sustaining students' *attention span*. It is known that human attention span, is no more than

10–12 minutes. This means that for a typical lecture of 55–60 minutes, the instructor must include some strategies to sustain student's attention span. In Section 5, we have learned how the *change of activity* (from listening to doing) can help resolve this issue (Fig. 5.5, p - 129). This *change of activity* may require the student to be engaged individually or collaboratively.

6.4.2   The Practical Perspective

Two clear directives emerging from the discussion on the theoretical perspective are: i) instruction should be so designed that students learn by *doing* (active) and not by just *listening or viewing* (passive), and ii) they get to work with their peers to develop and refine higher order thinking skills. Both these objectives are served when instructors make a conscious effort to design focused, interesting, and outcome-oriented activities that inspire students to get involved and collaborate actively.

To ensure result-oriented student engagement, the instructor must plan strategies that work at both the explicit and implicit levels. At the explicit level, the instructor needs to devise strategies that will allow the students to be actively involved in manipulating the learned content by discussing, analyzing, and applying it. At the implicit level, the instructor must ensure a pleasant, relaxed, and welcoming class environment where the affective filter is very low and the students feel comfortable discussing, asking questions, and expressing their opinions. Most effective strategies also offer students the opportunity to reflect and self-evaluate their own performance.

Depending on the schooling they have experienced, many undergrads are not keen on collaborating. To get the best results, it is important to first make students aware of the importance of collaboration for academic and professional success. It is a good idea to share the graphic on p -50 that scientifically explains the close connect between active engagement and learning. It is important to explain to the students how these activities also help in developing the 21st-century employability skills for becoming successful professionals. This will motivate them to participate more actively and draw the best benefits from collaborating with peers.

6.5   Active, Cooperative, and Collaborative Learning

In the domain of student engagement, one is often confused by terms like *active learning, collaborative learning,* and *cooperative learning.* The confusion arises because all three terms share the same conceptual origin, have many common features, and are used interchangeably in multiple, overlapping context. It is worth taking a few moments to clearly understand how these terms are generally defined and how they will be used in this book.

Active Learning, is a generic term that refers to an educational approach where students are involved in actively processing new knowledge by thinking, discussing, and manipulating it, as opposed to passively receiving it by listening to a lecture or viewing a video. It refers to "instructional activities involving students in doing things and thinking about what they are doing" *(Bonwell and Eison, 1991).* Research confirms that in comparison with conventional lecturing, active learning is much more effective in achieving learning outcomes, and improving retention *(Prince, 2004).*

Active learning activities are short (5–8 minutes) and designed to promote in-depth learning of the content being discussed during the lecture. These activities may be completed individually or in pairs, but they are generally not graded. These interventions are invaluable for the students (for sustaining attention span and promoting in-depth learning) as well as for instructors (for getting realistic feedback on how well the students have assimilated the content).

Collaborative Learning refers to a learning strategy where students are put in formal teams to work in a structured manner to achieve a well-defined goal. Collaboration has been defined as "*...an interactive process that engages two or more participants who work together to achieve outcomes they could not accomplish independently*" *(Salmons, 2011).* Collaborative activities where students work in formal teams, are invaluable in undergraduate teaching because they help to develop several of the graduate attributes that are indispensable for becoming employable. Research celebrates and strongly advocates the benefits of collaborative learning. A well-designed group task '*allows the group members to combine different abilities, skills, knowledge or* *other physical or cognitive resources that is more than any group member can produce alone' (Laughlin, 2011).*

Cooperative Learning, like collaborative learning is also an educational approach where students work in teams to complete on highly structured tasks. Both these terms, *Cooperative Learning* and *Collaborative Learning* share several common features and are often used interchangeably. Both are group activities where students work in pre-assigned teams on tasks that are graded. So, what is the difference? The difference lies in the approach and focus of the activities. *Collaborative Learning* is broader in approach and allows more autonomy to the team members. *Cooperative learning*, on the other hand, demands greater interdependence among team members, and the activities are generally conducted in class under the supervision of the instructor.

Looking at the above definitions, we can see that the distinction between *Cooperative* and *Collaborative Learning* is rather hazy. Both formats are highly structured, completed in formally created groups, and involve some form of evaluation. Moreover, these two terms are often used interchangeably for the same activity.

Bypassing the academic debate about *Collaborative* and *Cooperative Learning*, we will take a more practical approach, and discuss student engagement activities in two categories: ***Active Learning*** and ***Group-based Learning***. In this book, we will use the following working definitions for the two categories of student engagement activities:

- The term ***Active Learning*** will be used for short (3–8 minutes) ungraded activities that are woven into the lecture to promote in-depth learning and get effective feedback about how the new knowledge has been received and assimilated. These activities may be completed individually or by pairs (or threesomes) of students sitting together. Activities like *Think-Pair-Share* or *Verbal Quiz* fall into this category.

- The term ***Group-based Learning*** will be used for more structured activities that are completed by formally assigned teams independently or under the supervision of the instructor. Generally, students work on these activities for an extended period that may range from one class to several classes. In addition to ensuring in-depth learning, these activities are designed to encourage a healthy collaborative environment, leading to the bonding of the group and the growth of individual group members. Activities like *jigsaw* or *Teams-Games-Tournaments* (TGT), and *Project-based Learning*, fall into this category.

6.6   Managing Active Learning

Active learning activities, as defined above, are invaluable for stimulating the teaching-learning process. They are equally helpful to the students, the instructor, and the class environment. Active learning activities help the students to assimilate and internalize the new knowledge and help the instructors get instant feedback on how well the new knowledge is being understood. They energize the class environment by promoting active interaction and open communication. However, like every other aspect of classroom management, the successful incorporation of these activities into regular course delivery requires careful planning, preparation, and smart management of time. To make the best use of these activities, two points must be kept in mind: a) there are no formal teams, and b) there is no formal evaluation. The activities may be completed individually or by students sitting together. Several research studies confirm that active learning activities reinforce learning and construction of new knowledge through discussion and the active exchange of information *[Bodner G. M., 1986; Taber K. S., 2011]*.

6.6.1   Ten Effective Active Learning Activities

As mentioned earlier, active learning activities are very short (5-8 minutes) and are meant to be woven into the class session. There are no formal teams; students work with their immediate neighbors (pairs or threesomes). The focus is on the completion of a given task, resulting in a shared understanding of the content being covered in the lecture.

Active learning has been the subject of extensive research, and many interesting activities have been devised that work across disciplines. Here, we will discuss ten simple, well-researched, easy-to-implement activities. There are other activities that can be accessed through scholarly articles.

Step-by-step instructions for conducting each one of the ten activities summarized below are included so that a motivated instructor can start implementing them immediately.

Table 6.a – Ten Effective In-class Activities for Promoting Active Learning

Activity	Time Required	Intended Outcome
1. Class Polls	2 – 3 Minutes	To get realistic feedback about student learning by using technology/non-technology-based options. The feedback is anonymous,
2. Summarizing	3 – 5 minutes	To get immediate feedback
3. Minute Paper	3 – 4 minutes	To get realistic feedback and help the instructor to address both individual and collective student needs
4. Think-Pair-Share	5 – 6 minutes	To make students review part of the content covered by solving a question/problem, first individually and then by discussing with one or both neighbors
5. Think Aloud Pair Problem-Solving (TAPPS)	6 – 8 minutes	to identify gaps in learning and develop problem-solving skills. The activity is carried out in pairs and focuses on a logical progression of the problem-solving process.
6. Verbal Quiz	16 – 20 minutes	To revise an important concept or a completed unit. Pairs/Threesomes work together to arrive at the correct solution. Because of the time required, this activity needs to be well-planned and implemented judiciously.
7. Designing Questions	5 – 7 minutes	To promote in-depth learning & critical thinking. The activity reverses the students' role by asking them to create questions on the content covered in class.
8. Problem Solving activity	5 – 6 minutes	To promote problem-solving and critical thinking among students. Students are presented with a real-world problem/situation related to a concept, product, or process that they try to resolve working in pairs or threesomes.

Activity	Time Required	Intended Outcome
9. Critical thinking Activities	8 – 10 minutes	To promote reflection and develop critical thinking – students are required to analyze a given problem, examine all possible solutions choose the most appropriate one, and provide justification for the choice.
10. Concept Tests	8-10 minutes	To promote in-depth learning and develop problem-solving skills. Here, the students respond to multiple-choice questions either individually or with peers after discussion, analysis, and mutual agreement.

As can be seen from the above table, the first three activities – *Class Polls, Summarizing* and *Minute paper*—are individual activities mainly meant for getting feedback about student learning in a specific context. The other seven activities are conducted in pairs (or threesomes) and are focused on reinforcing learning and assimilation of new knowledge. Let us learn how to implement each one of these activities:

Activity #1 Class Polls

One of the most effective and efficient activities in this group is Class Poll. Experience shows that polls are loved alike by students and instructors because they are anonymous, fast, and easy-to-use. The best part is that they are simple and fast to implement. Conducting a poll should take no more than 3 minutes. Polls can be taken at the beginning (based on a previous lecture), in the middle, at the end of a lecture, or in a lab class.

Using technology to prepare and conduct class polls is the most effective and interesting mode for our Gen Z students who are ever so keen to use their cell phones. Several free software and apps are now available that can be downloaded to participate in these polls (pp - 209-212). The instructor must keep some time to explain the process for downloading and using the app or still better, run a trial session in class. It is worth spending the time to get the system going because this is one activity that you can use in almost every lecture.

If using technology is not viable, PowerPoint can be used quite effectively to get the same information. Come prepared with one slide (per poll) with a multiple-choice question on the portion covered, project it on the screen, and ask students to think for a minute and then vote for each option by *show of hands*. Please do not ask students to give the correct answer but try and get that information by asking them *"hands up for those who think option A is the right answer."* This way, you can get a clear idea of how many students have understood the content and, accordingly, make an educated decision about whether to go forward or spend some more time explaining the content.

Activity #2 Summarizing

A very simple, common-sense activity involves asking students to summarize the key takeaways from the part of the lecture just completed. This activity can be used at any time during the class – right in the beginning to summarize a previous segment or a previous lecture; in the middle to reinforce a completed segment of the lecture; or at the end of the lecture. To optimize time, ask specific students to respond. This generates energy and motivates students to pay attention, as they do not know who will be called upon to summarize. The activity is completed in two steps:

Step 1: Ask one of the students to summarize the content learned. You may intentionally choose to ask a shy student, a distracted student, or a diligent one to achieve additional student management objectives.

Step 2: Give 1 minute for a response. If the response is incomplete, ask other students to fill in the missing points.

Activity #3 One-Minute Paper

This is one of the most commonly used activities in the American universities. Even though the title says 'one-minute' paper, the activity normally takes 3 – 4 minutes. This is very effective for getting precise feedback about students' learning. It is also very easy-to-implement and can be done at the beginning, middle, or towards the end of a lecture. Using the minute paper helps the instructor to identify gaps in learning for individual students as well as the collective class. The activity involves the following steps:

Step 1: Students are asked to respond in writing (just one or two lines) to questions such as "which part of the concept is unclear to you"; "what part of the content/question you would like to be reviewed?".

Step 2: Students get one minute to write their responses (that is where the name of the activity comes from). It is more efficient if you can pass pre-cut pieces of paper to the students to write their responses.

Step 3: The instructor collects the papers, identifies the areas that need to be reviewed, and addresses them first thing in the next class meeting. This is the most important step. The students immediately see the value of the activity and are happy to participate in it. If the instructor is not serious about discussing the feedback, the students become reluctant to participate in it again.

Activity #4 Think-Pair-Share (TPS)

The activity was developed by Frank Lyman in 1981, and is recognized as one of the most effective, and easy-to-implement activities. It can be completed in a very short time (5 – 6 minutes). It is best used when a concept/or part-concept has been completed and the teacher wants to check how well the students have understood it. As the name suggests, this activity is completed in three steps.

Step 1: (Think): The instructor starts by asking a question or setting a problem based on the content just covered in the lecture. Make sure that the question is at least an application or analysis level question that requires thinking. Each student is asked to study the question and think quietly. Students can take 1-1:30 minute to think and write down their response.

Step 2: (Pair): Students are then asked to pair up with the neighbor and discuss their responses. For more complex problems or very large classes, you may have threesomes work together. The pair discusses and comes up with an agreed response. You will notice that the noise level will go up at this point, but you must keep a sharp eye on timing. Pairs may be given 2 minutes to complete this step. Everything tends to fall in place once the activity moves on to the next step.

Step 3: (*Share*) The instructor then asks (randomly) two or three pairs to give their responses. Other groups are asked to add if their responses are radically different. (2-3 minutes).

Activity #5 Thinking Aloud Pair Problem-Solving (TAPPS)

This activity is credited to Lochhead and Whimbe (1987). The activity is designed to develop problem-solving skills through discussion and the sharing of ideas. Here, partners construct a common contextual framework to understand the concept taught, and they do it by jointly solving a given problem based on the concept taught. The activity is conducted using the following steps:

Step 1: The instructor designs two questions. Each question has two parts presented in two different handouts: i) describing the problem or case study (based on the concept studied), and ii) showing the solution along with the steps required to arrive at the solution. The second question also has its own set of two handouts.

Step 2: Students are explained the activity and its importance. Students are asked to pair with their neighbor to play a specific role. Each pair is given the first set of problem-solution handout. The person with the problem acts as the *Solver* while the one holding the solution acts as the *Inquirer*.

Step 3: The *solver* reads the problem aloud and begins to work out the solution in steps. The inquirer follows *Solver*'s logic, catches any errors, or flaws, and asks questions if *Solver*'s begins to lose direction. The *inquirer* is not supposed to share the solution but guide the *solver* by pointing out the errors.

Step 4: The pair then works on the second problem with the reversed roles of the *Solver* and the *Inquirer*. At the end of the allocated time, the instructor takes verbal feedback and explains any gray areas.

Activity #6 Verbal Quiz

This activity is a big favorite with the students because it works like a game and evokes a sense of competition. It is best used after a substantial segment of the course, or an entire unit of the course has been completed. The activity is recognized for promoting student engagement and motivation and is considered ideal for reinforcing difficult concepts and energizing the class. It is especially helpful as a revision strategy just before the exams. The activity is conducted using the following steps:

Step 1: The class is divided into four large teams (A, B, C, and D) by an imaginary horizontal and vertical line across the class.

Step 2: The instructor comes prepared with eight questions (4 of medium difficulty and 4 of high difficulty) from the content completed in class.

Step 3: The instructor directs the first question (medium difficulty) to team A and gives them 2 minutes to work on it. Any member of the team can answer the question. If the answer is correct, the team gets 1 point; if the answer is wrong, they get 0, and the question passes to Team B. After that, the instructor gives the second question (medium difficulty) to Team B. The game goes on until all four teams have had their questions. The important point is that each team must get a chance to go first.

Step 4: The same process is followed for the second round of questions (high difficulty). The team with the highest total score after the two rounds is the winner.

Activity #7 Designing Questions

One way of ensuring higher-order learning is to make students formulate questions on the content studied in the current class or one of the previous classes. Asking the right questions is an important life skill that implicitly confirms the knowledge level of the learner. This activity becomes more enjoyable if done in pairs or threesomes.

Step 1: Identify a segment of the learning unit completed recently.

Step 2: Ask the students to work with their neighbor(s) and create one question in a given time slot, and hand it over to the instructor.

Step 3: The instructor picks one question randomly and asks the class to respond to it. If the question is unclear or poorly composed, ask the students to improve it. The most relevant and interesting questions can be recognized in class.

Another way of completing this activity is to ask students to create a team of three or four and work online to create a tricky/tough question from the identified portion(s) of the course. This activity is completed *outside of class*. Each group is asked to submit their question. This activity would be most useful just before the final exams. As a variation, different sets of pairs may be assigned different chapters to create questions. All questions created by the class can be posted in the virtual classroom for practice work.

Activity #8 Problem-Solving Exercises

In this activity, a problem is presented, and pairs or threesomes are asked to provide the solution along with the different steps required for solving the problem. The activity is time-bound.

To ensure the complete success of the activity, it is better to start by giving a small example on the board to demonstrate how the activity should be completed. Make sure to choose a problem that offers multiple approaches for arriving at the correct solution. You may even design a few different problems to be given to different groups.

At the end of the allocated time, call upon one or two groups to share their solutions and the process used to arrive at the solution. Make sure that a different group is approached every time.

Activity #9 Critical Thinking Exercise

The *Critical Thinking Exercise* is another very interesting and easy-to-implement activity that can be completed in the following steps:

Step 1: Come prepared with a case study to be projected/distributed in class. *The case study refers to a failed project.* The students are asked to work in pairs or threesomes.

Step 2: The pairs are asked to identify errors or deficiencies leading to the failure of the project. A time limit is set depending on the complexity of the project.

Step 3: At the end of the stipulated time, the pairs are provided with the solution, and asked to assess their performance and give themselves a grade (A, B, or C).

Step 4: Each pair is asked to call out their grade. Pairs with B/C grades are asked to discuss the solution and identify their faulty reasoning.

The activity may seem a bit complicated and time-consuming, but it is very powerful. It not only develops critical thinking skills but also promotes a reflective mindset.

Activity #10 Concept Tests

Originally popularized by Eric Mazur, professor of physics at Harvard University. The activity is designed for in-class use; *concept tests* are excellent for testing students understanding of a single concept. Questions are generally designed in multiple-choice mode and are built around an outcome, an application, a problem, or a situation.

The most suitable questions are those that require students to apply higher-order learning skills (analyzing, evaluating, and creating). The question may ask students to extend the concept to new situations, apply the concept to predict the outcome of an experiment, compare processes, make assumptions, identify errors, interpret data through numerical or graphs, etc. Concept tests can be used for any discipline and any level.

A Word of Caution

- While implementing active learning activities, do not expect 100% success the first time.

- Do not try all activities at once. Choose one or two simple ones, implement them once or twice for students to get familiar with them and see the expected results.

- If any activity does not work, do not condemn it outright. Identify the reason for its failure because each one of the activities included here is validated by research and active users.

6.6.2   Challenges of Implementing Active Learning

Despite recognizing the value of active learning, instructors are often apprehensive about using it. Some of the well-known concerns are:

- Activities will eat up too much of class time.

- All students will not participate in the activities.

- There will be too much noise.

- Disruption caused by the activities will make it hard to get the class back on track.

Sure, all these challenges are real, but they can be addressed successfully with careful planning and smart execution. The benefits of incorporating active learning are worth all the time and effort. Let's examine each one of these challenges and look at strategies for countering them.

Too Time Consuming

It is true that these activities are designed to be completed in 5-8 minutes, but in the beginning, when both the instructor and the students are new to the experience, you should expect them to take a little longer. However, experience shows that with each implementation, the control over time gets better, and the activities can be completed in the stipulated time. Here are a few tips for managing this challenge:

- Bring a timer or a bell to class to monitor the time.

- Plan the duration of the activity carefully. If the responses are subjective and open to discussion, you naturally need to give them more time. The time allocated for the activity should be announced at the beginning and strictly adhered to, even if only a few students have completed it. Close the activity by giving the correct response. Some learning will take place, but more importantly, the students will learn to push themselves to work within the time limit.

- Make sure that the students work only with their neighbors. Avoid any movement in class because that is a big drain on time.

- At the end of the activity, do not ask students to volunteer responses. It is best to choose two or three pairs to give their response. You should announce in advance that you will be asking two or three pairs to share their answer and how they derived the answer. If any other group has a different response, they should be given a chance to share, and a few minutes should be kept for discussing the correct answer.

The above recommendations are time-tested and should help in managing time.

All students will not participate.

This is bound to happen, but remember, in any class, there are around 4 to 5% of students who because of different reasons, do not participate in class work. However, as the activities are mostly completed in pairs or threesomes, the non-participating students are still learning something from the exercise. Experience shows that if these activities are conducted regularly, most students eventually get involved.

The best way to counter this is to avoid asking for volunteers or 'show of hands' for getting responses to the activity. Instead, announce that you will be asking two or three students to respond. This will put almost the entire class is on alert, as they do not know who will be called upon.

Too Much Noise in the Class

It is true that when you start the activity, there is an immediate burst of excitement, and the noise level goes high as the pairs or threesomes begin to actively discuss the given task. But this is a good problem – as long as the noise level does not disturb the class next door. This sudden burst of energy and accompanying noise are quite healthy and signify active participation. We should not forget that these are young people who have been listening to lectures for hours and are happy to interact with their peers.

To keep the noise under control, a couple of strategies can be adopted. In addition to reminding the students to keep the volume low so that the other classes are not disturbed, two strategies can be used to keep noise under control. The first is to use a bell to warn the students when the level gets higher than acceptable. The second strategy is to use a PPT slide with a big picture of the traffic light to monitor the level of noise. Explain to the students that when they see an amber or red light, they need to lower their volume. Of course, with practice, the instructor and the students generally find an optimal level to keep the noise at an acceptable level.

Hard to Get Students Back on Track After the Activity

This challenge can be easily countered by coming back with an interesting opening for the next segment of the lecture. In Section 5, a number of strategies for making an engaging opening were discussed including the inductive style of introducing a new topic that helps to get immediate attention of the students (pp -126-127). As soon as the activity is over, begin the new segment by using a pre-planned opening strategy. Depending on the topic, strategies such as *asking a question*, *projecting an image or graphic*, or *taking a poll* can be used to get students' attention back immediately. The instructors are advised to plan this ahead of time. will have to plan this.

6.7 Managing Group-Based Learning Activities

Earlier in this section we established the working definition of group-based learning as it will be used in this book. Instead of getting lost in the maze of *Cooperative Learning* and *Collaborative Learning*, we will study them as group-based learning activities. The group-based activities can come in different shapes and forms ranging from simple, short *activities* completed by formally created teams to highly structured long-duration *projects* also completed by formally created teams. We may distinguish them as *group-based activities* and *group-based projects*. Whether we are planning short group-based activities or long, highly structured projects, six standard steps shown in Fig, 6.3 need to be planned. Let us learn about each of these steps.

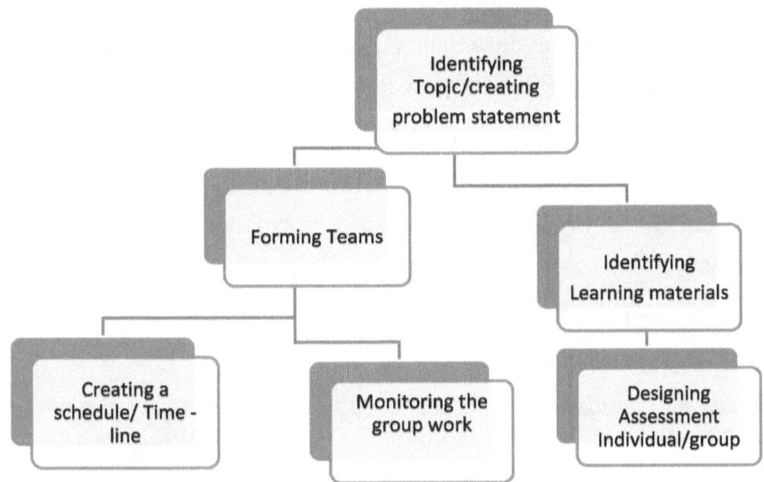

Fig. 6.3 – Steps for Planning and Implementing Group-based Activities.

6.7.1   Identifying a Topic and Creating a Problem Statement

The planning must start with identifying the topic(s) and listing specific learning outcomes. To ensure attainment of the outcome, it is best to create a problem statement. The problem statement must be open-ended, with several different pathways to the solution. Whether the groups are working on the same problem or different problems, the instructor must explain to the students the *why* and *how* of different steps for completing the activity. This becomes even more important if the students are doing a group activity for the first time. One important tip is to ensure that all instructions are given out in writing and made available to individual students either as a hard copy or posted in the virtual classroom.

6.7.2   Forming Teams

This is an important step for the successful completion of the collaboration process. The recommended group size is between 3-5 (2 is too small, 6 is rather big). An effort should be made to see that the task defined in the problem statement can be further divided into sub-tasks so that the responsibilities can be subdivided amongst the group members. This ensures the serious participation of individual group members.

There are four main types of groups that you can create. Each of these options has its own advantages and drawbacks. For someone who is just starting to use group learning activities, this step needs to be planned very carefully with a specific objective in mind:

- *Heterogeneous Groups* – have members of mixed-ability that are chosen based on their academic performance, demographic profile, gender, etc.

- *Homogeneous Groups* – have members of similar ability and a similar demographic profile.

- *Random Groups* – are created by the instructor using the roster or the computer.

- *Voluntary Groups* – are created by students choosing their own teammates.

Heterogeneous Groups are the most difficult to create, but they are also the most productive. The advantage here is that the lower-ability students get to learn from the more advanced ones. Also, working in a mixed-profile group can be interesting and motivating. The only disadvantage is that low-ability students are likely to feel uncomfortable and dominated. If you plan to form heterogeneous groups, you will need to make high-ability members aware of this issue and make them responsible for maintaining democratic and harmonious interactions.

Homogeneous groups can also be very productive. When you opt for homogeneous groups, you can vary the complexity of the tasks according to the cumulative ability of the group. High-performing groups can be given more challenging tasks on the same topic. The advantage is that members are emotionally more comfortable and feel more accountable for the success of the collaboration.

Random groups are created when the instructor uses a computer or the class roster to form groups. This form of grouping has advantages as well as disadvantages. There are two main advantages: i) the method needs the least amount of time and effort to form groups, and ii) it replicates the real-world workplace scenario where people with different abilities, profiles, and ideologies are required to work together.

Voluntary Groups are viable if the students in your class are experienced team workers and have the maturity to take personal responsibility. For undergraduate students, this may be a bit tricky. It can be disappointing for some students who are not picked to join any group. While working in *Voluntary Groups* may be more joyful for some students, it becomes more arduous for the instructor to monitor them, and the pedagogical effectiveness is questionable.

If you plan to use group-based activities on a regular basis, it is recommended that you create the groups early in the semester and post the list in the virtual classroom. This motivates the students to begin the interaction early.

6.7.3   Identifying the Learning Materials

The success of the group-based activities also depends on the care with which the learning resources are chosen and presented to the students. Instructors can choose ready resources (book chapters, articles, excerpts from a chosen MOOC, YouTube videos, etc.) or develop their own materials in the form of video lectures, PowerPoint presentations, and notes. These resources must be posted in a common area, like the virtual classroom. The most important points to keep in mind are: i) create introductory instructions about how to use each of the listed resources; and ii) acknowledge all materials chosen as learning resources.

6.7.4   Creating a Schedule or Timeline

One important criterion for measuring the success of group activities is that they must be completed within the stipulated time. A common mistake made by many instructors is not having a well-defined timeline for the completion of the activity/project. The instructor must draw up (or ask the group to submit) a detailed schedule with deadlines for mini milestones from the start to the end of the project. The instructor can then design assessments (qualitative or quantitative) around these mini milestones.

6.7.5   Monitoring Group Work

Once the timeline is finalized, the instructor must put in place a plan for monitoring the groups. Having a clear timeline helps the group monitor their own progress, but it is the responsibility of the instructor to set up a clear process for reporting the progress of the activity/project. In fact, the monitoring process can be set up to serve as the formative assessment process for both the group and individual members. A very effective and efficient method for monitoring group activities is to become a *silent member* of each team. This allows the instructor to closely monitor the group interaction (the frequency and quality of meetings and conversations) and intervene if an individual member or the group is headed in the wrong direction. When the instructor requires the group to submit mini progress reports, the group members are acquiring different skills like reflection, self-evaluation, and communication. Experience shows that in every group activity, there are always a few points where the group is likely to get stuck or face a deadlock. The instructor needs to preempt these points and provide guidance for managing them. Timely and constructive feedback from the instructor not only provides direction to the group members, but it also keeps them encouraged.

6.7.6   Assessing Group-Based Activities

One of the most complex tasks in implementing group-based activities is designing assessment because we want to assess the performance of both the group and the individual members. Evaluating the performance of the group is relatively easier than evaluating the performance of individual members. Strategies have to be put in place right in the beginning to ensure a fair evaluation of each member of the team *(Kaufman, Felder & Fuller, 2000.)* Depending on the complexity of the activity, the assessment can range from a simple quiz at the end of activity to a series of short assessment events across the duration of the activity.

Fig. 6.3 presents a model for designing assessment for complex, long-duration projects to assess the performance of the group as well as of individual members at the formative and the summative levels. Depending on the discipline and the type of activity/project the assessment may need to include both qualitative and quantitative components.

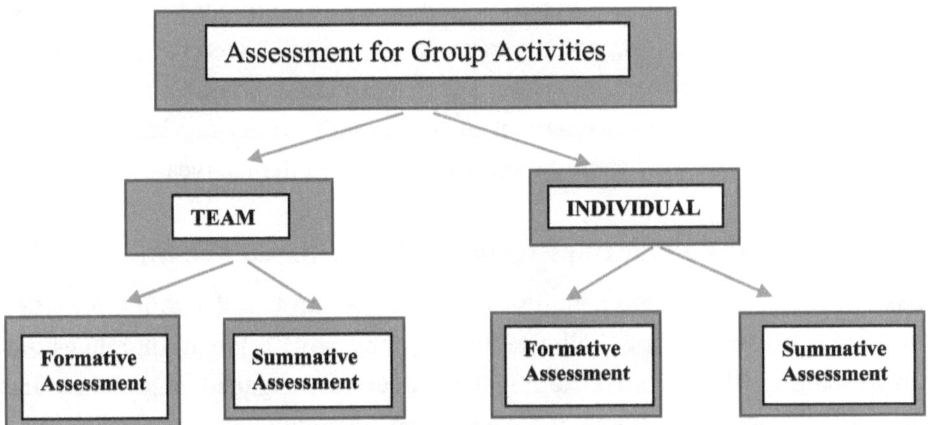

Fig. 6.3 – Designing Assessment for Group-based Activities.

To assess whether the set outcomes were achieved by the group and individual members, the instructor needs to develop appropriate rubrics. It is important for the instructor to clearly explain to the students how they will be assessed and share the rubric. The assessment must include possibilities for students to evaluate themselves and their groupmates. All this must be planned before the start of the activity/project.

For assessing the performance of individual members, the instructor may ask them to submit short reports about the progress of the specific tasks assigned to them or any one of the milestones. A rubric or grading scheme for the mini report will be very helpful. One big advantage of the instructor becoming a silent member of the group is that he or she can use personal observations to assess individual contributions. For summative assessment of individual group members, they may be asked to submit a short reflective report at the end of the activity/project about their personal contribution and experience of participating in the activity (qualitative). A very popular and effective technique is giving an end-of-project quiz on the concept or course content covered in the activity. This helps to ascertain how well individual members have mastered the concept or content.

For assessing the performance of the group, the quality of the completed activity/project itself is the main tool. A rubric must be created around the key performance indicators like *organization* (assignment of roles, communication, meeting deadlines, etc.), *group interaction* (communication, decision-making, conflict resolution, etc.), *achievement of the stated outcome/s, quality of reports and presentations*, etc. Here, again, individual members can be asked to submit their personal assessment of the group's work, key learnings, and contributions made by different members, including themselves.

6.7.7   Concerns about Implementing Group-Based Activities

Even though the enormous benefits of including group-based learning activities in regular instruction are well-established, they have a lot of apprehensions that discourage them from becoming wholeheartedly engaged in implementing group-based activities. Some of the apprehensions include:

- How long will it take to plan and monitor the activity?
- What type of instruments will be best for evaluating the activity?
- What types of groups will work best for the activity?
- Will the students follow instructions?
- Will I end up resolving all the differences and serious conflicts?

At the same time, the students have their own fears, and many of them resist participating in group work without even trying it. The following concerns have been reported by most students:

- Will my grades be jeopardized? Will I get my due recognition for the work I put in?
- Will every member contribute honestly, or will I have to cope with the *freeloaders*?
- Will the project be well-organized with clear instructions and a fair distribution of work?
- Will the team have a congenial atmosphere, or will I have to deal with bullies?
- Will we be able to complete the project on time and to the expected standard?

As always, the burden of successfully implementing group-based learning activities/projects lies squarely on the shoulders of the instructors. It is important to anticipate student concerns and address them before the start of the activity. If the students know how exactly the activity will be implemented, what will be their specific responsibilities, and, most importantly, how they will be evaluated as a group and as individual members, their fears can be transformed into excitement. Successful implementation of group-based activities requires meticulous planning so that maximum support is provided to both the individual team members and the groups (*Berkley, Major and Cross, 2014*)

Recommendations for the Instructor

- Always share your plan/expectations with the students and what they will gain from participating in the activity.

- Explain how they will be graded. Involve them in the evaluation process by allocating a small part of the grade for self or group evaluation.

- Create a short but effective questionnaire with qualitative and quantitative questions for collecting feedback from individual students.

- Technology can be a great partner in this process. It can help you in making groups, setting up the communication channel, monitoring, conducting evaluation and collecting feedback.

6.8 Some Effective Group-Based Activities and Mini-Projects

Table 6.b lists five short group-based activities that can be completed in about 45 minutes (one class), and two longer projects that may need one to several classes. Each of these activities/projects serves very specific objectives and are found to be very effective for undergraduate students.

Table 6.b – Some Effective Group-based Activities.

Activity	Duration	Target outcomes/special advantages
Jigsaw	40-45 minutes – can be completed in one class.	Excellent for in-depth learning topics that have multiple aspects/sub-topics.
Team Achievement Individualization (TAI)	40-45 minutes – can be completed in one class.	Excellent for consolidating learning and getting ready for exams.
Teams – Games-Tournaments (TGT)	40-45 minutes – can be completed in one class.	Excellent for in-depth learning and building team spirit and confidence.
Student Team Achievement Divisions (STAD)	40-45 minutes – can be completed in one class.	Excellent for consolidating learning and getting ready for exams.
Team-based Learning	25 – 30 minutes – can be completed in one class.	Excellent for in-depth learning & group interaction.
Problem-based Learning	One to several classes	Excellent for developing problem-solving and team building skills.
Project-based Learning	A few classes to an entire course	Excellent for developing problem-solving, critical thinking, management, and team building skills.

All the above-listed activities help to reinforce the learning of core concepts and to develop lifelong learning skills. All the activities have been extensively researched and are found to be very helpful in promoting in-depth learning and acquiring several of the graduate attributes. Each format aims to generate peer interaction, build teams, develop critical thinking skills, and enhance spoken and written communication. Students find each one of these activities very interesting because they generate a lot of energy while keeping the class environment very relaxed. This helps the students learn together, internalize, and master complex course content.

Unlike active learning activities, group-based activities involve several steps that need to be planned meticulously and implemented flawlessly. Even though each of these activities has its own format, they share three common features. First, almost all these activities are completed *after* the related course content has been taught in class or studied individually by students. Second, each activity is completed by pre-assigned teams under the supervision of the instructor, and finally, each of them has a mechanism to assess the performance of both the group and the individual members.

Let us learn the step-by-step process for planning and implementing each of these activities. Please note that step 0 refers to activities that the instructor must complete before implementing the activity.

Activity #1 JIGSAW

This activity is ideal for reinforcing complex concepts that have several sub-sections, aspects, or segments. For example, a topic such as *Impact of Recycling* can be studied through different aspects, such as environment, economy, technology, and society.

Table 6.c – Steps for planning & implementing *Jigsaw*

Steps	Implementation
Step 0	• Explain the activity to students and mentally prepare them and get them excited about working with their peers. • Pick the topic and finalize the sub-topics. Let us say that the topic has 4 sub-topics. • Display the topic and the 4 sub-topics with numbers (1, 2, 3..) on a PowerPoint slide.
Step 1	***Create Teams*** • For this activity, it is best to make random groups. • The size of the group must be the same as the number of subtopics e.g., if you have 4 subtopics, each team should have 4 members. Each group will work on the same main topic through the sub-topics. • Let each member pick a subtopic and hold the same number – 1, 2,3, 4. The team members will serve as EXPERTS for the chosen subtopic in their respective groups.

Steps	Implementation
Step 2	***Create Expert Groups*** • Now it is time to separate out the groups. No. 1 from each group will go to one corner of the classroom and make an expert group for the subtopic no. 1. Similarly, all no. 2s, 3s, and 4s will go to different sections of the classroom to form their specific expert group. • Let each Expert group discuss the chosen subtopic for an allocated time (say 6 – 8 minutes depending on the members in the expert group). Let everyone participate in the discussion and take notes.
Step 3	***Reporting Back to the Group*** • At the end of the allocated time, the experts get back to their original group. • The original group will now prepare a final report/presentation on the complete topic using the contribution of each member.
Step 4	***Final /Report/Presentation*** • Each group will be asked to submit a report on the topic covering all four sub-topics. Many instructors ask each group to make a 5-minute presentation but that can be very time-consuming if the class is large with many groups. To save time, the groups can be asked to upload the presentations/reports in the virtual classroom and the winning teams are announced in class. • Giving a short quiz on the topic in the next class is highly recommended. This will provide realistic feedback about individual learning.

Activity #2 Teams, Games, and Tournaments (TGT)

This activity is very popular with students because it is more like a competition. The activity requires careful planning and preparation. Ideal for revising important core, relatively more complex concepts that students need to master. Research claims that this activity is good for building confidence because the students are exposed to reviewing the same content through different questions.

Table 6.d – Steps for planning & implementing *TGT*

Steps	Implementation
Step 0	• Explain the activity to students and mentally prepare them and get them excited about working with their peers. • Teach the main topic. • Give a short class quiz and note down the scores carefully. • Ask students to come prepare to discuss the unit/chapter. • Create Heterogeneous groups – 4 students of different academic abilities. If the group has 4 members, choose one low – performing student, (No. A) one high-performing student (No. D), and two average (No. B & No. C). It is a good practice to give highest title to the low-performing members. The groups along with the number each member carries should be announced early (or posted in virtual classroom). This facilitates students to sit with their group as soon as they arrive and save a lot of time. • Prepare revision materials that the group will study in class. This may comprise of summary sheets, handouts, prompts for discussion etc. • Create questions for the activity. The number of questions should be same as the number of groups. For example, for a class of 50 – 52 and groups of 4, you will have 13 groups and 13 questions. Put correct answers to all questions on a separate sheet. The questions should range from easy-to-medium – to – high difficulty levels.
Step 1	***Revision of the content*** Give each group about 10 – 12 minutes to review the material studied. Let the group work with the materials you have prepared for revision to streamline the process. The teacher should walk around to see if any group has questions.
Step 2	***Regrouping for the Tournament*** After students have reviewed the material, they are now put into four *Homogeneous* groups taking one member from each group. At this point, each group will have students of the same academic level – all 1s will be one group, and similarly all 2s, 3s & 4s will be in separate groups. At this point, your entire class is divided in to 4 large groups with all as in one group, Bs in another etc.

Steps	Implementation
Step 3	***The Tournament*** Each group will choose three leaders – i) Organizer, ii) Checker & iii) Scorer. The organizer will start asking the questions whichever student gives the correct answer gets 1 point. The checker has the list of correct answers and checks the answer. The scorer keeps the score. If no one can answer the question, it is kept aside to be handed over to the instructor for explaining it to the class at the end of the activity.
Step 4	***Back to the Group*** Students return to their groups and report their scores – Group with the highest total score is the winner.
Step 5	***Closing Quiz*** The entire class is given another quiz. If there is no time, the quiz should be given in the next class. Depending on the topic, the teacher may choose to give the same quiz given at the beginning of the class. The activity provides an individual score and a group score.

Activity #3 Student Team Achievement Divisions (STAD)

This highly motivating and enjoyable activity is very popular for assuring in-depth learning. This activity is particularly effective if a lot of students in class have difficulty understanding a particular concept or have not done well in an assignment or assessment, and the instructor wants to review the content. The activity is conducted in the following steps:

Table 6.e – Steps for planning & implementing *STAD* activity

Steps	Implementations
Step 0	• Explain the activity to students and mentally prepare them and get them excited about working with their peers. • Teach the main topic in the class. In some cases, the instructor may ask students to come prepared with the basic reading. • Prepare revision materials (handouts, summaries, discussion prompts) that the group will work with in class. • Give a short quiz and ask students to keep their scores from the quiz.
Step 1	***Create Groups*** For this activity, heterogeneous groups work better. To optimize time, the groups should be made in advance and posted in the virtual classroom.

Steps	Implementations
	Students in each group calculate their team score by adding the individual scores from the quiz. Now, they study together, focusing on the content that different members of the group did not understand as shown by the quiz.
Step 2	*Group Study (20 – 25 minutes)* The group is given time to revise/study the content using the materials/exercises prepared by the teacher and identified from the quiz score. During this time, the instructor actively walks around to monitor and support the groups.
Step 3	*Evaluation of Group Performance* • At the end of the stipulated time, students are dispersed throughout the class and given a second quiz. • Scores of individual members are added to get a second group score. The two scores are compared and the Group that makes the most improvement is the winners.

Activity #4 Team-Assisted Individualization (TAI)

Team-Assisted Individualization is especially helpful in facilitating in-depth learning and developing team spirit. The high-performing students in the group take on the responsibility of teaching the low-performers. The activity allows the instructor to closely interact with the students and focus on students needing assistance. This activity has been found to be very useful for teaching subjects in mathematics and basic sciences. Many steps for this activity are common to other cooperative activities. The main difference is that here, individual scores are dependent on the group score which is the opposite of what is done in the STAD activity.

Table 6.f – Steps for planning & implementing *TAI*

Steps	Implementation
Step 0	• Explain the activity to students and mentally prepare them and get them excited about working with their peers. • Emphasize the fact their individual scores will be determined by the score of their group. • The main topic is taught in an earlier class or students are asked to come prepared with the prescribed reading.

Steps	Implementation
	• Prepare revision materials that the group will study in class. • Prepare handouts/exercise sheets for group work.
Step 1	*Class Quiz* – start the activity by giving the entire class a short quiz and carefully recording the scores obtained by each student. The quiz may be given in an earlier class rather than on the day of the activity.
Step 2	*Creating Groups.* Students are put in small, heterogeneous groups of 4-5 with different academic level and gender. It is recommended that the instructor does this ahead of time and posts the groups in virtual classroom so that students can get into their groups as soon as they arrive.
Step 3	*Group Study (20 – 25 minutes)* The group is given time to revise/study the content using the textbook or materials/exercises prepared by the instructor. During this time, the instructor is actively monitoring and providing help.
Step 4	*Closing Quiz* The entire class is given another quiz. For more complex subjects, the instructor may choose to give the same quiz given earlier.
Step 5	*Evaluation, Announcing Scores, and Team Recognition* Group scores are calculated. Students scoring 100% marks get 3 points bonus points; students scoring 90% marks get 2 bonus points, and students scoring 80 % get 1 bonus point. This is a very sensitive time. The instructor must praise the winners and encourage the losers. If some groups fail, the instructor may offer to work with them separately and/or give them a make-up test.

Activity #5 Team-based Learning

Team-based learning was developed by a professor at the University of Oklahoma and used for the MBA classes. Later, the concept was tried and found to be equally effective for other disciplines at the undergraduate level. The concept is very similar to that of the flipped class. Here, the students complete the assigned reading before coming to class. In class, the students are placed in random groups and asked to work together on a multiple question test. This is often done in the open-book-open notes format. After the allocated time, the instructor presents the correct solutions and questions are discussed. Team-based Learning has become very popular for STEM disciplines.

Activities #6 Problem-Based and Project-Based Learning

Both Instructors and students are generally confused about these two terms – *Problem-based Learning and Project-based Learning* because there is a lot of haziness in the usage of these two terms. Both activities are group-based activities and share a lot of common features. Most important, both are known by the same acronym, PBL. Recently, there has been a welcome trend of using a different acronym, PjBL, for project-based learning, and that is what we will follow here.

Both PBL and PjBL are group learning approaches that have been extensively researched and are considered to be eminently suitable for undergraduate instruction. Both approaches are student-centric and are credited with promoting in-depth learning and developing several of the 21st-century employability skills (pp - 67-69). Both formats require students to resolve a real-world problem which makes the instructional experience more relevant, meaningful, and joyful. Both PBL and PjBL offer students the opportunity to examine the problem from different perspectives and find a viable solution using critical thinking and problem-solving skills. The activities are designed to train students to manage diverse responsibilities that lead to enhanced self-confidence and self-esteem. Contrary to common apprehension, both PBL and PjBL can be conducted effectively in large classes too. These two activities differ from other group-based activities discussed earlier because they allow a lot more independence to the group, and a large part of the collaborative work is completed outside the class.

However, both approaches are different in focus and scope. The focus of PBL is to train students to examine a given problem from all different perspectives, explore all possible solutions, and use a scientific process to choose the most suitable one. The focus of PjBL, on the other hand, is on achieving diverse outcomes, mostly ending in a tangible product or a process. The two differ in scope as well. PBL concentrates on one central problem, and therefore the duration can be quite short. PjBL may or may not be centered on one problem. The outcomes here can be multifaceted and require work on different aspects (analysis, design, and implementation) completed over an extended period of time. Another major difference is in the design of assessment: in PBL, the evaluation is based on the quality of the solution selected and its justification. Assessment of PjBL is designed to evaluate not only the achievement of outcomes but also the process components such as the quality of design, research, illustration of rationale, presentation, etc.

Table 6.g – Steps in Planning and Implementing PBL and PjBL

Steps	PBL	PBjL
Format	Students work in a group to study a given problem, research different possible solutions and select the most suitable one.	Students work in a group to resolve a complex or extended real-world problem/issue that they may choose themselves. The project may involve designing a new product, or a process, or enhancing an existing one.
Step 1	Create a problem statement and define the outcome.	Create a problem statement, specify the outcomes, and list the deliverables.
Step 2	Conducting analytical research and examine different aspects of the given problem	Analyzing the problem/issue from different perspectives, identifying different steps for completing the project, and examining the available options and solutions including the failed ones.
Step 3	Evaluating different possible solutions and selecting the most suitable one.	Dividing the task into mini milestones with deadlines for completing each milestone.
Step 4	Completing the set evaluation process which may be in the form of a group presentation or a written report.	Completing a multi-part assessment that is designed to assess different components of the project and the performance of the group as well as individual members.

Steps	PBL	PBjL
Step 5	Collecting student feedback by using a specially designed instrument that includes both qualitative and quantitative questions.	Collecting student feedback by using specially designed, multi-part instruments to collect feedback on different components of the project.

It is easy to see that both strategies share a number of common features, but the differences are also very clear. Both these strategies are very effective for undergraduate instruction.

6.9   Student Engagement in Large Classes

Most undergraduate classes are large with an average of 50 to 70 students. One question that often comes up in training workshops is how to ensure student engagement in large classes. Planning and implementing student engagement activities in large classes is not easy but certainly viable. Most instructors who have large classes do not even want to consider including these strategies in their courses because of fear of losing control of the class. Implementing student engagement activities in a large class requires you to be creative and flexible to accommodate the different learning needs and attitudes of your students. Clearly, you need to be very well-prepared for running the activity, managing time, and keeping students involved. Here are a few tips that may be helpful:

- Some of the active learning activities, like *Polls, Think-pair-share* or *One – minute paper* can be easily implemented in threesomes. Creating a seating chart where mixed-ability students are made to sit together makes active learning very productive.

- One strategy that keeps students alert and involved is to call them by name to provide their response to the active learning activity. Make sure to ask different students to share their response, even if they have not raised their hands.

- Team-based *learning* is especially effective for large classes. Even though some students may not seem to be fully engaged, they are learning by simply going through the activity.

- If you want to run any of the other group-based activities, you may try to get help from colleagues, teaching assistants. If your institution does not provide teaching assistants, you can approach some of the course alumni who are always very eager to contribute.

- Allow some flexibility for students to choose their teammates. If you want to make heterogeneous groups, a good solution is to divide the class into four groups (A, B, C, D) according to their academic performance and ask students to create their own groups by taking one member from each group. Proactively monitor that all students are accommodated properly.

- Wherever possible, take help from technology. In the next section, several easy-to-use, free tools have been discussed that can be used for supporting student engagement in regular classes.

- While using PBL and PjB, an effective strategy is to set up an online project dossier in the virtual classroom and become a silent member of each group. This allows you to stay in communication, monitor progress, and provide timely support. Make sure that all instructions are clearly written out and posted in the virtual classroom.

6.10   Section 6: Wrap-Up and Tips for Ensuring Student Engagement

This section is devoted to one of the most important components of undergraduate instruction: student engagement. We have seen how student motivation and engagement are interconnected and have a direct impact on students' academic performance. This means that the instructor's responsibility is limited not only to designing good lectures supported by good explanations and examples but also to designing activities that will help the students master the content and develop essential employability skills. A strong theoretical framework confirms that well-designed peer interaction promotes skills like in-depth analysis, critical thinking, problem-solving, team building, and lifelong learning.

There are three dimensions to student engagement: cognitive, behavioral, and emotional, and all three-impact learning in different ways. To ensure student engagement, the instructor needs to design activities where students are actively involved in processing the new knowledge received during class sessions. These activities have been broadly classified as Active learning and Group-based activities.

Active learning activities are short (5–8 minute) interventions used in class. The activities require the students to work on the content completed in class. The activities may be completed individually or in small groups. These activities are generally not graded. Ten such activities are discussed in detail.

The term *group-based learning activities* is used for all kinds of activities that are more structured, completed in formally constituted groups, and involve some form of evaluation. The objective is to develop an in-depth understanding of the course content. Seven group-based activities are discussed along with step-by-step instructions for implementing them.

Table 6.h – Tips for Ensuring Effective Student Engagement

Tip No.	Recommendations
1.	On day 1 of your course talk about the connect between learning and student engagement. If possible, share the graphic showing the process of learning (p - 50). Share your expectations of active participation in different activities that you plan to incorporate in your classroom teaching.
2.	Explain the importance of all four dimensions of student engagement with i) Coursework; ii) Peers; iii) Instructor and iv) Self. Ensure that the ambiance in your class is welcoming and encourages students to interact comfortably with you, and their peers. Include activities where students can self-assess their performance.
3.	Early in the course, take the time to explain to the students the difference between active and group-based learning and how these will help them in not only mastering the course content but also in developing employability skills.
4.	Plan each activity meticulously and make sure that the task to be completed during the activity is challenging but well within the competency of the average students in class. Always be clear about the objective before selecting an activity.

5.	Use a variety of activities. You have learned many activities in this section so avoid using the same activity all the time. It is important to keep your students surprised and looking forward to each class.
6.	Always begin by explaining the objective and the implementation plan of the activity. Experience shows that the best results can be achieved if the students know what they are expected to do and why.
7.	For active learning activities, keep an eye on time. One way to optimize time is to avoid any kind of movement/relocation of students. Make them work exclusively with their neighbors.
8.	Implementing student engagement in the form of active learning and group-based learning activities presents several challenges. Please review p – and p – to learn more about these apprehensions and how to overcome them.
9.	Planning assessment for group-based activities is quite challenging because both the teams and the individual team members need to be assessed. One of the common errors made by instructors is that they do not plan assessments before the start of the activity. Once the outcomes and assessment are planned, you can share the details with the students and the entire implementation process becomes easy and manageable.

<table><tr><td>7</td></tr></table>

7 Partnering with Technology

7.1 Technology and Undergraduate Instruction

Any discussion about undergraduate instruction in the year 2024 must acknowledge the significant role that technology can play in making it more effective and engaging. Even though technology has been a part of higher education since the past fifty years, its presence has been mainly in online instruction. Online instruction is now established as an important discipline but outside the scope of this discussion. The focus of this book is on conventional classroom teaching, and the purpose is to explore how technology can be used to make it more effective, robust, engaging, and productive. It is hard to deny that the recent innovations in technology and pedagogy have made technology a highly potential player in the traditional classroom arena. Even a few years ago, we would have been very apprehensive about considering technology as an active partner in classroom teaching. But the scenario has changed radically. Today, we have access to several effective, free (or, very inexpensive), and user-friendly tools that that instructors can comfortably use in class because they do not require sophisticated infrastructure or specialized training.

It was during 2020–21, when the academic world came to a standstill due to the unfortunate disruption caused by COVID-19, that the real potential of technology was recognized. In all its brutality, the period offered an opportunity to all stakeholders – students, instructors, and administrator – to discover the strengths and capabilities of technology to address multiple facets of higher education. We have seen that the Gen Z students have a strong affinity for technology that can be fruitfully harnessed to support their learning process. In addition to stimulating regular classroom instruction, technology helps the instructor be better organized and efficient. Technology offers a lot of potential options for enriching instruction and making it more accessible, engaging, and productive.

In undergraduate instruction, technology contributes in three different modes: *Multiplicative, Prescriptive,* and *Supportive.*

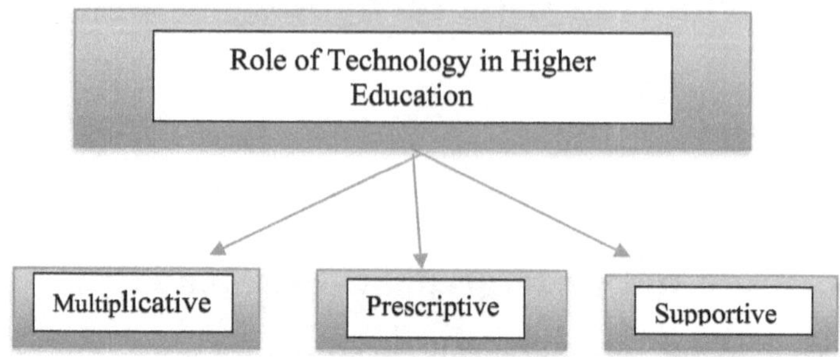

Fig. 7.1 – How Technology Supports Higher Education

In its ***multiplicative role***, technology contributes both quantitatively and qualitatively. Quantitively, technology can play a huge role in making higher education accessible to a much larger population by making it flexible and financially more viable. It can make instruction personalized and, at the same time, scalable. With the help of technology, the instructor can create, download, and record learning materials that can then be made accessible to an unlimited number of students across the globe.

Qualitatively, technology offers the opportunity for the instructors and the students to learn from the best. By allowing access to recorded lectures delivered by renowned experts, technology allows instructors to enrich their content and sharpen their delivery. For undergraduate students, technology offers the possibility to review the same course content delivered by different experts. The fact that students can access the recorded study materials at their own convenience and pace, along with the possibility of reviewing them as many times as needed, facilitates the learning process. Thanks to technology, today, the students have the choice to learn anything from world-class experts according to their own schedule.

In the ***prescriptive role,*** technology offers solutions for specific pedagogical and administrative issues. Technology offers effective solutions for addressing issues such as gaps in base knowledge, course planning, designing, and implementing student engagement, managing scheduling conflicts, etc. Technology also provides flexibility in terms of time, pace, and space. It helps in optimizing teaching time and standardizing the delivery of instruction. The opportunity to set up a virtual classroom (through an LMS or an online platform) helps the instructors be present and available beyond the regular class hours. Technology offers instructors a great blend of flexibility and structure to make instruction more personalized and focused. It also helps the instructor plan a multi-sensory delivery of content catering to different learning styles, making instruction more stimulating and joyful. The use of technology can help in promoting better student-to-teacher and student-to-student interaction and communication.

Technology is most powerful in a ***supportive role***. It offers multiple options for instructors to identify and support the learning needs of different sets of students. It helps to provide customized learning materials, handouts, and practice quizzes designed to fill specific gaps. It can add a lot of value by enhancing the overall quality of learning and making the role of the instructor more positive and the teaching-learning process more collaborative, interactive, and productive.

However, the skeptics have their own list of constraints and challenges related to using technology in instruction. Technology in education is still seen as something of an *elitist* activity and is considered to unfavorable for less privileged students. The digital divide exists not only in *'have'* and *'have-nots'* but also in *'know' and 'know-nots'*. In higher education, there is also worry about technology encouraging *surface processing*. Academicians are worried that the availability of ready information and solutions can discourage research, creativity, and original thinking. The increased temptation to plagiarize also cannot be underestimated.

Another major concern is instructors' preparedness to use technology efficiently. Institutions can provide good technology infrastructure and facilities for using technology in classrooms, but will the faculty have the incentive and motivation to invest the time and effort needed to incorporate these resources into mainstream teaching? Of course, this also puts more pressure on colleges and universities to provide the required training and incentives to the instructors for investing the time and effort to harvest the best benefits of partnering with technology.

7.2 Bringing Technology into the Classroom

Today, the time is ripe for bringing technology out of the computer labs and into the classrooms. We know that almost all undergraduate students are ready mentally (proficiency and motivation) as well as materially (smartphones and free apps). An aware and engaged instructor can take her class to another level by effectively incorporating technology to sharpen the learning process. There are three main avenues through which technology can make a substantial contribution to enriching classroom instruction by:

- Creating a dedicated course website or virtual classroom to support in-class teaching.

- Providing a vast array of customized, visually rich and animated learning and practice resources.

- Using simple ICT tools for promoting student engagement and creating a dynamic learning community.

In other words, to take full advantage of technology, instructors must develop the requisite skills to i) create a virtual classroom, ii) select or prepare video-based learning materials for supporting different student needs, and iii) using simple (and free) ICT tools to make learning more effective and joyful.

7.3 Creating a Virtual Classroom

One of the most powerful technology-based tools that can support in-class teaching is a dedicated *Virtual Classroom* for the course being taught in a regular classroom. The virtual classroom serves as an annex to the main classroom. Let us understand what a virtual classroom is, how to set it up and use it to enhance the quality of instruction, as well as what are some of the known challenges for doing that.

A dedicated virtual classroom is an additional *private space* meant exclusively for students enrolled in your course. These days, most colleges and universities offer an LMS that hosts the college website to provide general information such as the academic calendar, department-wise courses, institute events, etc. This website is available to all faculty, students, and administration across the institute. Your dedicated virtual classroom is different—it is exclusive and private. You can use the college LMS to create it or use any of the free LMS (Canvas, Edmodo, Skype, etc.) to create it. This is a private space created by you and is accessible *only* to you and the students registered in your course.

A virtual classroom allows you to stay connected with your students and provide academic support in and outside the class. Here, you can post specially selected or created learning materials, practice exercises and quizzes, details about collaborative projects, and class policy documents. This space is invaluable in building a private learning community of students enrolled in your course. The most encouraging part here is that setting up a virtual classroom using an LMS is quite easy. This is a very simple process and does not require any special infrastructure or equipment – most resources needed are readily available, and mostly free of cost. Moreover, setting up this facility does not require any specialized skills or training. If you can use a computer, you can set up your virtual classroom. Moreover, every LMS offers a lot of support in the form of free, user-friendly tutorials. You can set up your virtual classroom by following the three main steps discussed below:

Step 1: Choosing a Learning Management System (LMS)

The first step is to choose a suitable LMS platform. Some of the better-known LMSs used by institutions are **Blackboard, Teams, Google Classroom, E-College, Moodle, CAMU** etc. All these are commercial platforms that offer a free version for instructors and students. The paid version has some additional, more sophisticated features and technical support. For our purpose of having an auxiliary virtual classroom, the free version works perfectly well. If the students are already proficient in using a certain LMS, choose that one. If you think that students may have difficulty navigating the virtual classroom, it is worth spending a few minutes to walk them through it. Fortunately, most LMS come with very reader-friendly tutorials.

Step 2: Setting up the classroom.

Once you have chosen the LMS, login to the main website, download the teacher version, and set up the different sections of the virtual classroom.

Typically, every LMS offers all the following features with detailed instructions or tutorials. Most virtual classrooms allow you to:

- Post announcements and keep the class communication alive.

- Create discussion threads to promote student-to-student and student-to-instructor communication.

- Upload learning materials: pdf copies of lessons, handouts, PowerPoint presentations, mini-lectures, simulations, video clips, etc.

- View and monitor class participation. The instructor can create groups and assign tasks to them.

- Create assessment: in the form of different types of quizzes, self-correcting exercises, p assignments, and rubrics.

- Post grades: every LMS offers a gradebook or some efficient mechanisms for viewing and grading assignments and posting comments.

Step 3: Setting up the Roster and Giving Access to the Students

This feature allows you to enroll your students in the virtual class. The roster displays the names, e-mails, and status. (student, teacher, TA, etc.). Once the roster is ready, you need to send an invitation to the students, instructing them to *accept* the invitation. Once the students accept the invitation, they are automatically enrolled in the virtual class. The roaster allows the instructor to send an email to a single student, a selected group of students, or the entire class. The roster also helps you form groups and manage office hours. Once your students have accepted the invitation, they have access to the virtual classroom and all the content presented by you. The best part of a virtual classroom is that you can control what you want students to see. It is possible to upload a lot of materials ahead of time and *publish* only the content you want them to see. The uploaded materials remain invisible till they are published by you.

7.3.1 Using the Virtual Classroom to Enhance Classroom Instruction

The virtual classroom works as a powerful space that allows the instructor to accomplish a number of tasks that are generally difficult to accomplish in regular class. Most of these tasks are related to customized activities for addressing the academic needs of different sets of students. Given below are *five* areas in which a virtual classroom supports the instructor to optimize time and enhance student learning:

- Advance course planning

- Hosting customized learning materials

- Providing academic support

- Promoting student engagement and interpersonal communication

- Managing evaluation

Let us discuss each of these in more detail.

Advance Course Planning

The virtual classroom is an invaluable tool that puts the instructor in the driver's seat and allows her to get better organized even before the start of the semester. Based on the learning in sections 4 and 5, the instructor can prepare a detailed plan (week-wise or unit-wise) for the entire course and keep it ready and uploaded in the virtual classroom and publish only the portions you want students to see and work on. This is extremely useful if you are likely to teach the same course again.

Table 7.a – Using Virtual Classroom for Advance Course Preparation

Capability	How it helps the instructor
Pre-preparation of the course before the start of the semester	The most useful feature of the virtual classroom is that it allows the instructor to pre-plan the entire course, select, and prepare all learning resources before the start of the semester, and publish the materials as and when required. Note that the students can see materials *only* when they are published. The pre-planning can be tentative or very complete. It can include highlights of the lectures, handouts, simulations, practice exercises, activities, and assessments. You also have the facility to update content on the go. This saves an enormous amount of time and gives you better control over the course.

Capability	How it helps the instructor
Preparing support materials for mastering Prerequisites	One area where the virtual classroom can support the instructor is in managing gaps in students' background knowledge which is one of the biggest challenges faced by undergraduate instructors. This is because many students have not mastered the concepts covered in pre-requisite courses. Once the semester starts, there is very little time to take care of anything beyond the course. A well-organized instructor can prepare to address this issue before the start of the semester with the help of the virtual classroom. The instructor can identify concepts that are generally difficult to understand in the pre-requisite course, and create mini-lectures, handouts, and practice tests in the self-correcting format to review and reinforce them. These can then be published as and when needed.
Posting pre-prepared policy documents and schedule of academic events.	Posting class policies and ground rules as well as the schedule for major academic events (tests, project work, invited lectures, site visits etc.) is very practical for keeping the class well-organized throughout the semester.

Hosting Learning Materials

In addition to the prescribed textbook, an undergraduate student is expected to refer to different learning materials. In addition, the instructor may provide additional customized learning materials like chosen scholarly articles, chapters from other books, research articles, video clips etc. The virtual classroom is an ideal place to post these.

Table 7.b – Virtual Classroom for Hosting Learning Materials

Capability	How it helps the instructor
Posting customized, specially created learning materials	The virtual classroom allows the instructor to post customized, specially created learning materials for each unit/lecture. This is very helpful for the students who can review the material at their own pace and time to prepare for different class tests as well as summative assessments.

Capability	How it helps the instructor
Posting media-based resources	The virtual classroom allows the instructor to add media-based materials such as pictures, audio, videos, simulations, experiments, etc. We know that making these digital, visually – rich resources available to students in any other form is almost impossible. These additional resources help the students to understand the principles and processes being taught in class. This is also very useful for Lab. courses because students can see the upcoming experiments as simulations/virtual labs before performing the experiments in the lab.
Posting Additional Scholarly Resources	This space can also be used for uploading additional reading or reference materials, excerpts from MOOCs for Flipped Class or the PSIS activity.

Supporting Academic Needs of Different Sets of Students

In addition to supplementing and enriching the quality of classroom instruction, a virtual classroom is invaluable for providing student support. In Section 3, (P –). we have learned about the learning and emotional needs of different sets of students in our classes, and this space can be used to provide quality support to the different sets of students. This space helps the instructor to connect with students and provide support to both the low-performing and high-performing students. The best part is that technology helps the instructor maintain privacy and confidentiality. It is possible to post readings, quizzes, and other preparatory materials to materials that are accessible only to the selected set of students.

Table 7.c – Providing academic support to different sets of students in your class.

Capability	How it helps the instructor
Supporting Low-performing Students	To support the low-performing students, the virtual classroom can be used to: • Post additional resources and exercises/self-correcting quizzes to master complex content or prerequisites. • Post specially designed study guides, revision notes, and sample tests to prepare for class tests, mid-term, and final exams. • Organize dedicated office hours or study groups for this group of students.

Capability	How it helps the instructor
Supporting High – performing Students	It is true that in most of our classes, the high-performing students generally do not get their share of attention because our attention is mainly focused on the average or low-performing students. Often, the high-performing students find classes uninteresting and boring and are demotivated because of lack of challenge. Once the virtual classroom is set-up, the instructor can use some very simple strategies to keep them challenged and fully engaged in the course. Some of the activities that the instructor can accomplish through the virtual classroom, are: • Assign special/advanced reading/ video materials related to the coursework for them to summarize/critique and present to class. • Ask high-performing students to work in small groups to undertake research in selected concepts being studied in the course. The groups can publish their findings in the virtual classroom. Or, time permitting, present them in class. This encourages the students to get an early initiation into research. • Participate as a *Buddy* to help one or two low-performing peers. • Prepare advanced students for regional, national, or international competitions.
Preparing them to participate in important, academic and competitive events	Identify events at the university or regional level that some of these students can participate in individually or in small groups. You can help them in this journey from start to end using the virtual classroom.

Promoting Student Engagement and Interpersonal Communication

The virtual classroom offers a dynamic space for establishing student-to-student and student-to-instructor communication and thereby promoting student engagement. Given below are some of the features of the virtual classroom that can be used very efficiently to achieve these objectives.

Table 7.d – Promoting Student Engagement & Interpersonal Communication

Capability	How it helps the instructor
Posting Announcements	The instructor can keep constant touch with the students by using the *Announcements* feature. In addition to providing general information about the course, the Announcements section can be used for posting tips and strategies for students to manage their learning. The instructor may choose to post some interesting quotes, or greetings for festivals/special days that may occur during the semester.
Promoting Discussions	A very exciting feature of the virtual classroom is the *Discussion Forum*. This very powerful tool helps not only to enliven the class but also promote in-depth learning. Using the virtual classroom to host a weekly discussion is found to be an extremely productive practice.
Creating a Q/A thread	Like the discussion thread, the instructor can create a permanent Q/A thread where students can post their questions and anyone (instructor or other students), respond to them. Research confirms that having a Q/A thread is extremely beneficial for the entire class.
Creating a Dynamic Learning Community	The virtual classroom offers a private, secure space for students to connect with other students as well with their instructor. The constant presence and easy access to the instructor make the students feel more secure and valued. The online roster facilitates the instructor to keep ready contact with individual students as well as with different sets of students. Two strategies help in setting up the learning communities: *Online Office Hours* – The virtual classroom allows the instructor to set-up office hours (in-person or online) that can be very helpful for students. We know that during college hours, most students are very busy attending courses/labs. Online office hours can be set-up even on the weekends. *Online Study Groups* – In addition to office hours, the instructor can set-up online *study groups* where small groups of students can be scheduled to work together and/or with the instructor. The instructor may take additional sessions with low-performing students to prepare them for exams etc.

Capability	How it helps the instructor
Managing Group Projects	The virtual classroom is invaluable for managing group activities. Starting with posting initial instructions, formation of groups, mentoring the groups and evaluating group performances, the course website can assist in every task.

Creating and Implementing Evaluation

One of the most important contributions that a virtual classroom can make is in the area of designing and implementing assessment. Most LMSs offer the facility to create different types of questions and quizzes. The fact that the instructor can create and store assignments, quizzes, tests, etc. ahead of time and make them available as per schedule is an amazing opportunity for instructors to not only review and refine the assessment instruments but also optimize their time and effort.

Table 7.e – Virtual Classroom for Creating & implementing Assessment.

Capability	How it helps the instructor
Quizzes & Short Assignments	Almost all LMSs offer the facility to create different types of assessments – quizzes, short answer questions as well as long essay type questions. The value-addition here is that different versions of the same quiz can be created and posted randomly so that the students are forced to prepare well and the temptation to plagiarize is minimized. In addition, the instructor can post templates, brainstorming sheets, rubrics, and highest-scoring assignments to encourage students and promote reflection and self-assessment.
Evaluating Group Projects	Experience shows that evaluating class projects eats up a lot of class time. Using the virtual classroom to do that is an ideal solution. Once the projects are submitted in the virtual classroom, many interesting formats can be used for evaluating them. If you have created a rubric, you can ask a colleague, alumnus, or students themselves to evaluate the projects. The winners can then be celebrated in class.

Capability	How it helps the instructor
Conducting Surveys	The virtual classroom offers excellent facilities for conducting surveys. The class surveys can help the instructor to get feedback in different areas. The anonymity offered by the online medium encourages students to participate confidently. Surveys also help to develop reflective and critical thinking skills that are so important for undergraduate students. Conducting a survey about the course halfway through the semester is found to be a very effective practice for the instructors.

7.4   Developing Customized Audio/Video-Based Resources

In this digital era, with all the professionally designed books, high quality research documents, and free multi-media resources, do we really need to bother developing customized resources? The answer is *yes*! Each author has his or her own unique way of explaining content. As the instructor, you know your students better than anyone else, and the learning resources generated by you are certainly most effective for ensuring that learning happens. Even when you identify a text or audio/video resource authored by other experts that you really want your students to use, you must create a short audio/video message explaining the best way to study the given learning resource.

When we think of developing audio and video-based resources, we think of a sophisticated studio equipped with fancy lighting, cameras, headphones, etc. In reality, we do not need any of these; it is a lot easier than it sounds. No one is expecting a professional quality video. Remember, the quality of the video is judged on the content of the lecture (explanation, example, etc.), and not on quality of the recording. All you need is a decent camera, a microphone to do the basic recording. The camera and microphone on most smartphones and laptops have adequate capabilities for recording your lecture. In the worst-case scenario, you may need to invest in a webcam, a piece of equipment that is readily available at reasonable prices. In addition, you will need an editing tool. *Active Presenter* is a popular editing tool that is easy to use. It is free for personal and non-commercial use and very suitable for our purpose. Here are a few tips for creating your own customized, audio and video-based learning materials.

Table 7.f – Tips for developing customized audio/video resources

Tip no.	Strategy
1.	The audio/video content should not be too long. If you have a lot to share, create multiple shorter videos or break it in smaller segments by inserting a question, a graphic or a short exercise. *Later in this chapter, we will talk about how this can be done effectively with the help of a technology option called Edpuzzle.* This can be also done when you are using audio/video resources authored by other experts.
2.	Start by preparing the content well. While you may like to write out what you want to say, it is a bad idea to read from a written script. It not only distorts your eye contact, but it also hinders the flow of speech which in turn reflects poorly on your control of the subject and your confidence level.
3.	If you are planning to use a video lecture or podcast by another author, it is best to create a short introductory brief explaining to the students what to focus on in the lecture. It would be even better if you could give the exact portions (with minutes/seconds) to be studied. This optimizes the students' time and effort and helps to customize the resource.
4.	Choose the location carefully. Recordings are generally done indoors – make sure to pick a background that conveys the desired ambiance – an academic backdrop (a set of books) or a neutral-colored wall works best. If you are doing a series of lectures, try to change the backdrop.
5.	Lighting is important, make sure there is enough lighting coming from in front of you. Avoid sitting in front of a window, as the glare will distort the picture.
6.	Look right into the camera lens. If you are using a laptop to record. Cover the laptop screen so that you do not get distracted by the image on the screen.
7.	Position the camera slightly higher than your eye level so that you look up a little. If you are using a laptop, place it higher so that your eyes don't look closed.

Tip no.	Strategy
8.	Do not bother planning special effects. Remember, it is the quality of the content/explanation that is important and not special effects. If you are using a PowerPoint presentation, keep it as simple as possible, and avoid using too many colors, ornamentation, or animation.
9.	Make sure that your voice is well-paced, relaxed, and pleasant. A pleasant, smiling disposition is always very helpful.

Publishing Your Videos

Once you have prepared the audio/video materials you need to make them accessible to the students. If the file size is within the limit allowed by your LMS, you should post these in your virtual classroom but if the video file is very large as it can happen when we include simulations or virtual labs, you will need to create a YouTube channel, upload the content, and share the link in virtual classroom. There are three easy tasks to be accomplished:

   i)   Create a YouTube channel,

   ii)   Upload the prepared audio/video materials, and

   iii)   Share the link to access the materials.

Creating a personal YouTube Channel

We need to begin by creating a personal channel. It is not very complicated. After signing into your Google account, click on YouTube and click on your profile. Select "Create a Channel' option. You will need to give it a name – you can create a new name or keep the existing one that you use for your Google account. Voila! you now have a channel of your own that you can personalize further by clicking on *"Customize Channel"*. You can add a profile picture or a relevant

Uploading the prepared video materials

Once the channel is ready, you are all set to upload materials. This is not a very complex task. Click on the *Camera icon* (usually located at the top), then the *Upload Video* tab. Select the video file/files you want to upload, add a caption and a brief description, and click *Upload* to submit. If you are ready, choose the setting "privacy" and click. The video file will get published.

Sharing the link

This is the link that your students or general viewers will click on to view the video and further share it with others. Go to the channel and click on the specific video you want to share. You will see a video player and a *Share* button under that. When you click on it, several options for sharing the video like e-mail, text, social media, WhatsApp, share the link etc. will pop up. Choose *Share the Link* option and paste it in the virtual classroom.

7.5 Using Information and Communication Technology (ICT) Tools for Student Engagement

It is very heartening to see that more and more technology experts and companies are now focusing on developing new *Information and Communication Technology* (ICT) tools for enriching higher education. Almost every day, new apps are being launched to enhance class dynamics and/or solve some common problems faced by the instructors in their traditional classes. Most of these ICT tools are found to be equally effective for traditional as well as online instruction.

Let us discuss some of the popular ICT tools being used for achieving specific objectives. All options recommended here are free and user-friendly. They are designed to be simple, effective, and platform-independent and do not require any special skills to use them. It is important that you experiment with them and learn to use them proficiently before using them in class. Even though new software and apps are being developed every day, mastering the use of even one ICT tool can give you enough confidence to experiment with new and different ones. The 21st century university educator needs to develop proficiency in this area because of the speed with which new developments are taking place. Chances are that by the time you read this, many of the options mentioned here will have been updated or replaced by new, more powerful ones. For undergraduate teaching, the use of ICT tools is most effective for attaining the following two objectives:

- Getting realistic and measurable student feedback during the

- Enriching lectures and classroom and lab instruction by incorporating practical components like simulations, demonstrations, etc.

7.5.1   Using ICT Tools for Getting Measurable Student Feedback

As the lecture or class instruction progresses, it is normal for instructors to ascertain how the new knowledge is being received, understood, and assimilated by the students. We know that the general practice of stopping and asking, 'Any questions?' or 'Understood?' does not get us any dependable response. Instead, using a poll question or a short problem-saving activity based on what has just been taught can give clarity about i) how many students have or have not understood the content, and ii) which part of the content has not been understood well and needs to be reviewed. Listed below are some free and user-friendly technology options that can be used successfully to collect feedback for any discipline.

Table 7.g – Technology Options for Collecting Student Feedback

Resource	URL – Application – Usage
Mentimeter	**https://www.mentimeter.com** The *Mentimeter* is a practical interactive tool that you can use to create polls, quizzes, and surveys for collecting student feedback. Follow the steps given below to use the App. 1. Log into the URL and creating an account. 2. Prepare the desired instrument – poll, quiz, survey. Explain to the students the importance of the activity, and what they are expected to do in the given time. 3. Share the link with the students and let them participate in the activity using their laptops or smartphones. 4. Share the results with class. The *Mentimeter* has the possibility to show the results in a variety of formats including graphs or a word cloud. Since this is for in-class use, make sure that the instruments are short and focused to elicit the desired information. This very realistic feedback guides you to decide whether you need to repeat anything or go to the next teaching point.

Resource	URL – Application – Usage
Kahoot	**https://kahoot.it** *Kahoot* is actually a gaming tool that can be used not only for collecting student feedback but also for conducting formative assessments and promoting student engagement. Kahoot can be played in two formats: *Classic* (instructor-controlled) and *Self-paced* (student-controlled). To create and play Kahoot in class, use the following steps: 1. Login to download the App. Create an account using your email or social media address. It works equally well on all platforms. 2. Click the *Create* button to create the desired Kahoot (Multiple-choice, Open-ended questions, or video-based questions). Since it is planned as a game, you must assign points and specify a time for completion. Save the Kahoot to be used in class and note the generated PIN. 3. When ready to play, share the PIN with the students. Start the game by displaying the questions through a slide projector for students to respond by choosing the correct option. 4. Share the results consolidated by Kahoot. Like the Mentimeter, Kahoot can also provide analytics about the overall performance and question-wise performance of the students.
Quizizz	**www.quizizz.com** *Quizizz*.is another free and easy-to-use option for implementing in-class quizzes. Like Kahoot, Quizizz it is designed as a game, and shares many features with other options discussed here. To use it effectively, follow the steps given below: • Login and create an account using your email or social media account. • Click the *Create* button to create the desired instrument (MCQ or True-false format). Specify the time allocation. At this point, you can decide whether you want students to see the correct answer at the end of each question, or at the end of the quiz. Do not forget to note the *code* generated by the App. • Share the unique game code with the students. They will need to log in to the website and enter the unique code to access the quiz. • Review the performance of the students to draw conclusions about how well they have internalized the new knowledge.

Resource	URL – Application – Usage
Socrative	**https://www.socrative.com/apps/** *Socrative* is a powerful tool that can be used to gather detailed feedback. Like the *Mentimeter* and *Kahoot*, Socrative can be used to create polls, quizzes, and surveys and get very detailed feedback. Follow the steps given below: 1. Download the App and create an account as the *Teacher*. 2. Create the desired instruments – polls, quizzes, multiple-choice questions, or open-ended questions. Do not forget to add time for completion. Note the *code* generated by the App. 3. Share the code with the students and let them access the activity. You can see the responses in real-time as students work on their devices. 4. Socrative provides very detailed feedback about the class and individual performance. The information provided by the results guides the instructor in moving forward.
Edpuzzle	**http:// edpuzzle.com/** *Edpuzzle* is an amazing tool that allows the instructor to enhance the learning effectiveness of video lectures by adding many features such as voiceover, audio comments, and inserting questions at the chosen points. We know that in undergraduate instruction, video lectures (recorded by the instructor or selected from a MOOC) are a valuable resource that helps to attain a variety of objectives (Flipped Class, PSIS activity, Self-study for exam preparation). To use *Edpuzzle* effectively follow the steps given below. Step 1 – Login and create an account. Click *Create* and upload the video (created by you or taken from another source). Click the *Add Notes* button to add instructions or short explanations. Step 2 – Customize the use of the video lecture by using the different options provided. The video lecture can be open to the entire class (set to *public*) or made accessible to only chosen students *(set to Private)*. The instructor can may allow the students to review the entire video and then answer questions or require them to answer the question at specific points before moving forward.

Resource	URL – Application – Usage
	Step 3 – For adding questions, click *Add Question* at the bottom. You can add different types of questions (MCQ, True-False, or open-ended). As a good practice, specify a time limit for responding to the question or completing the activity.
	Step 4 – Use the A*ssign* button to open the video lecture to the students (all or selected). The responses to the inserted questions can be analyzed to get realistic feedback on students' understanding of the content presented in the video lecture.

All these ICT options work well for conducting formative assessments and providing clear, measurable feedback to the instructor. As the participation is anonymous, the students feel very comfortable participating, as opposed to the conventional way of raising their hands or standing up to respond in class. It is also possible for the instructor to get detailed analytics like how many students got which part of the question wrong etc.

7.5.2   ICT Tools for Supporting Lectures and Lab. Sessions

The ability to support in-class lectures with simulations, demonstrations, animated graphics, or dynamic visuals for explaining complex processes and phenomena is perhaps the most powerful contribution that the ICT tools have made to undergraduate instruction. Even though the popular belief is that ICT tools are more useful for courses in the STEM disciplines, the reality is that they have been used very successfully in other disciplines like Humanities, Social Sciences, Management or even Fine Arts. Irrespective of the discipline, the use of simulation, demonstration, or animated visuals is invaluable for promoting in-depth understanding, motivation, and the joy of learning.

ICT tools help us to bring animated visuals and simulations into the conventional classroom. It is true that creating simulations or animated visuals is not within the competency level of most of us instructors, but the good thing is that today, a large inventory of simulations or demonstrations in a huge array of disciplines is readily available. The instructor can use these readily available and free (for personal or non-commercial purposes) resources for classroom use. Please make sure to *clearly acknowledge each source*. What is even better is that once you have identified a suitable simulation, demonstration, or animated visual representation, there are tools you can use to customize them and make them more interactive.

There are different ways in which simulations, demonstrations, and animated visuals can be used effectively. One well-recognized methodology for incorporating demonstrations and simulations in regular lectures is ***Process Oriented Guided Inquiry Learning*** (POGIL). The strategy, developed in late 1990s, requires students (alone or in small groups) to understand concepts by studying and analyzing the given simulations and demonstrations. The process helps students to build knowledge through prompts, cues, and questions provided by the instructor in the form of a handout.

Listed below are some inventories of simulations and virtual labs that can be used very effectively by an undergraduate instructor to enhance the quality of their lectures.

Table 7.h – Some Technology Options for incorporating Virtual Labs and Simulations

Resource	Access & Features
PhET interactive simulations (website)	**http://phet.colorado.edu/** Excellent resource for STEM disciplines like Physics, Chemistry, Mathematics, Engineering, Biology, Earth sciences, etc. The inventory of simulations is available on the PhET website. Detailed instructions, manuals, and worksheets are also available. More interactivity can be added by the instructor.
Matlab	**http://www.mathworks.com/** Excellent for Engineering, Mathematics, and Physics courses. It is a programming language that helps students to create mathematical models and analyze data. However, this software is not free, and your institution needs to get a paid license for use across the institution. But the good news is that most institutions that run programs in STEM subscribe to it. So, in all probability, your institution will have this option available to you.

Resource	Access & Features
GeoGebra	**http://www.geogebra.org/** Excellent for Math, Geometry and Algebra. Equally effective for traditional as well as online teaching. Simulations help students to internalize concepts through visualization and active engagement.
Virtual Tours through Museums & Art Galleries	**http://www.moma.org** Museum of Modern Art (MOMA), New York, USA. Like most reputed museums, MOMA offers virtual tours that can be accessed through the museum website. The experience can help students to be seriously engaged in academic as well as cultural education.
NetLogo	**http://ccl.northwestern.edu/netlogo/** An excellent App for courses in Social Sciences. NetLogo is also a programming language that can help to build models to study phenomena related to complex systems.
Scratch	**http://scratch.mit.edu/** Excellent resource for Computer Science courses. This is a visual programming language that can create interactive games, stories, and animations. This is found to be especially useful for introductory courses. Students create simulations by dragging and dropping blocks of codes.
GAMS (General Algebriac Modeling System)	**http://www.gam.com/** A sophisticated, high-level modeling system commonly used for studying Econometrics. Use of simulations and virtual reality (VR) can provide students with first-hand experience of different economic scenarios including a virtual tour of the stock exchange.
Labster	**http://www.labster.com** A commercial provider of virtual lab simulations in different science disciplines like Biology, Life Sciences, Chemistry, etc. It allows students to experience live experiments. Again, the instructor can customize the lab by introducing different types of interactivities and evaluation.
Language learning Software	Simulations are very effective for language learning. They provide students first-hand exposure to pronunciation as well

Resource	Access & Features
	as cultural dynamics. Explaining cultural practices verbally can be very tedious but students can be made to experience it through animated visual representations. Simulations have been found to be invaluable for teaching phonology and pronunciation (showing the position and movement of the tongue, lips, etc. for creating a specific sound). Some currently popular language learning software using simulation are *Rosetta Stone, Duolingo, Babbel, FluentU, and HelloTalk.*

Recommendations for the Instructor

- All these simple ICT tools are very potent and can help you to make teaching more dynamic, motivating, and joyful. Be open to experimentation. Most Apps/software offer well-developed video tutorials that can help you to master the tool/strategy.

- Identify course content that can be better explained with the help of simulations, and search for an appropriate resource that can help you resolve the problem.

- Make it a point to always check that the source has been properly acknowledged.

- Be aware that every day, new, innovative, and more powerful tools are being added to the technology arsenal of the instructor. Do not be tempted to keep trying new tools in class just to impress your students. If something is working well for you and the students, just stick with it.

7.6.   Section 7: Wrap-Up and Tips for Incorporating Technology in Your Classroom

To sum up, technology has a lot of potential to make undergraduate teaching more effective, meaningful, and exciting. We have seen that in the academic context, technology is equally powerful in multiplicative, prescriptive, and supportive roles. The three areas where technology is most effective in undergraduate instruction are: creating and using a virtual classroom; creating and using instructor-designed audio/video resources; and using free and easy-to-use ICT tools to make class sessions more interactive, energetic, and meaningful.

Technology is powerful, but its effectiveness depends entirely on how its use is planned and executed by the instructor. Here are a few tips for harnessing the full power of technology.

Table 7.i – Tips for Effectively Using Technology in Classroom Teaching

Tip No.	Recommendations
1.	Remember, making effective use of technological options needs proper planning and preparation, and that takes time. The temptation to use technology options at the last minute can be disastrous and should be avoided.
2.	Even though most undergraduate students are technology-savvy, you must not expect them to understand everything intuitively. While using a new device or App proved detailed instructions. Experience shows that the most common reason why strategies involving technology fail, is rushed, unclear and confusing instructions. It is worth spending a few minutes to have a small trial in class. Provide the necessary instructions or lead them to resources for self-training (video – tutorials etc.)
3.	Be well-prepared. Make sure that the hardware (plugs, batteries, speed), and software (version compatibility) meet the requirements. Passwords are often a problem.
4.	Always have a backup plan because no matter how sophisticated the infrastructure may get, there will always be surprises and unseen failures. In many developing countries, unexpected power cuts can be an issue.
5.	Be very careful about the copyright rules and seek appropriate permissions wherever needed. It is also necessary to check the administrative rights etc. Once again, always acknowledge the source/s.

<table><tr><td>8</td><td></td></tr></table>

Planning and Implementing Effective Assessment

8.1   Assessment and Learning

This section focuses on designing and administering *Assessment* which is widely recognized as the most challenging aspect of university teaching. To begin with, it is important to understand the difference between the two terms *Evaluation* and *Assessment* which are *often* confused and used interchangeably. In fact, the two terms are different. The term *Assessment* refers to a systematic, continuous process for collecting information about student learning. *Evaluation,* on the other hand, refers to a one-time activity for analyzing and drawing conclusions with the intention of measuring the attainment of stated learning outcomes. (*Felder-Brent 2016*).

Assessment is the key component of the pedagogic process that impacts the effectiveness of both teaching and learning. Assessment allows the instructor to decide whether learners are ready to move on to the next segment of the course or some components need to be reviewed. Assessment is a powerful tool that directly impacts the learning process and student motivation (or demotivation).

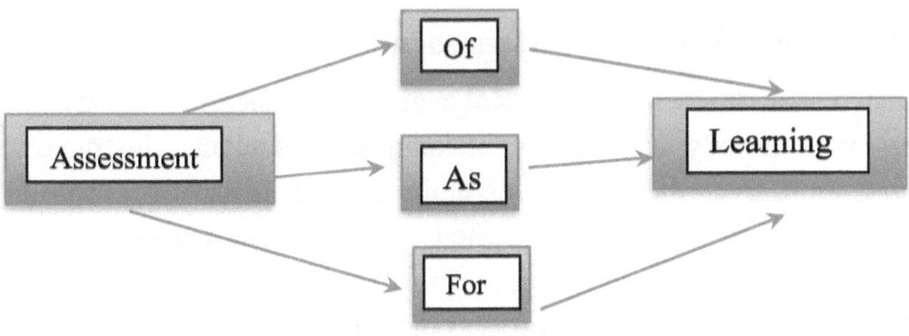

Fig. 8.1 – Assessment and Learning

Well-designed assessment helps to measure student learning as well as instructor proficiency. At the same time, feedback from assessment is a learning experience for the instructor. It educates the instructors about their own performance by identifying gaps in student learning, and areas where they need to sharpen their teaching. It is easy to see the three different roles assessment plays in *measuring* learning, *promoting learner motivation,* and *educating the instructor.* In other words, assessment helps the instructor to not only collect evidence of students' learning but also guide important instructional decisions.

8.2 Summative and Formative Assessment

There are two types of assessments that a university instructor needs to be concerned about: *Summative Assessment* and *Formative Assessment.* The summative assessment measures students' learning at the *completion* of a pre-defined segment or the entire course. The verdict comes in the form of final grades. Formative assessment, on the other hand, is an ongoing process that takes place during the entire course. It can be informal (non-graded, based on class performance and instructor observation) or formal (graded, based on home assignments, in-class quizzes, end-of-section/unit tests, etc.). Formative assessment generally has little to no emphasis on grades and is focused on getting feedback about student learning. Over the years, the focus has been shifting progressively from *summative* to *formative assessment.* However, both summative and formative forms of assessment are very important, and instructors need to develop full control over all aspects of designing and implementing them.

8.2.1 Planning Summative Assessment

Summative assessment is an important event in the undergraduate instructional process that directly impacts all stakeholders—students, instructors, and administration. Even though the university systems in most countries around the world still use a centralized system of having the end-of-term or final examinations set by external boards or agencies, more and more universities are moving towards an autonomous process of allowing departments or instructors to set their own exams. Whatever the situation, every undergraduate instructor needs to have the competency to plan, create, and implement summative assessment. This is important for preparing the students for success. The summative assessment requires planning at the *macro* and *micro* levels.

Macro-level Planning of summative assessments is mostly organizational. It is generally dictated by the institute's policies and includes three main decisions:

- How many assessment events (tests/exams) should be planned for the entire course?

- When these events should be scheduled?

- What should be the overall breakdown of marks between different assessment events?

Micro-level Planning of summative assessments is more involved. Starting with decisions about the number and format of questions for each exam and the criteria for designing each question. The quality of summative assessment depends on how well each individual question is formulated and written out. The following guidelines will help make the summative assessment more effective.

Table 8.a – Guidelines for Planning Effective Summative Assessment

Criteria	Guideline
Clear identification of the content being tested?	Clearly identify the portion/chapters of the course to be tested in each exam. Make sure that the content has been taught in class, and that the students are aware that it will be included in the summative exam.
Analysis of the Knowledge/Skills required to meet the outcomes.	Before composing each exam, study the stated learning outcomes for the identified content. List Bloom's taxonomy level/s of knowledge and skills required to attain them. This is especially important for courses that are expected to serve as prerequisites for the subsequent courses.
The complexity level of different questions in the instrument	It is important to ensure that questions for each exam are pitched at different complexity levels. A general recommendation is that about 15 – 20% of questions should be of *low* complexity level; about 60-70 % of questions should be pitched at a *medium* level of complexity; and about 15 – 20% of questions should be at a somewhat challenging level.

Criteria	Guideline
Alignment of the competence/skill and the stated outcomes	The alignment of the competence/skill level with the stated outcomes is ensured by pitching the questions at the appropriate level of Bloom's Taxonomy of Cognitive Objectives. The suggested verbs for each level can be helpful in achieving that alignment though the though the instructors must keep in mind that mere use of a verb does not automatically establish the level. To review *Bloom's Taxonomy of Cognitive Objectives* and the *List of Verbs* for each level (p - 102 -103).
Selection of question formats	A summative exam paper should have a good mix of different types of questions (short answers, multiple-choice, graphic-based, or long descriptive). This allows the instructor to test different cognitive/skill levels and cater to different learning preferences.
Time allocation for completing the question paper	This is a very important but much-neglected aspect. Most instructors tend to go by the expected number of questions in an exam without considering how much time an average student will need to respond to each one of them. Experts recommend that once the exam is created, the instructor should take the test herself to check the required time to respond to each question, and then allocate at least 30% more time for the students. *(Felder, 2002)*
Quality of composition of the question and instructions	The actual writing of the questions is equally important. Experience shows that many students are unable to achieve the deserved grade simply because they do not understand the question. The lacuna can be on the side of the student (lack of language competency or careless reading of the question) but, more often, it is because the instructions are unclear and confusing. Make sure that each question is written in simple, familiar words that clearly define the expectations.

8.2.2 Planning Formative Assessment

Unlike summative assessment, formative assessment is less focused on grades. Its main objective is to monitor student learning and therefore, needs to be implemented throughout the entire course session. We are told that "…to support learning, assessments must evolve from being isolated occasional events attached to the end of teaching to becoming an ongoing series of inter-related events that reveal changes in student learning over time" *(Stiggins, 2008)*.

The instructor has the total flexibility to plan, design, administer, and determine the number, format, and grade value of each intervention. Formative assessment is effective because it allows students to work on a small segment of knowledge acquired over a short period of time and helps them build their knowledge base, supported by prompt and effective feedback from the instructor or peers. With higher levels of awareness about how learning happens, the focus is shifting from summative to formative assessment. Instead of focusing on one of two summative exams, most colleges are now moving towards formative assessments, where student performance is assessed throughout the entire semester and only a small percentage of marks are assigned to the summative exam.

Formative assessment can be informal or formal. The informal formative assessment may include ungraded, regular, in-class questioning, while the formal formative assessment includes graded assessment conducted at the end of a short, a specific section or a unit. Both formats are important and serve different objectives. The objective of the first one is to get prompt feedback on how the content being taught in class is being assimilated by the class. The objective of the second format is to ensure that the students have mastered the key concepts covered in a specific section or a unit and are ready to move forward. Both these formats of formative assessment – ungraded in-class questioning and graded assessment at the end of a short, specified section or unit – are important and need to be designed and implemented carefully.

Informal Formative Assessment: Regular In-Class Questioning

In-class questioning promotes learning. Research tells us that the teacher does not transfer knowledge through instruction, but through asking 'good questions' that stimulate, analysis, synthesis and evaluation *(Petty, 2009)*. In-class questioning helps us to get effective feedback about how much of the content being discussed in class has been assimilated by the students. The questioning can be verbal or written; it can be completed individually or with peers. Normally, while teaching, we keep checking by asking questions like, "Is this clear? Or "Understood?" Or "Any Questions?" and we all know that the responses received do not provide any realistic feedback about how many students have understood the content, or which part of the content needs to be re-explained. In Section 6, we looked at many active learning activities (*class polls, minute papers, concept tests,* etc.) that also serve as very effective feedback tools. Some of the technology-based options (*Google Forms, Mentimeter,* and *Socrative,* etc.) discussed in Section 7, are also very effective as informal formative assessment tools. Given below are a few additional tips for successfully embedding informal assessment in regular classes.

Table 8.b – Tips for Incorporating Informal Formative Assessment in Regular Class Sessions

Tip No.	Recommendations
1.	Consider in-class questioning as a part of your lecture and plan the question/s or activity along with the point in the lecture when you want to use it.
2.	Remember to design the assessment for the content taught recently. Depending on the type and complexity of the content, you can decide whether the activity will be completed individual or paired activity.
3.	The assessment should use no more than a few minutes of class time. This means that the question/s or activity must be short, very focused, and managed very efficiently.
4.	Call on one or two students to share their responses. Discuss the correct answer explaining the finer points. Do not ask for volunteers because that eats up a lot of time.
5.	For verbal questions, make sure to ask one question at a time (*define X and how it impacts Y)* are two questions.
6.	Also, for verbal questions, give the students sufficient time to respond. It is observed that the time we typically give to a student to respond is much shorter than what we think it to be. The time given for response should match the cognitive complexity of the question.

Tip No.	Recommendations
7.	Create a respectful environment for responding to questions. Always, encourage the responder by recognizing the correct part of the answer, however small. If the responder is hesitating, provide additional prompts to help the student to scaffold the response.
8.	An effective variation is to ask students to work in pairs (or threesomes) to create questions about the concept studied.

Formal Formative Assessment

Formal formative assessment involves conducting short tests at the completion of a specific segment, section, or unit that are generally graded. This format offers a number of advantages to both the students and the instructors. The students get an opportunity to review and master the content in smaller segments, and the instructor gets clear indication about outcomes achieved during the course. Some colleges prefer to have fixed weekly or fortnightly tests, but most commonly, colleges prefer to hold formative assessments at the end of a learning unit with specified outcomes for the content covered in that segment, section, or unit. Given below are some tips for designing and implementing formal formative assessments.

Table 8.c – Tips for Designing and Implementing Formal Formative Assessment

Tip No.	Recommendations
1.	As the content being examined is small, the instrument must be short and focused.
2.	The questions should be in mixed format (MCQs and descriptive) and focused to assess the outcomes specified for the content.
3.	Even though the assessment instrument is short (3-5 questions), try to design questions with multiple parts. This helps to identify specific gaps in student understanding that may need to be reviewed in class.
4.	Make sure that the turnaround time for providing feedback (and grades) is very short. This is very important because as soon as the exam is over, you are addressing the content of a new segment, and students are likely to lose the context if feedback is delayed.

8.3 Different Types of Test Questions

We saw that an undergraduate-level question paper should present a good mix of different types of questions. Questions at the undergraduate level may be classified in four main categories: *Selection-based questions, Short Answer questions, Descriptive Essay Type questions,* and *Case Studies.* Each type of question serves a specific objective and should be used intentionally.

Selection-based type questions

This category includes questions where the responder has to select the correct option – Multiple-*choice Questions (MCQ), True or-False* or *Fill-in-the-Blank.* All types of questions, especially the MCQs are very popular with all instructors because the questions are easy to create and even easier to evaluate. The format can be used effectively for all disciplines and for both formative and summative assessments. However, questions in this category are ideal for testing mostly low to middle levels of Bloom's Cognitive Taxonomy (*Remembering, Understanding, Applying*).

Questions in this category have two parts: i) the *Stem* (the main question) and ii) the *Options.* Both parts need to be composed very carefully. While composing the *Stem,* simple and familiar words should be chosen, and the sentence structure should be as concise as possible. It is better to avoid the use of negatives, which can be unnecessarily confusing (e.g., distillation is not the best way to: a) purify water; b) create perfumes; c) refine oil). For composing the *Options,* keep the choices as close as possible, and ensure that all of them are in the same format e.g. all of them can be one word, a number, or a short phrase.

A very efficient way to create *Selection-based Questions* is by using a Learning Management System (LMS) like Canvas, Moodle, Google Classroom, Blackboard, etc. Most of these platforms offer the facility to not only create this type of question but also present the same question in multiple versions that can be distributed randomly to the students. Using an LMS to create questions serves several objectives: the instructor can prepare the questions ahead of time; create a question bank, and random distribution of different versions of the same MCQs helps to minimize plagiarism. The question bank can be invaluable for supporting low-performing students as well as for using in a future course.

Short Answer Questions

This is a very popular format that can be used for all disciplines. This type of question can be pitched at a higher complexity level, requiring students to demonstrate in-depth understanding, critical thinking, and creative problem-solving. The strength of this format is that it can be used to test learning at all six levels of Bloom's taxonomy.

Short answer questions also need to be designed carefully. The challenge is to frame the question in simple, direct language so that the desired response is elicited. The question should clearly specify the scope of the response (mentioning a word limit is very helpful). Short questions built around a picture, graphic, or diagram are also found to be very effective.

Descriptive (essay type) Questions

This category of questions should form the core part of undergraduate-level assessment, as they help to assess higher-order learning as well as problem-solving and critical thinking skills. Descriptive questions are most effective when they are open-ended, allowing the test-taker to discuss complex concepts from multiple points of view. This category of questions is not limited to long descriptions, depending in the discipline, the test takers may be asked to explain or evaluate a process, write algorithms or a computer program, or solve a given problem and give the rationale for the chosen solution.

The problem with descriptive questions is that they are challenging not only to create but also to evaluate. The instructions for this type of question must clearly state the expectations regarding the focus and depth of the response. For open-ended questions (questions that can have multiple pathways to a correct response as opposed to closed-ended questions that have a yes-no response), giving a word limit is recommended, and in all cases, providing an appropriate evaluation rubric is invaluable for both the test-taker and the instructor. How to create and use a rubric is discussed later in this section.

Case Studies

The use of case studies as an instructional tool in higher education is not new. The pedagogy was initially used in France in the early 20th century. Even though the case study method is more popularly used in disciplines such as Law, Management and Social Sciences, the method can be used effectively in any discipline where the instructor intends to evaluate classroom learning in the real-world context. The method uses actual or designed scenarios (situations) built around general or specific problems that allow students to observe, investigate, record, evaluate, and propose viable solutions using the concepts learned.

The case study method is a powerful strategy that promotes motivation and higher-order learning skills such as investigation, analysis, problem-solving and critical thinking effective for promoting learning and motivation. As most students like to work with problems that depict real-world issues, they help the students to visualize and experience the problem and get fully engaged. Whether they work alone or in teams, the strategy promotes higher-order thinking and accountability. However, the format requires carefully crafted scenarios and structured implementation. The first step is to identify and write the learning objective and create a scenario that presents a problem built to directly addresses the learning outcome. Implementing case studies requires the instructor to make several decisions, such as:

- Student/s submit the completed assignment—an in-class presentation, an online presentation, or a written Will the task set for the case study be completed by individual students or in groups?

- Will the case study be used in a regular class, as content for a flipped class, or as an assignment? If it is meant to be used as an in-class activity, it must be very short.

- When and how will the case study materials be shared with students?

- How much time should be given for completing the activity?

- In which format should the report?

- Finally, what criteria should be included in the assessment rubric?

8.4 Evaluating the Effectiveness of the Test/Exam Questions

It is a good practice to study the effectiveness of the tests or exams designed or administered by you. This is best done by comparing the <u>expected</u> student performance with the <u>actual</u> student performance. In addition to determining the extent to which the learning outcomes have been achieved, the exercise helps you to identify the sections of the course content that have not been fully understood and need to be reviewed. It is advisable to do this early in the semester so that the learning from the exercise can be used to bring in the required modifications in teaching within the semester. This exercise involves studying two indicators – i) *the overall class performance*, and ii) *the effectiveness of individual questions*.

The *overall class performance* reflects the overall quality of instruction. The best way to study this is to plot each student's grade as a graph. The curve gives a clear indication of the ratios between high, average, and low scores and informs us about the extent to which the outcomes specified for the portion covered in the test or exam have been achieved. It also indicates whether the numbers of high, average, and low performance align with the identified profiles of the different sets of students in your class.

At the *individual question* level, the test/exam is study to determine the extent to which each question has achieved the anticipated performance level. Earlier, we learned that a well-designed exam paper has questions set at different complexity levels. The recommended mix is that 15%–20% of questions should be simple enough to be answered by *all* students in class while most of the questions (60%–70%) should be targeted at average (or average +) students, and about 15%–20% of questions should be challenging enough to identify the high-performers.

Let us try and understand this two-part process with the help of an example, and analyze both *the overall class performance* and the effectiveness of *individual questions*. The scenario involves analyzing an *end of unit test comprising of 4 different types of questions carrying a total value of 24 marks. The total number of students in class is 73 and the pass mark is set at 45%.*

To get the *overall class performance,* it is best to plot a graph using the *marks* obtained by each of the 73 students as shown in Fig. 8.2.

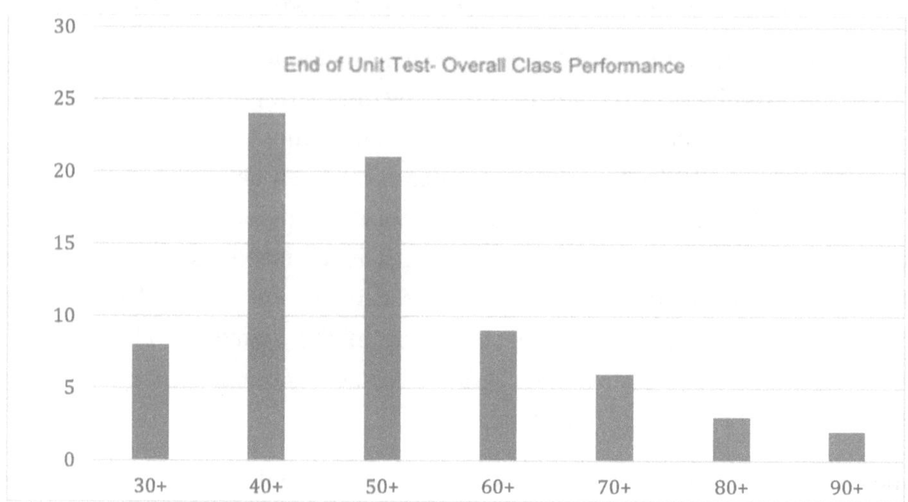

Fig. 8.2 – Analyzing the Overall Class Performance

The Fig. 8.2 shows that the class performance in the end of section/unit test is rather disappointing. Of the 73 students; 9 have failed (below 45+%) and 24 have barely made the pass mark (45+%); 21 students have an average grade of 55+%; while 9 students have made the 60+% mark, and only 11 students have scored over 70+% (5 above 70+, 3 above 80+% and only 2 students 90+%).

This disappointing result can be attributed to two reasons. Either the topics/concepts included in the test/exam were not fully understood by the students or, the questions were not composed clearly, or in the worst-case scenario, both the teaching of subject matter and the composition of test questions were not up to the mark. This result requires serious reflection on and remedial action the part of the instructor.

For analyzing the effectiveness of individual questions, student performance in *each question* needs to be analyzed. Here again, the student performance is a direct indicator of instructor's efficacy. If the student performance is below expectations in a certain question, it can be because either that part of the content was not understood well by the students or, the question was not framed clearly. In both cases, the feedback provided by this analysis can be very helpful for the instructor in identifying specific parts of the content that need to be reviewed, and refine the writing of the questions. The format given below can help to analyze the question-wise effectiveness of a question paper.

Table 8.d – Sample Format for Item-wise Analysis of a Test/Exam Paper

End of Section/Unit Test
No. of students – 73
M. Marks – 24; No. of Questions – 4; Pass marks 45%

Q.	Type/Marks	Difficulty Level	Performance in %age						Expectation Mapping
			<45	55+	65+	75+	85+	90+	
Q.1	Numerical (Applying level) (8)	Medium	*6*	*36*	19	8	4	0	***Expected performance*** – most students were expected to score 75+ – 85% ***Actual performance*** – data shows that 78% students scored between 55+ to 65+ %. **Conclusion** – Both the content covered in this part and the clarity of the question need to be reviewed,
Q.2	Short answer (Analyzing level) (8)	Medium	*2*	*47*	1	8	5	2	***Expected performance*** – most students were expected to score 75+ – 85% ***Actual performance*** – Data shows 64% students scored 55+% which is unacceptable. **Conclusion** – Both the content covered in this part and the clarity of the question need to be reviewed,
Q.3	MCQ (4)	Low	-	1	6	9	45	*12*	***Expected performance*** – most students were expected to score 75+% ***Actual performance*** – Data shows that over 86% students scored 75+% ***Conclusion*** – The question is well composed, and the students seem to have mastered the content well.

Q.	Type/Marks	Difficulty Level	Performance in %age						Expectation Mapping
			<45	55+	65+	75+	85+	90+	
Q.4	Short Answer (Evaluating level) (4)	High	2	7	26	22	10	6	**Expected performance –** most students were expected to score around 55+%. *Actual performance* – Data shows that over 87% students scored above 55+%. **Conclusion –** Unexpectedly good performance and the students can be challenged further. The question was well-composed.

It is evident from the above sample that student performance in questions 1 and 2 is not acceptable. Both the content covered in these portions and the writing of the questions need to be reviewed. Student performance in question 3 is as expected but, the performance in question 4 is positively surprising which means that majority of the students are ready for even more challenging questions in that specific topic.

An exercise like this keeps us connected with our students' performance and provides realistic feedback about our own performance as a teacher and a test-setter which in turn, helps us to finetune our pedagogy. This process of creating and evaluating tests can be made more efficient with the use of technology that can help us to analyze the effectiveness of an exam at the overall and item-wise levels. It also helps to create and store multiple different versions of the same questions.

8.5   About Assessment Rubrics

A *Rubric* may be defined as a shared system of evaluation that guides both the test-taker and the test-evaluator. A rubric is a tool that provides clear expectations of how an assignment, or an exam will be graded. for grading. Assessment rubrics are valuable for both the students and the teachers. For instructors, the rubrics promote transparency, make grading consistent and time-efficient, and provide informative feedback about specific gaps in student understanding. For students, the rubrics improve student preparation and performance by providing clear guidelines about the evaluation criteria as well as the grade value of each criterion. Rubrics are indispensable when the same course has to be taught by different instructors or when you want to engage students in self – or peer-evaluation.

8.6   Two Types of Rubrics

There are two types of rubrics: *Holistic* and *Analytical*. Both are equally important and are used to evaluate different types of questions.

Holistic Rubrics

Holistic rubrics are suitable for open-ended questions or tests that can have several possible correct responses or approaches for addressing the same question or problem. Here, the subjective opinion, judgement, rationale are pronounced. In other words, this type of rubric works best for questions or tasks like essays, critiquing a poem, commenting on socio-cultural situations, or ethical issues that do not have one standard correct response. The evaluation is based not on right or wrong but on how well the arguments are presented and justified. In Holistic rubrics, all criteria are evaluated collectively, and an overall grade is awarded.

Analytical Rubrics

The Analytical rubrics, on the other hand, are best suited for assignments/ questions that have a universally accepted response/solution, and the answers are more structured and specific as in the case of STEM courses. Here, each criterion is evaluated separately and assigned an individual score. These are then added to calculate a final grade. The feedback provided by an analytical rubric is more precise and allows the student to get a clear picture of where and why the marks were deducted. In the Analytical Rubric, the criteria and the performance level are separated, and each criterion is evaluated separately. The descriptors for each performance level allow the student to understand how their work has been evaluated. The process of creating a rubric is two-dimensional and involves i) setting criteria on which the response will be evaluated and ii) defining the levels of performance that are generally labeled as *Excellent, Good, Acceptable,*

Poor, or *A, B, C, D, etc.* Then, descriptors are created to describe the expected performance for each level – *A, B, C, D* etc.

Let us try and get a better understanding of these two types of rubrics and how to create them using a sample assignment – designing a project presentation. We will create both rubrics for evaluating the same assignment using five criteria: *content selection, content organization, quality of visuals, delivery of a presentation, and responding to audience questions.* Let us begin with creating a **Holistic Rubric** for the sample assignment using the five criteria.

Table 8.e – Sample Holistic Rubric for Evaluating a Project Presentation

Grade	Criteria and Performance
A	The presentation was well-organized, and the presenter showed excellent knowledge of the subject. The slides were well-designed. The presenter spoke clearly and maintained eye contact with the audience. The audience's questions were addressed confidently.
B	The presentation was quite well-organized. The presenter showed good knowledge of the subject. Most of the slides were well-designed. The presenter spoke clearly and maintained eye contact for most of the time. Most of the questions posed by the audience were addressed.
C	The presentation could be better organized. The presenter showed some knowledge of the subject. The slides could have been better designed. The presenter maintained limited eye contact and was not able to answer the audience's questions confidently.
D	The presentation was poorly organized. They showed little to no knowledge of the subject. The slides were poorly designed. The presenter maintained limited eye contact and was unable to answer any of the audience's questions.

In the **Analytical Rubric,** the criteria and the performance level are separated, and each criterion is evaluated separately. The descriptors for each performance level allow the students to clearly identify the criteria they scored poorly and why.

Table 8.f – Sample Analytical Rubric for Evaluating the Same Project Presentation

Criteria	Excellent	Good	Acceptable	Needs Improvement	20 Marks
Content Selection	The content of the presentation was focused and engaging. It raised many relevant questions. (5 – 4.5)	The content of the presentation was quite good. It kept the audience involved. (4.5 – 3.5)	A part of the presentation lacked focus. At times, the audience seemed confused. (3.5 – 2.25)	Most of the content of the presentation was confusing and irrelevant to the topic. (2.25 – 0)	5
Content Organization	The presentation was very well-organized. (4 – 3.5)	The presentation was fairly well-organized. (3.5 – 3.0)	The presentation could have been better organized. (3.0 – 2.0)	The presentation was poorly organized. (2.0 – 0)	4
Quality of Visuals	The visuals were very well-designed. (3 – 2.5)	The visuals were fairly well-designed. (2.5 – 2)	The visuals were unclear. and confusing (2 – 1.5)	The visuals were repetitive and/or poorly designed. (1.5 – 0)	3
Delivery – voice control/ eye contact	The delivery was flawless, clear delivery – consistent eye contact. (6 – 5)	The delivery was good, quite clear, eye – contact most of the time. (5 – 4)	The delivery was confusing – too fast/ slow limited eye – contact. (4 – 3)	Poor, unclear delivery. Little to no eye – contact (3 – 2)	6
Management of Audience Questions	All audience questions were answered clearly. (2 – 1.75)	Most of the audience questions were answered clearly. 1.75 – 1,5)	Some audience questions were answered but very hesitantly. (1.5 – 1.0)	Most audience questions remained unanswered. (1.0 – 0)	2
Total					20

8.7 The Role of Feedback in the Teaching-Learning Process

An active culture of collecting and providing feedback helps to make teaching more effective and learning more meaningful. Feedback is equally important for both the students and the instructor. Feedback makes assessment a powerful tool for learning and plays a key role in planning corrective action, providing reinforcement, increasing a sense of accountability, and sustaining motivation. To achieve all these objectives, *Feedback* must be viewed as an integral part of regular classroom teaching and should be planned as an important component of instruction.

The instructor may choose a *formal* or an *informal* process to collect student feedback. Formal feedback is taken after a predetermined chunk of content has been completed. Informal feedback, on the other hand, includes on-the-spot, ungraded, short activities planned to check understanding of the immediately covered content. The main objective for the instructor is to know whether he or she should stop to review some parts of it or continue teaching.

Formal feedback is taken using a structured, specifically designed instrument, and the results are shared with the students for a follow-up dialogue or action. To collect formal feedback, the instructor needs to design a formal instrument and devise a process for the students that is comfortable and secure. In a way, the grades obtained for assignments, class quizzes, etc., serve as formal feedback about student learning.

This is one area where technology can really help the instructor. Using an **Online Platform** to collect formal feedback is also a very practical option. It offers several advantages. It is flexible, secure, and private, and above all, it does not eat up class time. Your virtual classroom can serve as a powerful avenue for doing this. Especially just before the exams, you can ask students to post areas where they are having difficulty. You can then group them into two or three main areas and discuss them in class. In Section 7, we learned about a number of free and inexpensive technology-based tools that can be used effectively for getting feedback.

8.8   Formats of Feedback

For effective teaching, four forms of feedback—*student-to-student, student-to-instructor, reflective feedback, and instructor – to – student –* are essential and must be planned seriously.

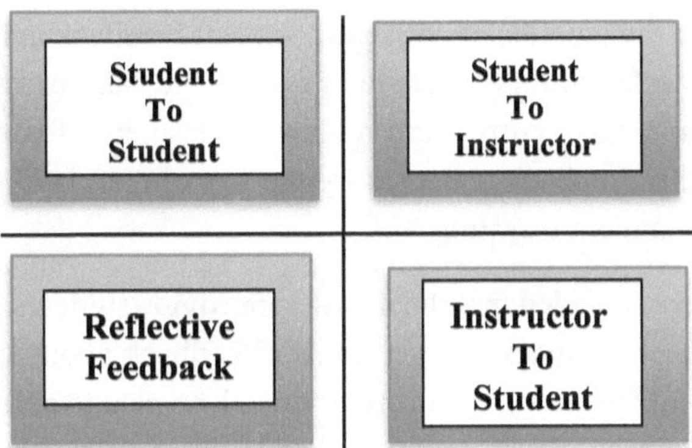

Fig. 8.3 – Different Forms of Feedback

Student-to-Student Feedback

This form of feedback is very valuable because it is candid, without any fear or apprehensions, and it is beneficial for both parties. Respecting each other's feedback is an important workplace skill that students must develop. However, not many undergraduate students have exposure to this activity and know how to give and receive feedback. Instructors must guide them. A possible solution is to create a handout sharing some of the tips provided under *Tips for Providing Constructive Feedback* (pp - 237-238). This is an important life skill that undergraduate students need to learn in order to be successful at the workplace.

One very simple and effective exercise for training students for providing constructive feedback, is peer-evaluation. Begin by creating a regular class assignment along with the rubric. As this will be the first time the students will be participating in such an exercise, it is better to keep the grade value low. Once the submissions come, each student is assigned one peer's assignment for grading using the rubric and submit a one-paragraph report justifying the grade. Every student gets two evaluations: one by the instructor and the other by the peer, both using the same rubric and supported by comments/justification.

Student-to-Instructor Feedback

Student-to-instructor feedback is well-recognized as an important tool for quality control in higher education. A discerning instructor is very sensitive to it and can get feedback from simple behaviors, including 'bored expressions in the eyes of the class in front of you!' *(Brennan J, & Williams R, 2004)*. Most institutions have the practice of collecting student feedback in the middle or at the end of a semester with the intention of using the data for various purposes like instructor appraisal, curriculum review, assessment of course popularity, etc. However, this feedback collected by the department is of little use to the instructor about student learning.

It is strongly recommended that the instructor provide students opportunity for providing frequent feedback. To get holistic feedback about student learning (and the quality of teaching), the instructor needs to plan to collect both formal and informal feedback. For informal feedback, the instructor can use activities like *polls,* a *one-minute paper,* or any other of the active learning activities discussed in Section 6. This immediate feedback informs the instructor what the students have understood or what needs to be repeated, which strategy worked well or did not work. To get more comprehensive feedback, the instructor must plan a brief (no more than 4-5 questions) survey and implement it from time to time. This will help to get very focused feedback about course content and teaching methodology. Moreover, the practice of collecting regular student feedback promotes a 'bond' between the instructor and her students. Students begin to acquire a sense of ownership of the course; they feel important and are likely to be more engaged in classwork.

Reflective Feedback – Training Students to Assess Themselves

The most effective form of feedback the students can get is through *reflective feedback* where they have the opportunity to assess their own performance. Being able to assess one's own performance and identify the pluses and minuses is an essential life skill that can be of immense value to undergraduate students. As instructors, we must provide opportunities for the students to self-evaluate themselves on a regular basis. When students become aware of their strengths and weaknesses, they learn to take ownership, and make important decisions about the modifications and refinements required to improve their performance. Finally, the practice of reflection and self-analysis helps students develop accountability for their own learning, which in turn helps to develop self-efficacy and self-confidence. To promote self-evaluation, some of the strategies mentioned below can be tried:

- Ask students to evaluate themselves on a class quiz and submit a report about where the points were lost. This is an excellent strategy for building trust and self-confidence. The same format can be used for peer-evaluating a home assignment.

- Advise students to keep a journal to monitor their progress.

- Teach students to write a reflective report about their learning and overall experience of being in the class and give suggestions for improving it.

Instructor-to-student feedback

Teacher-to-student feedback forms a crucial link between the different components of the instructional process. Instructor-to-student feedback has high impact on student motivation. While giving feedback, the instructor must be sensitive and choose the words carefully. The tone of the written and verbal feedback should be positive. Negative and poorly chosen words can be very de-motivating and can destroy a student's self-confidence. To be effective, instructor feedback must be timely and focused. The focus should be on the error and how it should have been addressed.

Another important point is to ensure that the privacy of the students is respected. Make it a point to never discuss a student's poor performance in class. Finally, all feedback provided to the students must be constructive, designed to address the errors and not the person. However, experience shows that the feedback provided by most instructors is rather sketchy and non-specific. Even though most instructors recognize the importance of providing detailed feedback, in practice, very few take the time to do so.

8.9 Providing Constructive Feedback

What is *constructive* feedback? Constructive feedback focuses on pointing out the errors and suggesting solutions for fixing them. Constructive feedback is worded carefully to keep the students informed, encouraged, and motivated.

Constructive feedback promotes reflective practices and self-assessment, which are essential lifelong learning skills for undergraduate students.

Table 8.g – Tips for Giving Constructive Feedback

Tip	Explanation
1.	Convey right from the beginning that you are sincerely interested in the success of your students, and for that their feedback is an important tool. Explain how you will be giving and taking feedback throughout the course.
2.	A very effective strategy is to ask the students to pick up their first assignment from the office (p - 67). This gives you the opportunity to start the learning process by giving personalized feedback and building mutual trust and confidence.
3.	Follow the famous 'feedback sandwich' model proposed by Celestine Chua *(Chua, 2012)* that recommends opening with a positive comment followed by corrective input and closing with another encouraging comment.
4.	Remember that the choice of words used to give feedback plays an important role in motivating or demotivating students. All feedback must be in positive terms (instead of saying this is wrong, it is better to say, this could have been done in another way). The words and phrases chosen must convey empathy and assurance that you are on the learner's side.
5.	Make sure that the comments focus on the error rather than on the student. Errors may refer to misinterpretation of the question, applying the wrong principle, faulty reasoning, miscalculation etc. Constructive feedback is non-judgmental, for example, it is better to say, *the question was misinterpreted* rather than saying *you misinterpreted the question*. Your feedback should communicate a sincere interest in seeing the students improve their performance.
6.	Constructive feedback targets specific issues/problems and provides viable solutions. Non-specific comments such as "great job." Or "could be better" are not helpful to learners. Constructive feedback helps identify specific parts of the knowledge or skill that need to be developed. It focuses on "what can be improved" rather than on "what is wrong."
7.	Feedback is useful when it is provided promptly. Effort should be made to provide the feedback while the test/home assignment is still fresh in the mind of the student.

8.10 Open Book Tests and Exams

Open-book exams are a type of assessment where students are allowed to bring and refer to textbooks, class notes, and other reference materials during the exam. Most instructors are apprehensive about the viability of the open-book format. However, there is sufficient evidence in favor of this format, provided the instructor puts in sufficient thought to designing questions to evaluate specific competencies. This format is particularly effective for testing higher-order learning, and as such, the open-book exams are more challenging for both the test-setter and the test-taker. While the concept is admired by both instructors and students, it has not really become mainstream in the undergraduate arena. The main reason for this is that most instructors do not feel confident about designing the right types of questions. On the other hand, the students have yet to get comfortable with the concept of open book exams.

8.10.1 Type of Questions Suitable for Open-Book Exams

Instructors often think that open-book exams are somewhat limiting, but that is not true. Many different types of questions can be used as long as they test higher-order competencies (analyzing, evaluating, or creating). Case studies are a popular choice for open-book tests because, once the context is established, the scope for creating questions at the analysis, evaluation, and creation stage is expanded. Any question that requires the students to resolve a given problem by applying a specific theory, concept, or formula is suitable for an open-book exam. The following question formats are found to be very effective:

- Ask the students to complete a part-process or a part-solution and explain the rationale for it.

- Ask the students to predict/calculate the outcome of the scenario given in the case study and what will happen if some of the parameters are changed. This format is very useful as it works across disciplines, whether it pertains to a policy, values, chemical agents, measurements, time duration, etc.

- Ask the students to identify the errors or gaps in a failed project or scenario, explain the analysis, and provide solutions.

8.10.2   Implementing Open-Book Exams

Designing questions for an open-book exam is, by default, very different from designing questions for a conventional exam. The starting point is still the pre-stated outcomes, but the nature of the tasks to be completed is very different. Here, the questions must be designed to test higher-order learning with active problem-solving, critical thinking, and manipulation of the learned information or/and data. Questions that require students to make decisions regarding the appropriate method or process and/or choosing and justifying the correct solutions are most effective. Three important considerations here are: i) preparing the students for managing open book/notes tests, ii) managing time, and iii) writing instructions.

If you are planning to introduce an open-book exam, the first thing you need to do is prepare the students both mentally and skill-wise. Begin by explaining the advantages of the format. Give them an idea of what type of questions to expect and what kind of materials to carry with them. Tell them how these exams are preparing them for life and their future professional lives. The main thing is to warn them that even though they will have their books and notes with them, they still need to know the concepts and processes, and for that they need to put in the time and effort to prepare well for the exam.

The other important thing is to teach the student how to manage *time*. Research shows that one of the main obstacles is time management. Generally, students spend a lot of time looking up or confirming information that they already know. Because they have the books and notes, they waste time adding unnecessary information. If you are planning to use the open-book format, it is best to organize a short open-book test in class to prepare them specially for managing time.

Another challenge is the actual composition of the questions. It is seen that because the context needs to be established, the instructions tend to be long, and students with limited language competency, get confused. It is a good practice to compose open-book test questions in two parts: the context and the task. It is observed that often, the main task is lost in the description of the context. It is best if the task comes at the end of the description or scenario, either as the last sentence or as a separate sentence. The general instructions related to policies or time allocation should be clearly separated from the questions and written in very simple, familiar words.

8.11 Combating Plagiarism

There is no denying the fact that, despite persistent efforts by the college/university administrations, incidents of plagiarism are quite high. This is true across the globe and across disciplines. However, it is an important responsibility of the instructor to ensure that plagiarism is controlled as much as possible.

Plagiarism is best defined as the act of presenting someone's words and ideas as your own, intentionally, or unintentionally. In the *MLA Style Manual and Guide to Scholarly Publishing*, Joseph Gibaldi describes plagiarism as an *intellectual theft* because one is presenting someone else's words or ideas as his or her own. *(Gibaldi, 1998).*

Controlling plagiarism must begin by first analyzing some of the reasons why students plagiarize. Very often, millennials and Generation Z students do not understand what constitutes plagiarism. They are so habituated to looking up everything on the internet. Moreover, very few colleges or individual instructors take the trouble to teach students how to cite sources. Other reasons include a lack of understanding of the content, a lack of interest in the subject, or sheer laziness. Plagiarism is facilitated when there are no well-defined policies regarding the penalties involved. In this case, students find copying an easy option with little or no penalties. It is important for colleges and universities to have a standard, well-advertised policy on plagiarism. Some students may enjoy beating the system. The instructor should make it a point to remind the students of the seriousness of the action and the penalties every time a formal exam is set.

Another important reason that tempts students to plagiarize is poorly designed assignments. It is not unusual for instructors to create tests or homework assignments in a hurry. These assignments are often unclear and confusing for students. Many different factors contribute to this confusion: the assignment may be too complex in comparison with what was taught in class; the instructions are confusing, poorly worded, or contradictory. Sometimes, the students cannot figure out what is expected of them.

Table 8.h – Tips for Combatting Plagiarism

Tip No.	Recommendations
1.	Take a few minutes to explain to students what constitutes plagiarism and what will be your policy for responding to it. Have a clear policy about penalties associated with plagiarism. Read out the policy in class and repeat it every time you set an assignment or a test/exam. This must be done as early in the course as possible. This is especially important for first year students who may have not been exposed to this rigor at school.
2.	Plan to take some form of commitment from the students that they will submit original work. Many colleges/universities have students sign an honor code such as: *"I confirm that this assignment presents my own work and all sources consulted for the purpose have been acknowledged. I understand that not following the policy entails serious penalties".*
3.	Find a slot (tutorial/office hour) to talk about the stylesheet you expect them to use for citing references. Give them a brief demo of how to cite sources from books, research articles and online sources.
4.	Create assignments on the portion that has been taught and reviewed in class. For mid-term/final exams, arrange class activities where students review and learn the content in small groups. You can also create a study-guide (post it in the virtual classroom) that will help them to prepare for the tests/exams. These strategies should help to minimize the temptation to plagiarize.
5.	Make sure that questions/instructions for assignments are written in simple, clear, and familiar words. If possible, assignments should be created using a learning management system that allows to creation of multiple versions of the same assignment, discouraging plagiarism.
6.	Make sure to provide sufficient time for completing the assignments. Very often, we do not give sufficient time and low-performing students are forced to look for help here and there.

8.12 Section 8: Wrap-Up and Tips for Designing and Implementing Effective Assessment

If you were to ask any undergraduate instructors to list three things, they find difficult in their profession, managing *assessment* would be on everyone's list. All aspects of assessment—designing, evaluating, and providing constructive feedback—are equally challenging. This section begins by establishing the impact of assessment on learning and learner motivation. Both *Summative* and *Formative* assessments are discussed in terms of their importance in the learning process. Guidelines for designing and implementing both types of assessments are discussed in detail.

The two-pronged approach has been adopted for discussing the assessment process. The first part deals with creating good tests and exams, and the second part deals with assessing and creating effective rubrics. Different types of questions and their effectiveness have been discussed, and the two types of rubrics – *Holistic* & *Analytical* are discussed, and a sample for each has been provided.

One part of the section that the instructors should find of special value deals with how to evaluate the effectiveness of the tests and exams they create. A template for undertaking this activity has been provided. The next important point taken up in the section is about the importance of feedback in the assessment process. The importance of all types of feedback received through *student-to-student, student-to-instructor, self-evaluation,* and *instructor-to-student,* is brought out clearly. Tips for giving and collecting feedback are included.

Designing and implementing *open book tests* that are of special significance for undergraduate students are discussed in detail. The section closes with a discussion about yet another important challenge: controlling plagiarism and developing ethical behavior.

Table 8.i – Tips for Designing & Implementing Effective Assessment

Tip No.	Recommendations
1.	Remember that *Assessment* is the most powerful instrument for motivating (or demotivating) students. Assessment is not only a medium for measuring learning, but also a valuable tool for promoting learning.

Tip No.	Recommendations
2.	Clearly understand the objectives, formats, and implementation of *Summative* and *Formative* assessment. Please review the recommendations given in Tables 8.1 (Summative Assessment) & 8.2 (Formative Assessment).
3.	While designing tests/exams. pay special attention the form and the difficulty level of the questions across the exam. Make sure that there is a good mix of both. As a general guideline, about 15% of the questions should be of basic level that everyone in class should be able to answer. About 70% questions should be of average difficulty level but requiring higher-order learning skills (application, analysis evaluation) and about 15% should be of high difficulty level.
4.	From time to time, review the tests/exams set by you to see if i) the questions are well-written and are easy to understand, ii) mostly involve higher-order learning skills, and iii) the planned difficulty levels are effective (this can be checked from the overall performance of the class and the grades obtained).
5.	Make sure that every assignment as well as test/exam has a well-designed rubric. The most important components of a rubric are the descriptor that explains the requirements for reaching a particular grade. Make sure that the descriptors are well composed and are as quantitative as possible. The rubrics must be made available to the students along with the assignments/tests.
6.	Receiving and giving *Feedback* is an essential part of assessment. All four forms of feedback (*Student-to-Student; Student-to-Instructor; Instructor to Student*; and S*elf-evaluation*) are important and should be made an integral part of classroom instruction. The manner in which the instructor provides feedback can kill or promote motivation. Please review Table 8.6 for tips for giving constructive feedback.
7.	A very engaging and effective format of assessment is *Open book/notes Exams*. When you introduce open-book assessment, you are telling your students that *you think they are responsible learners*, and that *you trust them*. Designing questions for an open-book test/exam is a very challenging activity. Here, all questions must be pitched at the *application* level and higher. Experience shows that students are generally ill-prepared for open-book tests, so, having a small practice session in class before the actual exam, is strongly recommended.

Tip No.	Recommendations
8.	An all-pervading issue related to assessment is controlling plagiarism. Which is becoming even more challenging after the arrival of ChatGPT. Experience shows that we also have a role in promoting plagiarism by designing assignments that are poorly written out, or beyond the reach of average students. We often do not give sufficient time to. Please review Table 8. g in this section for tips for controlling plagiarism.

<table><tr><td>9</td></tr></table>

The End Note: Monitoring Your Professional Growth

As we come to the end of this journey, it is important to review in what ways the *knowledge and practices* from this book have confirmed or modified our knowledge, skills, and attitude towards undergraduate teaching, and in what ways the input has refined our overall teaching practices and reinforced our confidence level. To get answers to all these questions, we need to look inward a second time, review the positive changes in our teaching, and underline the stubborn blockages that have obstructed progress. Regular self-appraisal and self-reflection are key practices for monitoring one's professional growth. Their importance cannot be overemphasized, irrespective of the number of years you have been teaching.

Self-appraisal is a process that allows individuals to identify their strengths and shortcomings. It is a very mature enterprise that demonstrates a person's commitment to developing a reflective mindset and self-efficacy irrespective of the nature of the profession. While the performance indicators for self-appraisal may vary according to the profession, the process of conducting self-appraisal remains the same. To conduct self-appraisal in a scientific manner, you need to pursue the following three steps:

- Collect objective feedback,
- Analyze the data objectively and
- Create a firm action plan.

9.1 Gathering Objective Feedback

Effectiveness of self-appraisal depends on the feedback we collect. All types of feedback is valuable whether it is formal or informal, explicit, or implicit. In addition to student feedback discussed earlier, feedback comes from two other sources – *institutional feedback*, and *self-evaluation*.

Institutional Feedback

Most institutions have some formal system for gathering feedback about instructors' performance. Occasionally, institutions may have a senior instructor observe classes to collect formal feedback. The most common practice, however, is to collect course feedback from students that includes a section on instructor engagement and performance through items such as *punctuality, class preparedness, timely grading, accessibility,* etc. However, the institutions collect this feedback mostly for specific purposes like tenure granting, nomination for promotion, awards, allocating administrative responsibilities, etc. This feedback is rarely shared with instructors except when it is very negative, and the institution wants to take punitive steps against the instructor. The objective of collecting feedback here is for a totally different purpose – to use it for planning professional development.

Feedback from Self-evaluation

The more effective feedback comes from self-evaluation both informal and formal. The advantage of self-evaluation is that the conclusions are undisputed, and more forceful. You see the gaps yourself and are motivated to take action to come up to your own expectations. Informal feedback about your performance comes intuitively through observations. If the attendance or participation drops, we know that something is not right. Unfortunately, we often take the easy route to blame the students, but we know very well that we are the one who need to address this.

More concrete feedback can be obtained from formal instruments of self-evaluation because you are the assesses as well as assessors. Before starting work with **Undergraduate Teaching**, we worked with two formal instruments to assess our existing competencies.

- Instrument I: ***Evaluating Teaching Effectiveness Using the Matrix Based on Lowman's 2D Model of Teacher Effectiveness*** (p –), and

- Instrument II: ***The Seven Attributes of Outstanding Undergraduate Instructors*** (pp - 29-30).

Both these instruments give a comprehensive evaluation of the competencies considered essential for becoming an outstanding undergraduate educator. This may be a good time to re-do the exercise and re-evaluate ourselves. This will certainly help in updating status about current competencies and making a plan for self-development. Another very efficient mode for collecting formal feedback is designing and using an end-of-semester self-appraisal form.

9.2   Analyzing the Feedback – End-of-Semester Self-Appraisal

Self-appraisal is an effective strategy for getting constructive feedback about your own performance even though keeping an objective stance is not easy because we always tend to overrate our own effort and defend our lapses, especially when things do not work as expected. To facilitate the self-appraisal process, a simple *end-of-semester self-evaluation form* is provided below. The form is built around a set of prompts that should help the brainstorming process. Seven basic aspects have been included in the self-appraisal form, but you can modify or add criteria according to the specific needs of your course or/and teaching environment. Clearly, components where you scored an A are excellent and do not need any intervention. Areas that got a B-, B, and C need to be reviewed more closely. Remember, our main objective is to get clarity about the areas that need to be improved.

Table 9.a – End-of-Semester Self-Appraisal Form

Criteria	Brainstorming Prompts	Performance				Analysis & Conclusion
		A	B	B	C	
Managing Time	Was the course and all planned academic events completed as scheduled?					*Identify which unit/ topic took more time than planned? What other factors caused delay, and need attention?*

Criteria	Brainstorming Prompts	Performance				Analysis & Conclusion
		A	B	B	C	
Quality of Course Plan	How well the course was structured? Were all key concepts covered?					*Which parts of the course were not well-prepared, and need attention? What modifications are required?*
Quality of the Course Delivery	How satisfactory were my lectures on the whole? Were introduction of the topics and closures of the lectures impressive? Did the students enjoy the classes?					*Which part/s of my lectures need to be modified? Which examples/support materials worked well, and which did not? Which activities/ practices failed completely, and must be avoided?*
Student Engagement	How was the class attendance? Was I able to get most of the students fully engaged in the course work?					*Which active & cooperative activities did not work well? What changes in preparation or approach are needed?*
Student Support	Was I able to provide the planned level of support to each set of students? How effective were the online sessions?					*How effective were the office hours? What modifications need to be made? What other support strategies can be tried next semester?*

Criteria	Brainstorming Prompts	Performance				Analysis & Conclusion
		A	B	B	C	
Quality of Assessment	*Formative Assessment* – To what extent the frequency and quality of formative assessment was effective in providing feedback and promoting learning? *Summative Assessment-* How effective were the questions for summative assessment? To what extent the class performance and the quality of individual questions met expectations?					*Based on the analysis, how can the instruments or the process for formative assessment can be made better?* *Based on the analysis, what improvements need to be made to make summative assessment more effective?*
Use of Technology	How well technology was used to support my teaching and student interaction?					*How well the virtual classroom was managed to support my in-class instruction. What other operations can be added? Which ICT tools were most or least effective?*

In addition to the above-mentioned criteria, you can add any other parameters that are relevant for your course. The most important requirement is that your assessment is as objective as possible. Please use a copy of the blank format provided on P – to complete this exercise at the end of each semester.

9.3 Creating an Action Plan

Based on the cumulative feedback from different sources, you can get a clear picture of your performance in different areas. This exercise will allow you to take stock and prioritize your time and effort for fine-tuning your personal performance. Data from overall class performance will give you a general idea of your performance as a teacher, and the end-of-semester self-appraisal form will provide more specific information about the gaps that need attention. These two evaluations will help you to identify the strengths and the weaknesses of your teaching style – strategies that worked well and need to be reinforced, and strategies that did not work and need to be modified or dropped.

Once the areas needing attention have been identified, you need to examine each component more closely to analyze the source of weakness and create an action plan. In order to be well-prepared for the coming semester, you will need to take a number of decisions regarding structuring and delivering your course and refining the student support practices. Developing professional excellence is an ongoing process. It needs time, effort, and persistence. In the words of Pele, the greatest football player of our time, *"Success is no accident; it is hard work, perseverance, learning, studying, sacrifice, and most of all, love for what you are doing or learning to do."*

Good luck for your onward journey!!

Practice Worksheets

In this section, three formats are provided for you to monitor your personal progress. Each format has two parts : 1) the *Blank Format* (the components have been explained in the respective sections, and ii) a *Reflective Summary*. Please feel free to copy the formats to self-evaluate yourself regularly. Do not forget to note the date every time you complete self-evaluation.

Worksheet	Title	Instructions
1a	**Self-assess on Seven Attributes of Outstanding Educators**	Please self-evaluate yourself on the *Seven Attributes of Outstanding Educators*. Before responding to the questionnaire, please review the description of each attribute (p –). Do not forget to complete the reflective summary and create an action plan.
1b	**Reflective Summary**	Save the reflective summary for record. Create a plan for the areas needing attention.

Worksheet	Title	Instructions
2a	**Self-assess Your spoken Image**	Take a few minutes to self-evaluate your spoken and non-verbal communication using the format given below. Please review the explanation of each component (p –) before taking the survey. Based on the results obtained, please complete the reflective summary, and create an action plan.
2b	**Reflective Summary**	Save the reflective summary for record. Create a plan for the areas needing attention.

Worksheet	Title	Instructions
3a.	**End-of-Semester Self-appraisal**	Make it a practice to complete the end of semester self-appraisal form. The form is built around a set of prompts discussed on p – . Seven basic aspects have been included in the self-appraisal form, but you can modify or add criteria according to the specific needs of your course or/and teaching environment. Remember, our main objective is to get clarity about the areas that need to be improved.
3 b.	**Reflective Summary**	Save the reflective summary for record. Create a plan for working on the areas needing attention.

<u>Practice Worksheet No. 1a</u>   **Date:**

Seven Attributes of an Outstanding University Educator

Read carefully the requirements for each attribute explained on P – , and evaluate yourself on each attribute on a **scale of 1 to 4 where <u>1 is the lowest and 4 is the best.</u>** Reflect objectively and give yourself a score. After completing the self-appraisal, complete the Reflective Summary.

No.	Attribute	1	2	3	4
1.	Content Expertise				
2.	Accessibility & Connect with Students				
3.	Good organization				
4.	Using Innovative Methodologies				
5.	Effective Communication				
6.	Positive Approach to Technology				
7.	Passion for Excellence				

<u>Practice Worksheet No. 1b</u>   **Date:**

Reflective Summary – Self-evaluation Seven Attributes of Outstanding Educators

<u>Observations:</u>

<u>Action Plan:</u>

<u>Practice Worksheet No. 2a</u>   **Date:**

Self-evaluating Your Spoken Image

Component	Description	Good	Acceptable	Needs Attention
Energy Level	How is your energy level in class? Are you able to sustain the same level of energy throughout the class?			
Clarity of Speech	Are your students able to understand each word is pronounced clearly?			
Pace	How would you rate the pace at which you speak?			
Modulation	Is your speech well-modulated? And, do you use modulation as a highlighter to emphasize parts of speech by using a higher or slower pace.			
Projection	Do you project your voice well so that students sitting in the last row can follow what you are saying?			
Eye Contact	How would you rate your eye contact with students?			
Facial Expression	Are you particular about keeping a pleasant, happy disposition in class? your students' facial expressions. A smile goes a long way!			
Posture	How would you evaluate your posture throughout the class?			

Practice Worksheet No. 2b   Date:

Reflective Summary – Your Spoken Image

Observations:

Action Plan:

Practice Worksheet No. 3a   **Date:**

End-of-Semester Self-Appraisal Form

Performance Indicator	Brainstorming Prompts	Performance			
		A	B	B	C
Time management	Were you able to complete all planned academic events as scheduled?				
Quality of Course Plan & Structure	Were you satisfied with the way you had planned the course and structured all the different components?				
Quality of the Course Delivery	Were you satisfied with How satisfied are you with your preparation? Did the students enjoy the classes?				
Student Engagement	How will you rate student attendance? Were you satisfied with the level of students' engagement and participation?				
Student Support	Are you satisfied with the level of support you were able to provide support to different sets of students in your class?				
Quality of Assessment	How satisfied are you with the number and quality of tests created by you? Did you evaluate the overall and item-wise effectiveness of the tests?				
Use of Technology	Were you satisfied with your use of virtual classroom? Were you happy with the ICT tools used by you?				

Practice Worksheet No. 3b   Date:

Reflective Summary – End-of-Semester Self-Appraisal Form

Observations:

Action Plan:

References

Adam, S. (2004). Using learning outcomes. A consideration of the nature, role, application and implications for European education of employing 'learning outcomes' at local, national and international levels. (pp. 1–2) [Conference Background Report, UNITED KINGDOM BOLOGNA SEMINAR]. Heriot-Watt University. http://aic.lv/bolona/Bologna/Bol_semin/Edinburgh/S_Adam_Bacgrerep_presentation.pdf

Ambrose, S. A., Bridges, M. W., DiPietro, M., Lovett, M. C., & Norman, M. K. (2010). How learning works: Seven research-based principles for smart teaching (1st ed). Jossey-Bass.

Anderson, L. W., & Krathwohl, D. R. (Eds.). (2001). A taxonomy for learning, teaching, and assessing: A revision of Bloom's taxonomy of educational objectives (Complete ed). Longman.

Bandura, A. (1977). Social learning theory. Prentice-Hall.

Barkley, E. F., Cross, K. P., & Major, C. H. (2005). Collaborative learning techniques: A handbook for college faculty (1st ed). Jossey-Bass.

Bauersfeld, H. (1995). 'Language Games' in the mathematics classroom: Their function and their effects. In P. Cobb & H. Bauersfeld (Eds.), *The emergence of mathematical meaning: Interaction in classroom cultures* (pp. 211-292). Hillsdale, NJ: Lawrence Erlbaum

Bodner, G. M. (1986). Constructivism: A theory of knowledge. Journal of Chemical Education, 63(10), 873. https://doi.org/10.1021/ed063p873

Bonwell, C. C., & Eison, J. A. (1991). Active learning: Creating excitement in the classroom. School of Education and Human Development, George Washington University.

Brennan, J., & Williams, R. (2004). *Collecting and using student feedback: A guide to good practice*. Learning and Teaching Support Network.

Brownstein, B. (2001). Collaboration: The Foundation of Learning in the Future. Education, 122(2), 240–247.

Caine, R. N., & Caine, G., (2005), *12 Brain/Mind Learning Principles in Action: The Fieldbook for Making Connections, Teaching, and the Human Brain*. California, USA

Celestine, C. (2012, May 15). *How To Give Constructive Criticism: 6 Helpful Tips*. https://personalexcellence.co/blog/constructive-criticism/

Chandler, C. (2021, May 12). How Can Teachers Determine Whether Students Are Engaged? https://www.middleweb.com/45104/can-teachers-measure-student-engagement/

Chi, M. (1994). Eliciting self-explanations improves understanding. Cognitive Science, 18(3), 439–477. https://doi.org/10.1016/0364-0213(94)90016-7

Elbow, P. (1987). Embracing Contraries. Explorations in Learning and Teaching. Oxford University Press.

Felder, R. M. (2002). Teaching Lessons Learned. Designing Tests to Maximize Learning. Journal of Professional Issues in Engineering Education and Practice, 128(1), 1–3. https://doi.org/10.1061/(ASCE)1052-3928 (2002)128:1(1)

Felder, R. M., & Brent, R. (2016). Teaching and learning in STEM: A practical guide. Jossey-Bass.

Felder, R. M., & Silverman, L. K. (1988). Learning and Teaching Styles in Engineering Education. Engr. Education, 78(7), 674–681.

Fosnot, C. T. (2015). Constructivism: Theory, Perspectives, and Practice (2nd ed (Online-ausg.)). Teachers College Press.

Gardner, H. (1983). Frames of mind: The theory of multiple intelligences. Basic Books.

Gibaldi, J. (2003). MLA handbook for writers of research papers (6th ed). Modern Language Association of America.

Goleman, D. (2005). Emotional intelligence (10th anniversary trade pbk. ed). Bantam Books.

Hammer, T. R. (2011). Social Learning Theory. In S. Goldstein & J. A. Naglieri (Eds.), Encyclopedia of Child Behavior and Development (pp. 1396–1397). Springer US. https://doi.org/10.1007/978-0-387-79061-9_2695

Hilgard, E. R., & Bower, G. H. (1975). Theories of learning (4th ed). Prentice-Hall.

Israel, M. J. (2015). Effectiveness of Integrating MOOCs in Traditional Classrooms for Undergraduate Students. The International Review of Research in Open and Distributed Learning, 16(5). https://doi.org/10.19173/irrodl.v16i5.2222

Jensen, E., & McConchie, L. (2020). Brain-based learning: Teaching the way students really learn (Third edition). Corwin Press.

Kaufman, D. B., Felder, R. M., & Fuller, H. (2000). Accounting for Individual Effort in Cooperative Learning Teams. Journal of Engineering Education, 89(2), 133–140. https://doi.org/10.1002/j.2168-9830.2000.tb00507.x

Kumar, V. (2023). Peer-supported Independent Study (psis)—An Effective Model for Enhancing Student Engagement and Optimizing Class Time in Engineering Courses – A Case Study from India. Journal of Engineering Education Transformations, 36(3), 77–84. https://doi.org/10.16920/jeet/2023/v36i3/23100

Laughlin, P. R. (2011). Group Problem Solving: Princeton University Press. https://doi.org/10.1515/9781400836673

Lowman, J. (1995). Mastering the techniques of teaching (2nd ed). Jossey-Bass Publishers.

MacGregor, D. (1960). The human side of enterprise. McGraw-Hill.

Mascolo, M. F., & Fischer, K. W. (2004). Constructivist theories. In Hopkins, B., Barre, R. G., Michel, G. F., Rochat, P. (Eds.). Cambridge encyclopedia of child development (pp. 49–63). Cambridge University Press.

Mastascusa, E. J., Snyder, W. J., & Hoyt, B. S. (2011). Effective instruction for STEM disciplines: From learning theory to college teaching. Jossey-Bass.

Mazur, E. (1997). Peer Instruction: A User's Manual. In Series in Educational Innovation (p. 253). Prentice Hall. /files/mazur/files/rep_0.pdf

Morse, A., Millerick, K., Tindle, K., Cremeans, L., & Jones, S. (2017). Lowman's 2D Model of Effective College Teaching: Justifying the Need for Faculty Diversity. 2017 ASEE Annual Conference & Exposition Proceedings, 28635. https://doi.org/10.18260/1-2--28635

Paris, S. G., & Turner, J. C. (1994). Situated Motivation. In W. J. McKeachie, P. R. Pintrich, D. R. Brown, & C. E. Weinstein, Student motivation, cognition, and learning: Essays in honor of Wilbert J. McKeachie (pp. 213–237). L. Erlbaum.

Petty, G. (2009) Teaching Today, 4th ed. London: Nelson Thrones

Prince, M. J. (2004). Does Active Learning Work? A Review of the Research. Journal of Engineering Education, 93(3), 223–231. https://doi.org/10.1002/j.2168-9830.2004.tb00809.x

Salmons, J. E. (2008). Taxonomy of Collaborative E-Learning: In L. A. Tomei (Ed.), Encyclopedia of Information Technology Curriculum Integration (pp. 839–846). IGI Global. https://doi.org/10.4018/978-1-59904-881-9.ch132

Sass, Edmund J, (1989), Motivation in College Classroom; What Students Tell Us, Volume16, Issue 2, http://journals.sagepub/doi.org/abs/10.1207/s1538023 top1602_15

Schlechty, P. C. (2001). Shaking up the schoolhouse: How to support and sustain educational innovation. Jossey-Bass.

Schunk, D. H., & Usher, E. L. (2012). Social Cognitive Theory and Motivation. In R. M. Ryan (Ed.), The Oxford Handbook of Human Motivation (1ˢᵗ ed., pp. 13–27). Oxford University Press. https://doi.org/10.1093/oxfordhb/9780195399820.013.0002

Smedshammer, M. (2017). 10 Tips for Creating Effective Instructional Videos. https://www.facultyfocus.com/articles/teaching-with-technology-articles/10-tips-creating-effective-instructional-videos/

Sousa, D. A. (2011). How the brain learns (4ᵗʰ ed). Corwin Press.

Stiggins, R. (2008). Assessment Manifesto: A Call of Balanced Assessment Systems (pp. 1–12). ETS Assessment Training Institute. http://www.ebecplc.org/uploads/2/1/9/4/21941210/assessmentmanifesto08-1.pdf

Taber, K. S. (2011). In J. Hassaskhah (Ed.), Educational theory (pp. 39–61). Nova Science Publishers.

Vygotskij, L. S., & Cole, M. (1981). Interaction between learning and development. In Mind in society: The development of higher psychological processes (Nachdr., pp. 79–91). Harvard Univ. Press.

World Economic Forum. (2016). Global Challenge Insight Report. The Future of Jobs Employment, Skills and Workforce Strategy for the Fourth Industrial Revolution. https://www3.weforum.org/docs/WEF_Future_of_Jobs.pdf

Glossary

Acknowledgement – most of the definitions/explanations are based on the information derived from diverse sources, especially from and *The Glossary of Education Reform (https://www.edglossary.org)* and *Wikipedia.*

Teaching, like every other profession, depends on key terms and expressions to describe/explain the theoretical framework, principles, specific methodologies, and learning strategies. It is important for a learned and well-trained instructor to be conversant with them. This section is designed with this end in mind. Simple explanations of the key technical terms are provided so that the meaning, scope, context, and usage of these terms/acronyms become clear.

- **Action Research** – the term refers to research undertaken to solve a problem. The problem may be from any domain, simple or complex; related to a process, phenomenon, or system.

- **Affective Domain**– the term refers to a domain of learning that is associated with a student's emotional response to the instructional process at large (ideas, content, peers, instructors, and the process). In this context, the term **Affective Filter** is commonly used to describe **the** n*egative* feelings like fear, anxiety, discomfort, lack of confidence and motivation that act as a filter and obstructs student learning. Instructors are advised are to keep the affective filter low by ensuring an open, welcoming, and relaxed class environment.

- **Advance Organizer** – the term refers to a framework that the instructors create to share the order in which learning will take place in a session, a term, or a semester. An advanced organizer helps both the instructor (to structure delivery of new input) and the student (to prepare to receive the new input). to structure learning place the new knowledge logical the order in which the teacher organizes the learning tasks are organized given to the students ahead of class or at the beginning of the class.

- **Andragogy**: the term refers to the theoretical and practical aspects of adult learning. The specialized used of the term recognize and highlight the fact adults learn differently from how children learn. However, the term *pedagogy* continues to be the popular term to describe the learning-teaching practices.

- **Aptitude** – the term may be defined as a person's natural talent, competence, and inclination to learn or accomplish a targeted skill. Aptitude might be physical or mental, or both. It is inherent and varies from student to student, or from professional to professional.

- **Asynchronous Learning** – the term refers to a learning environment where learning materials, tools and assessment are made available to the students through an online platform for flexible learning at their own time and pace. The system is student-centric and requires students to take ownership for their own learning.

- **Attention Span** – the term refers to the amount of time a person spends concentrating on a task before becoming distracted. Distraction happens when a person's attention is involuntarily diverted to another activity or feeling. It is well-recognized that humans have a limited attention span.

- **Backward Course Design** – the term refers to a method for structuring curriculum of individual courses that reverses the traditional method by putting assessment right in the beginning of the course planning process. Backward course design begins by designing assessment tools that will provide the evidence of attainment of outcomes.

- **Blended Learning** – the term refers to a teaching practice that includes the use of digital learning tools with traditional face to face classroom teaching. As opposed to remote teaching, blended learning requires the physical presence of both the instructor and the student.

- **Brain-based Learning** – the term refers to a theory based on research findings in neuroscience that propagate that "…*learning in accordance* *with the way the brain is naturally designed to learn"* *(Jensen, 1995/2000)*. Brain-based learning confirms that aligning teaching to the recommendations made by brain-based learning can greatly enhances the students' potential for learning.

- **Brainstorming** – the term refers to an approach that promotes open and free generation of ideas to address a specific problem, issue, or challenge. Brainstorming activity can be conducted individually or in small groups. The process involves initial acceptance of every idea or suggestion without any criticism or interruption. The proposed ideas/suggestions are then reviewed individually to evaluate their viability for addressing the specific problem, issue, or a challenge.

- **Collaborative Learning** – the term refers to a specific approach in education where students are encouraged to work with their peers. Collaborative learning may be spontaneous or highly structured; it can refer to completing a short activity to a long multi-stage project.

- **Concept map** – the term refers to visual representation of knowledge in the form of charts, tables, flowcharts, Venn Diagrams, etc. designed to help students to understand complex concepts graphically. And by placing new knowledge in the context of their pre-existing knowledge base.

- **Cognitive Map** – the term refers to a visual representation of a person's (or a group's) mental model of knowledge about a process, or a concept. A cognitive map has no fixed structure. It lays out complex ideas, processes, patterns, and relationships in simple graphic formats to facilitate understanding.

- **Cognitive Overload** – the term refers to a situation where a person is given too much information or asked to complete several different tasks at the same time.

- **Critical Thinking** – the term refers to mental exercise that involves evaluating information through reflection, examination, and formation of judgement. To achieve this, logical information is collected and analyzed through observation, reasoning, and inference.

- **Clustering** – the term refers to a process of grouping ideas for creating concept maps or planning a study. When a topic is being studied, the scholars may choose a system for clustering the constituents. For example, music may be studied in *clusters* such as *classical, folk, instrumental* etc. Clustering is commonly used in fields such as statistical analysis, image processing, machine learning etc.

- **Constructivism** – the term refers to a learning theory that claims that learning happens when learners have an opportunity to construct knowledge rather than just receiving it passively (listening to a lecture or viewing a video etc.). The theory proposes that when people internalize learning, it gets integrated into their pre-existing knowledge base (*Schema*). Two phenomena are associated with constructivism – *Assimilation* (new knowledge is incorporated in the existing schema) and *Accommodation* (new knowledge effects revision of the existing schema).

- **Course Learning Outcomes (CLO)** – the term refers to clear and concrete statements that define what learners will be able to *do* at the end of the learning activity. To be effective, the CLOs must be written using action verbs that are observable and measurable. Verbs like *know, understand, appreciate, realize* must be avoided as they cannot be measured.

- **Criterion-referenced Grading** – the term refers to the evaluation process based on pre-determined criteria that is shared with the student before the assessment is undertaken. Standardized tests fall under this category.

- **Design Thinking – the term refers to** both an ideology and a method that is used for creative problem-solving. The process involves five steps (empathize, define, ideate, prototype, and test). This approach places the human interest at the center and is effective in developing skills like critical thinking and problem-solving.

- **Differentiated Instruction** – the term refers to a system where the curriculum offers the possibility to design lectures that offer different learning experiences and cater to different learning needs of the students (like for students with disability). Terms such as *Individualized* or *Customized* instruction are also used for this method.

- **Deductive and Inductive Mode of Teaching** – these two terms refer to the two opposing methods of teaching new content/concept. In the deductive mode, the instructor starts by explaining the main concept and then supports it by giving specific examples. In the inductive mode the instructor starts by presenting specific examples/observations and uses them to arrive at the principles/definitions of the new content/concept. Both modes are effective but inductive mode is found to be more engaging.

- **Domains of Learning:** There are three domains of learning:

    i) *Cognitive Domain of Learning* – refers to learning through processing new information using mental skills like remembering, *applying, analyzing, evaluating* etc.

    ii) *Affective Domain of Learning* – refers to learning through *emotions, attitude, values etc.* Educationists claim that holistic learning happens when the cognitive domain is complimented by affective domain.

    iii) *Psychomotor Domain of Learning* – refers to learning through motor skills like alacrity and coordination in *physical movement, and manual dexterity.* This domain is important in disciplines that require hands-on activities, procedures, or techniques in execution.

- **Educational Research** – the term refers to the type of research that investigates the theories, systems, processes, and issues related to education. It aims to study the policies and practices to enhance the quality of the teaching-learning process.

- **Epistemology** – the term refers to a branch of philosophy that aspires to decipher the mysteries of knowledge by exploring questions such as – what is the foundation and process of knowledge, how it is acquired, what is its relation to notions such as truth, belief, reason, evidence, justification etc. The subject has been of great interest to researchers since the ancient times.

- **Experiential Learning** – the term refers to a process by which students develop knowledge and skills from direct experience, usually outside the traditional classroom. The concept combines both a cognitive and behavioral approach to learning *(Kolb 1984)*. Learning gained through internships, study abroad, community-based learning, service learning, and research projects fall under experiential learning.

- **Flipped Class** – the term refers to a teaching strategy that reverses the conventional teaching-learning sequence. In a conventional class, the students learn the content with the instructor in class and then work on follow-up exercises and assignments at home to internalize the new knowledge. In the *flipped class*, student learn the new content by themselves, and work in small groups on application-based activities in class under the supervision of the instructor to internalize the new knowledge.

- **Formative Assessment** – the term refers to a process of *ongoing* assessment that aims to provide feedback to both the instructor and the learners during the learning process. Formative assessment may or may not be graded. Using in-class activities, quizzes, weekly tests, or draft submissions are some of the examples of formative assessment.

- **Inclusive Teaching** – the term refers to an approach that aims to create a learning environment where all students irrespective of their academic performance, socio-cultural background, and life experiences are made to feel equally respected, valued, and supported for academic success.

- **Information Processing Approaches** – the term refers to the approach students use to process information presented to them during the course. There are three different ways in which the students may process information:

    i) *In-depth Processing* – the learner works with the objective of mastering the content. The learner is fully engaged using higher order learning strategies.

ii) ***Surface Processing*** – the learner works with the objective of getting only the basic level information about the content. Here, the learner is minimally engaged and is satisfied with getting just the overall idea of the topic.

iii) ***Strategic processing*** – the learner works with the objective of sifting/selecting course content to determine the amount of effort and time to be devoted to content needing in-depth or surface processing.

All three approaches are important, and the instructor must guide the students to effectively manage the different sections of the course content.

- **Inquiry-based learning** – the term refers to an instructional strategy that focuses on student exploration, reflection and raising questions to understand the issue at hand. Much like the inductive approach, inquiry-based instruction begins by raising questions that are followed by explanations. Inquiry-based activities, designed as individual, peer or group activities offer opportunity to students for developing problem-solving and critical thinking skills.

- **Learning Management System (LMS)** – the term refers to a technology platform designed to deliver instruction online in synchronous and asynchronous mode. The LMS offers the instructor facilities to run a regular classroom online using facilities such as managing the class roster and posting announcements, reading materials, assignments, quizzes, and grades. Today, instructors have access to several free LMSs to choose from and set up a virtual classroom to teach online or/and supplement their regular classes.

- **Learning Styles** – the term refers to different modes that learners prefer to receive, interpret, organize, and store information. At least seven different learning styles have been identified and several instruments have been developed that learners or instructors can use to assess their own learning style. Instructors are advised to deliver instruction using different modes to accommodate a maximum number of learning preferences.

- **Learning Objective/Outcome** – the term refers to carefully designed statements that specify skills, knowledge and attitudes the students are expected to attain at the end of a learning event or a complete course. Learning objectives help instructors to organize their teaching, as well as design assessment. They are equally helpful for students in discerning the relative importance of different course components and acquiring the requisite skills.

- **Learning Taxonomies** – the term *taxonomy* is most commonly used by scientists to classify species. Following that, the term learning taxonomies refers to the act of classifying different types and levels of learning skills (applying, analyzing, manipulation etc.) in the three different domains of learning – *Cognitive, Psychomotor, Affective.*

- **Liberal Arts** – the term refers to the field of study that focuses on broader education and aspires to develop psychological and intellectual skills leading to a comprehensive world view. Liberal Arts comprise disciplines related to *Humanities, Psychology, Social Sciences, Philosophy, Fine Arts* etc.

- **Lifelong Learning** – the term refers to the philosophical concept that suggests that "learning' is forever. There is no age, time, or place for learning. Given the fact that knowledge is becoming obsolete so fast, developing lifelong learning skills has become a priority for undergraduate education. Most educational programs now-a-days include components of curriculum and assessment that promote lifelong learning.

- **Long-term Memory** – the term refers to a system for permanently storing learned knowledge. As opposed to short-term memory, long-term memory has the capacity to hold information indefinitely, and retrieving the stored knowledge as and when needed.

- **Massive Open Online Course (MOOC):** The term refers to open-source video courses delivered by distinguished professors from well-known universities and made available free to public for wider participation. Most MOOCs serve as an excellent resource that the instructors can use to upgrade their own knowledge as well as enrich their teaching.

In the present time, researchers are busy experimenting with different modes of incorporating MOOCs in online or in-class instruction.

- **Metacognition** – the term refers to a person's knowledge about his/her own cognitive abilities and thinking processes. Metacognition helps to monitor one's learning, problem-solving, critical-thinking, and decision-making skills.

- **Mind Map** – the term refers to a visual format for organizing concepts, patterns, information, ideas in relation to a central topic/theme. Creating a mind map is an effective strategy for brainstorming, planning a process or a product by placing different components/steps in a creative and interconnected manner.

- **Norm-referenced Grading** – the term refers to a grading system where student performance is evaluated by measuring it against that of other students in the class. In this system all papers are corrected and then a graph is plotted where the biggest cluster represents the <u>average grade</u> (C in most cases). The other grade values are determined around the average grade. This system is mostly used in competitive exams/selections.

- **One Minute Paper** – the term refers to a popular active learning technique that requires students to reflect on their learning in a lecture and provide brief feedback (just one or two sentence) on what they did not understand or would like more clarification about.

- **Outcome-Based Education (OBE)** – The term refers to a method for designing instruction where different aspects of the teaching-learning process are organized around well-defined outcomes. Lecture input and learning activities are designed to ensure that students are able to achieve the pre-set outcomes. In the OBE format, assessment is also aligned to the outcomes.

- **Peer-supported Independent Study (PSIS)** – the term refers to an instructional strategy to address two most common challenges faced by university instructors: optimizing class instruction time and stimulating student engagement. The PSIS is conducted online and requires the instructor to identify portions of the regular coursework that students can manage by themselves. Most university instructors agree that about 15% to 20% of the course content regularly taught in classes can be managed by students on their own and is hence suitable for PSIS. The instructor creates tasks based on the identified course content that are completed independently by peer groups (3-5 students) and submitted online as an assignment. The topics identified for PSIS are expected to be included in the regular summative assessment.

- **Problem-Based Learning** – the term refers to a form of student-cantered, experiential pedagogy that focuses on having students work in small groups on real-world, open-ended problems. Minimal information is provided, and the students are expected to understand the problem, conduct research, identify possible solutions, and select the most viable one.

- **Project-Based Learning** – the term refers to an instructional method where students work in small groups to work through a complex project. These projects may be built around a product, a process, or a real-world problem. This methodology encourages team building, interpersonal communication, and interdisciplinary conversations.

- **Reliability** – The term is used in the context of assessment. An assessment instrument is considered to be *reliable* when it yields the same results every time it is administered in the same conditions with similar profile learners.

- **Reflective Mindset** – the term refers to one's effort to analyze, interpret, and assess personal experiences with the objective of learning from them. A reflective mindset is a pathway that leads to positive personal and professional growth.

- **Rubric** – the term refers to a 'grading' tool designed to guide both the test taker and the test evaluator. Here, the evaluator sets criteria for expected correct response. Once the criteria are established, the evaluator sets levels of performance that are generally defined as *Excellent, Good, Acceptable, Needs improvement*. Some evaluators may use numbers (1,2,3,4) to describe the level of performance.

Rubrics are of two types – *Analytical* and *Holistic*. Each serves a specific objective and is designed differently.

- **Scaffolding** – the term refers to an instructional technique used by teachers to help students move progressively toward stronger understanding and, ultimately, greater independence in the learning process. The basic objective of scaffolding is to support the students to bridge the gap between what they know and are expected to know.

- **Schema** (Plural – **Schemata**) – the term refers to cognitive framework or a pattern of thought or behavior used to organize information, processes, pre-conceived ideas, or concepts. The term schema is also used in the context of databases.

- **Self-Efficacy** – the term was coined by Albert Bandura in 1977 and refers to an attribute that describes a person's belief in his/her ability to acquire knowledge or skills that may be required to cope with any new or unknown situations. Self-efficacy leads to self-confidence.

- **Self-Esteem** – the term refers to the value a person attaches to himself or herself. It is a kind of self-appraisal (or self-worth) that can be positive or negative; exaggerated, or diminutive. It is different from self-efficacy though the two are related. Self-esteem is how a person feels about himself/herself whereas self-efficacy is how a person feels about his/her capabilities. One may be a terrible cook but that does not necessarily lower the person's self-esteem.

- **Service Learning** – the term refers to a system of education where academic curriculum and evaluation include community service. Service learning also falls in the category of experiential learning. By combining instruction with hands-on application and its visible impact, *Service Learning* not only promotes social responsibility and life-long learning but also provides emotional satisfaction.

- **Short-term Memory** – the term refers to the capacity of the brain for holding a small amount of information in an active, ready-to – retrieve state for a short period of time. This is also known as *primary* or *active* memory.

- **Social-Emotional Learning (SEL)** – the term refers to an educational method that attempts to combine instruction with awareness about the importance of finer human attributes like empathy, interpersonal communication, civic responsibility etc.

- **STEM Disciplines** – the term STEM is the acronym for *Science, Technology, Engineering,* and *Mathematics* disciplines, that are considered core subjects of higher order learning for a technological society. STEM disciplines are a priority with most educational systems that prepare workforce for technological advancement, self-reliance, and sustainability.

- **Student Motivation** – the term refers to the phenomenon of *motivation* in the specific context of the instructional process. A simple and well-accepted definition of student motivation is students' desire to make personal investment of time and effort to achieve their academic goals. A topic of extensive research, studies on student motivation bring valuable guidance to the instructor for sustaining student motivation which has a direct impact on student success.

- **Summative Assessment** – the term refers to a method of evaluation that measures students' learning at the completion of a session or a course. The objective of the summative assessment is to award a final grade based on a student's performance in specially designed instruments quiz, exams, term-papers.

- **Teaching Philosophy Statement** – the term refers to a narrative that shares your personal vision about teaching and learning. It describes your ambitions, goals, and values as a teacher at specific level you are teaching. A good example of a teaching philosophy statement is by Einstein when he says, "*I never teach my pupils; I only attempt to provide the conditions in which they can learn.*" It is important for every serious university instructor to create a well-reflected teaching philosophy statement and use it to navigate her approach, work plan, and future growth.

- **Validity** – the term is used in the context of assessment. A test is said to be *valid* when it evaluates set criteria. In other words, the validity of a test depends on the extent to which each criterion is achieved.

- **Working memory** – the term refers to type of human memory which much like the short-term memory holds information for a short duration but allows easy manipulation and application as opposed to just storing information.